Atonement a

Atonement as Gift

Re-Imagining the Cross for the Church and the World

Edited by
Katie M. Heffelfinger
and
Patrick G. McGlinchey

Paternoster:
thinking faith

20 19 18 17 16 15 14   7 6 5 4 3 2 1

First published 2014 by Paternoster
Paternoster is an imprint of Authentic Media Limited
52 Presley Way, Crownhill, Milton Keynes, MK8 0ES.
authenticmedia.co.uk

British Library Cataloguing in Publication Data
A catalogue record for this book is available from the British Library
ISBN 978-1-84227-816-1
978-1-84227-862-8 (e-book)

Cover Design by David McNeill (www.revocreative.co.uk)
Printed and bound by CPI Group (UK) Ltd., Croydon, CR0 4YY

Contents

List of Contributors   vii
List of Abbreviations   ix
Permissions   xi
Preface: Katie M. Heffelfinger and Patrick G. McGlinchey xiii
Foreword: Christina Baxter   xv
Introduction: Katie M. Heffelfinger and
    Patrick G. McGlinchey   xvii

Section 1: The Cross and Reality   1
1. Where Are We in Relation to Atonement?
    Stephen N. Williams   3
    Responses:
    Does Christianity Really Need a Doctrine of the Atonement?
        Richard Clutterbuck   16
    Reconciliation between Blame and Lament
        Cathriona Russell   24
2. The Cross and the Redemption of the Cosmos
    Ron Elsdon   31
3. The Cross and God's Embrace of Suffering
    Richard Bauckham   49
    Spiritual Exercise: Engaging Lament   61
    Suggestions for the Use of Integrative Silence 63

Section 2: Broken Relationships in a Fractured World   65
4. The Cross and the Reconciliation of Enemies
    David Tombs   67
5. The Cross and the Reconciliation of Gender
    Elaine Storkey   79

Group Activity: Letter Writing   93
6. The Cross and Our Aspiration for a Common Doctrine of
   Redemption: A Dialogue
       Con Casey and Stephen N. Williams   95
7. The Cross and Eucharistic Sacrifice: A Personal Reflection on
   an Ecumenical Struggle
       Patrick G. McGlinchey   114
   Suggestions for the Use of Integrative Silence   132

Section 3: Re-Imagining the Self in the Light of the Cross   133
8. The Cross and Our Captivity to Shame
       Robin Stockitt   135
   Exercise: Bibliodrama   150
9. The Cross and the Poetic Imagination
       Katie M. Heffelfinger   152
10. The Cross and the Healing of the Self
       Heather Morris   167
   Exercise: Prayer Clinic   178
   Suggestions for the Use of Integrative Silence   181

Section 4: Conclusions   183
Responses to the Chapters
       Katie M. Heffelfinger and Patrick G. McGlinchey 185
Continuing the Conversation
       Katie M. Heffelfinger and Patrick G. McGlinchey 197
Bibliography   199
Endnotes   215
General Index   244

CONTRIBUTORS

Dr Richard Bauckham is Emeritus Professor of New Testament, University of St Andrews.

Rev. Dr Con Casey is Director of the Loyola Institute, Trinity College Dublin.

Rev. Dr Richard Clutterbuck is Principal of Edgehill Theological College, Belfast.

Rev. Dr Ron Elsdon is former Lecturer in Geology, University College Dublin and is recently retired as Rector of St Bartholomew's Church, Belfast.

Dr Katie M. Heffelfinger is Lecturer in Biblical Studies and Hermeneutics at the Church of Ireland Theological Institute.

Rev. Dr Patrick G. McGlinchey is Lecturer in Missiology and Pastoral Studies at the Church of Ireland Theological Institute.

Rev. Dr Heather Morris is President of the Irish Methodist Church and Director of Ministry at Edgehill Theological College, Belfast.

Dr Cathriona Russell is the Dungannon and Beresford Adjunct Assistant Professor in Theology in the Department of Religions and Theology, Trinity College Dublin.

Rev. Dr Robin Stockitt is Minister of the Anglican Church in Freiburg.

Dr Elaine Storkey is Co-Founder of and Lecturer in the postgraduate Christian Mind Course at Oxford University.

Dr David Tombs is Assistant Professor in Conflict Resolution and Reconciliation at the Irish School of Ecumenics, Trinity College Dublin.

Rev. Dr Stephen N. Williams is Professor of Systematic Theology at Union Theological College, The Queen's University of Belfast Institute of Theology.

ABBREVIATIONS

Ann.	Tacitus, *Annals*
AB	Anchor Bible
ARCIC	Anglican–Roman Catholic International Commission
CDF	Congregation for the Doctrine of the Faith
CSI	Crime Scene Investigation
CUP	Cambridge University Press
Haer.	Irenaeus, *Adversus haereses*
HUDF	Hubble Ultra Deep Field
IBC	Interpretation: A Bible Commentary for Teaching and Preaching
IVP	InterVarsity Press
JSOT	*Journal for the Study of the Old Testament*
JSOTSup	Journal for the Study of the Old Testament: Supplement Series
KJV	King James Version
Lib. spect.	Martial, *Liber spectaculorum*
LXX	Septuagint
NAS	New American Standard
NCB	New Century Bible
NET	New English Translation
NICNT	New International Commentary on the New Testament
NIGTC	New International Greek Testament Commentary
NIV	New International Version
NLT	New Living Translation
NRSV	New Revised Standard Version

OFM	Order of the Friars Minor
OTL	Old Testament Library
OUP	Oxford University Press
SBL	Society of Biblical Literature
SJ	Society of Jesus
TS	*Theological Studies*
WBC	Word Biblical Commentary
WCC	World Council of Churches

PERMISSIONS

PREFACE

This book originated as a symposium held at the Church of Ireland Theological Institute in May 2011. We are grateful to the wonderful scholars who took part and contributed such richness through their varied areas of expertise. The book has grown directly out of our work as teachers in a close-knit learning community. At every stage it is fair to say that this work would not have gone ahead without the support of both students and colleagues. Our students, both past and present, are the inspiration for this work. We are particularly grateful for the administrative help we have received from Lynda Levis and Daphne Metcalfe, whose expert and gracious handling of many details made the seminar and this publication run more smoothly than we could have hoped. A special word of thanks is owed to the Director of the Theological Institute, Rev. Dr Maurice Elliott, who delegated to us the task of preparing an integrative seminar within the Institute's curriculum and who has given us unfailing encouragement to follow our vision for this project. Finally, we would especially like to thank our spouses, Jamie and Helen, who have truly gone the extra mile for this book: listening, encouraging and giving up their time to give us time to work. Without the two of them, this project would not have happened.

Katie M. Heffelfinger and Patrick G. McGlinchey

FOREWORD

Over many years, a former colleague would ask all potential theological teachers whom we interviewed, 'What, in a sentence, is the heart of the gospel?' It produced a huge variety of answers and not a little struggle in the candidates before us. Those who are Christians assume that they know what the gospel is or what atonement means, though they may find a one-sentence summary beyond them. Many of those who are not the disciples of Jesus find the cross, this heart of the gospel, incomprehensible, nonsense or offensive. Whichever kind of reader you may be, there will be perspectives in these essays to clarify, transform or challenge previous presuppositions so as to deepen your understanding.

In this volume, there is a fresh approach to the question which the first disciples of Jesus faced, as they sought to understand the cross/resurrection events to which they were witnesses. The question is answered in a way which attempts to open new windows into the mystery for those outside the faith who have never found traditional explanations illuminating. The fact that these chapters have been written contextually, consciously taking into account the history of conflict in Ireland, or the need for healing of memories, is itself a challenge to both readers and writers. This has been underpinned by a determination to address not only the individual but also the communal, to explore not only consequences for human persons but the consequences of God's action in atonement for the whole of the created order. And the arguments are developed in a way which takes account of the whole perspective of theology; setting the cross in Trinitarian and christological perspective, so that warped presentations are corrected. The essays are helpfully painted on a broad canvas.

Many people who do grasp something of the significance of the atonement do so by a sudden conversion or a long period of dawning realization. Once that has happened, it can be tempting to think that one can move on from there. These writers are convinced that we should never 'move on', because we could (and should) fruitfully live our whole lives in the light of this theology which touches not only individuals, but communities and creation itself. Perhaps most instructive is the way that the authors are determined that the cross of Jesus Christ is not to be understood only as an historic event, but as something to be appropriated in prayer, imagination, poetry, drama and real life – joyfully, painfully and transformatively, and always with the assistance of the Holy Spirit. In order to help that to happen, there are suggestions of ways in which readers may reflect on what they have learned, based on the ways in which those who participated in the original seminars were enabled to take their questions into discussion, their prayers into worship, their life issues into drama or Bible study. This is a book which could give rise to some parish or ecumenical study groups, for those who want to deepen their commitment to understanding and living out their Christian faith.

There are certainly themes and insights here which will repay longer reflection; for instance I will return to the meditation on what it means to enter into the servant song of Isaiah 53 as the church's prayer of confession; I will want to engage with those who do not yet have faith from the starting point of shame (instead of starting with sin) which may be more readily appreciated by contemporary western people with whom we talk in the church's mission. I will want to work through the processes delineated in the chapter on reconciliation in order to understand what is happening when civil wars or church disagreements break out. I will want to practise the careful listening to different others which is modelled in the dialogue between two traditions. These authors imaginatively unwrap the gift of the atonement for church and world in a way which will enable us all to appreciate the gift afresh. This is a book which gives an agenda for living, for acting, for praying and for preaching. I hope and pray that we will allow it to direct us afresh to the gift of God which is for each one of us.

Christina Baxter
The Circumcision of Christ, 2014

INTRODUCTION

Katie M. Heffelfinger and Patrick G. McGlinchey

We live and work in a small community. Conversations about life, work and faith take many forms, and happen on all kinds of occasions. Some are more memorable than others. Some change our lives more than others. One stands out as being particularly memorable.

I (Katie) was walking past Paddy's office one afternoon when he bounced an idea off me. Since what is most memorable is the result of the conversation, rather than the conversation itself, I am afraid I will have to approximate the dialogue. His question was something like 'Would the New Testament view of atonement match up with an account that says atonement is about overcoming shame?'[1] My almost unthinking response was something quite typical of biblical specialists asked such a question. 'Well, that all depends,' I replied. I was thinking about biblical books each having their own individual emphases, and of the well-trodden dictum that none of the classic atonement theories appear in anything like as systematic a form in the pages of the New Testament. What my response did not result in was the dropping of the subject. Instead, an interesting conversation developed. It was a conversation in which we each learned something about how a systematic theologian and a biblical scholar look at the same question from different angles. It was a conversation that piqued my curiosity about this way of thinking about atonement and eventually led us to conclude that the atonement had implications we had not explicitly considered. It was a conversation that we together concluded was exactly the sort of thing Christians generally, and our community in particular, should be thinking and talking about. It is a conversation that is still ongoing and this book is part of that conversation. We invite you to be a part of it.

Atonement as Christian Threshold

The claim that the cross lies close to the heart of Christian theology is, perhaps, relatively uncontroversial. Early creeds refer to the crucifixion, and the church has focused its worship and liturgy on the cross for centuries.[2] However, in this book, we would like to claim more than that for the cross. We propose that it is among those truths without which we cannot think, reason or reflect in a distinctively Christian manner. If theology's primary way of being is 'reflective engagement with situations under the Gospel', then the cross is an indispensable element of such engagement.[3] More than that, this task is not limited to clergy or professional theologians. Reflection on life and faith in light of the claims of the Christian message is central to what believers are called to do and to be. The atonement constitutes, within Christian disciple-ship, what educational theorists call a 'threshold concept'.[4] This is an idea whose mastery opens up a way of thinking necessary for full functioning within an area of study, or in this case, within a community of living practice.

Teachers who write about threshold concepts often point out the metaphor in the concept's name. Thresholds are doorways. One must pass through to access what is beyond the doorway, and once one passes through, a new vista emerges.[5] Because they are foundational, threshold concepts change our perspective in a way that cannot be easily undone and show us connections we had not previously realized.[6] For the earliest Christians no less than for us, the cross represents the doorway to a transformed worldview. The New Testament shows us various key figures in early Christianity reflecting profoundly on how the world, life and faith must be reinterpreted in light of the cross.[7]

Along with radically impacting the whole of life, such a shift of worldview brings its own difficulties. Threshold concepts are potentially 'troublesome'.[8] As windows into a previously unac-cessed way of viewing a subject, they can be difficult to grasp and appear 'counter-intuitive'.[9] Certainly, within Christian tradition the cross stands as both 'stumbling-block' (1 Cor. 1:23) and subject of seemingly ceaseless speculative theology. It is an intellectual conundrum and foolishness (1 Cor. 1:18). We cannot articulate to our own satisfaction all of the details of how it is that Jesus' death and resurrection constitute our deliverance, though we can agree that they do. And, as this book proposes, our preoccupation with the important task of getting the details of the threshold itself right has meant that we have not stepped regularly and fully into the new way of viewing the world that the atonement offers us.[10] The goal of this volume is to engage the task of thinking under the influence of the gospel, especially as that gospel is expressed in the Christian doctrine of the atonement. We will not spend much time on the issue of which classical atonement theory offers the best explanation of the New Testament's testimonies; many such books have been written before this one.[11] Rather, our authors will contribute to a conversation about what it means to re-imagine the world, the cosmos, ourselves and each other in light of the atonement.

An Anti-Polemical Response to Polemical Approaches to the Atonement

It is impossible to read the Christian press or visit Christian websites without being aware of how divisive the doctrine of atonement has become. Steve Chalke's depiction of penal substitution as 'cosmic child abuse' has caused anger among some Christians while confirming the suspicions of others that all is not right with traditional Christian language about the cross.[12] The result has been a series of scholarly responses either questioning or defending the validity of penal substitution.[13] These are understandable developments but they cannot determine all that is said about the cross and its meaning for human beings.

The time is ripe to complement these recent polemical treatments of the cross with a consciously eirenic approach which bypasses controversy and seeks to identify areas of common ground. A vital grid for understanding the cross is that of a *gift* given by God to the church and the world. This way of conceptualizing the atonement is embedded in the scriptural witness and warrants investigation in the same way that other more contentious themes related to the cross need exploration. While argument and debate may shed light on the degree to which certain theological propositions about the atonement are justified, they do rather less to flesh out what else may have been accomplished by that ultimate act of self-giving love.

The perspective underlying this collection of essays is that the cross is multifaceted in its achievements and a rich gift to individuals and the world at large. It is a profound act whose contemplation will inspire faith and gratitude, and whose breadth and overall significance is not best grasped in the heat of battle. Thus we invite readers to lay to one side polemical considerations and to view the cross as the wide-ranging and far-reaching gift that it is. If current debates about the cross focus on its objective nature and the manner in which it has achieved the eternal salvation of individual souls (the vertical dimension, so to speak), then let us widen our purview so that we see its impact on human relationships, people groups and even the physical creation. This holistic approach allows us to think of the cross in wider categories than those defined by recent debate.

This book, and the mode of theology it engages, is not just, or even primarily, for the clergy and those who teach them, though it admittedly emerges from that context. Christian discipleship includes learning to think under the influence of the gospel and is something for all of us. Thus, atonement-shaped reflection on a whole range of issues facing our world is indispensable to Christian living in it.

An Integrative Approach

As we thought about how best to invite our community into the conversation, it struck me (Paddy) that what made this theme so relevant was its implications for many aspects of Christian life and mission. I approached Katie with an idea. Why not expand our annual Integrative Seminar into a multi-day event with key scholars addressing the question of how the cross spoke to their own areas of knowledge and concern. So, we began to brainstorm a list of things that could be re-imagined in the light of the cross. The cosmos and suffering emerged as major themes about which the cross has something to say, even if this is often overlooked in traditional atonement theology. We also recognized that the cross impacted on intensely personal matters such as shame and emotional woundedness, and thus was a much neglected pastoral tool. Finally, taking our lead from St Paul, we identified interpersonal issues such as gender relationships and conflict to which the cross supplied a way forward. Moreover, for some of these areas, such as reconciliation and ecumenism, our particular Irish location seemed to offer a distinctive and important window.[14]

In this way, the approaches of different disciplines became the crucial component in viewing the 'troublesome' concept of the cross in an integrative manner.[15] We also saw the work of the seminar, and thus the work of the volume that has grown out of it, moving outward from the cross to the ways the cross makes a difference to our Christian life and practice. However, we were always hopeful that the movement would not be solely in one direction. We hoped that by examining the cross from the perspective of our 'engaged theology', we might better understand its core meaning. Our commitment was that one should not start from purely philosophical theology and then move on to what often goes under the name of practical or pastoral theology.[16] Rather, both of these approaches enrich and inform each other. As the various essays point to the same theme from different angles, the cross becomes visible from many different perspectives. These perspectives together give us an increasingly clear picture of what the cross means and is. Thus, this discussion of the cross is more than the sum of its parts.

It was also clear that the integration we were aiming for was more than an interdisciplinary one. We did not just want to combine insights from different fields and perspectives. We wanted students to interact with the doctrine in a holistic way that engaged the heart as much as the head. As the seminar took shape, it became important to embed it within the prayer and worship life of the community. So we planned special services of worship themed around the various emphases of each day with the concluding daily activity being a celebration of the Eucharist. We also incorporated discussion questions, exercises and activities as opportunities to further integrate ideas presented in the lectures. We have included these prompts in the volume so that the individual reader or group working through the material may interact with them as tools for engaging the topic. Finally, it became clear that integration of the sort we were hoping for demanded space and dedicated time. We adapted a practice from our spirituality curriculum to create this intentional space – that of community silence. Each day during the seminar, one hour was set aside as reflective time. Ideas for working at integrating the day's focus both intellectually and spiritually were supplied. We have included a sampling of these suggestions at the end of each of the major sections of this book. Silence creates space for reflective Christians to allow God's Holy Spirit to put pieces together within them. It is a devotional practice, a way of spending time with God, and we offer it as a way into a properly holistic approach to Christian doctrine. It is all part of our claim that the devotional can inform the academic and vice versa.

The Scope of the Book

In its first major section, the book examines the theme of the cross and reality. An opening chapter by Prof. Stephen Williams lays the groundwork for many of the subsequent chapters. It gives an overview of the current state of atonement thinking in the academy. Williams introduces some of the classic definitions of the atonement and explores them, particularly in light of the contemporary concern about violence and its relationship to the cross. The chapter traces the history of these classic theories and highlights the importance of the idea of penal substitution to current discussion. The discussion continues with responses to Williams by Dr Richard Clutterbuck and Dr Cathriona Russell. The reality of the cross is then applied to the physical creation by Dr Ron Elsdon, who challenges the notion that God's eschatological purposes are concerned solely with the salvation of individual human beings. Thus, he explores the implications of redemption on a cosmic scale and introduces the notion that the transformation of the cosmos should be understood diachronically rather than synchronically. The section concludes with an essay by Prof. Richard Bauckham which examines the view that the cross is God's act of solidarity with all who suffer. Beginning with a brief overview of the history of discussion about theodicy, Bauckham makes the point that in the twenty-first century this conversation has focused primarily on the problem of natural evil. He deals with the gospel passion accounts that link the cross to suffering, particularly in their citation of the Psalms of Lament. He then considers the relevance of the incarnation and divine impassibility to any discussion of theodicy and the cross.

The second major section holds together around its relational emphasis. The 'Broken Relationships in a Fractured World' section begins with a chapter by Dr David Tombs, who draws upon his knowledge of conflict in Northern Ireland to explain the structural nature of violence and the need for reconciliation. In this context, the cross functions as a powerful dissuasive against the violence which is rooted in the dehumanization of the other. The section continues with a chapter by Dr Elaine Storkey on 'The Cross and the Reconciliation of Gender'. Beginning with the early feminist critique of androcentric readings of the cross, Storkey proceeds to suggest that some feminist rejection of the cross is unwarranted. She proposes that Christ's self-emptying at the cross opens the possibility of female embrace of the atonement and the healing of gender relationships. Next, the transcript of a dialogue between a leading Irish Roman Catholic theologian (Dr Con Casey) and a leading Irish-based Protestant theologian (Prof. Stephen Williams) raises the question of what hope the doctrine of the cross might offer for inter-church dialogue and common theological thinking. Finally, Dr Patrick McGlinchey explores the doctrine of eucharistic sacrifice as a possible barrier to ecumenical rapprochement and asks whether the theology of Joseph Ratzinger (Pope Emeritus Benedict XVI) offers a way forward.

The book takes a more personal turn in its final major section which focuses on 'Re-Imagining the Self in the Light of the Cross'. Dr Robin Stockitt's essay addresses an issue deeply rooted in the human condition but rarely discussed or acknowledged. In this chapter, he reflects on how the cross might function as an antidote to shame. Stockitt demonstrates how central that emotion is to human identity and how God's embrace of shame in the cross functions to restore the shamed. Picking up the emotional thread, Dr Katie Heffelfinger's chapter asks how a Christian and poetic approach to an iconic Old Testament atonement passage (Isaiah 52:13 – 53:12) can open out our imaginations and form our emotions. Finally, in a narrative vein, Dr Heather Morris reflects on the nature of personal healing and selfhood as viewed through the lens of the cross.

In the book's conclusion, the editors offer a synthesis of the major themes that emerge from reading the chapters in light of each other, and make some suggestions about how readers might draw upon the book in practical ministry, church mission and theological education.

SECTION 1

THE CROSS AND REALITY

It is to the Cross that the Christian is challenged to follow his master: no path of redemption can make a detour around it.[1]

1

WHERE ARE WE IN RELATION TO ATONEMENT?

Stephen N. Williams

Introduction

Some years ago, I exchanged correspondence with a prominent militant 'new atheist' scientist, during the course of which he asked a question to this effect: 'By what method do theologians settle their differences? Scientists have a method for doing so and this establishes the rationality of their discipline. Do theologians? If so, how do they proceed?' The implication was: they do not and, thus, theology is not a rational enterprise.

Waiving the question of the extent to which he was right in rela-tion to science, and so setting aside questions in the philosophy of science, one answer which I could have given him was: 'Theolo-gians have no such method; but, while that may tell you a lot about theologians, it actually tells you little about their subject-matter.' Of course, that answer might be sufficient of itself to establish clear water between theologians and scientists. However, whether or not it does and, if it does, what significance this has is not a matter for exploration here. If we treat as 'theologians' all those who so describe themselves, and treat as 'theology' all which goes under that name, we seem to have no possible way of resolving disagreements, even in principle. There is no agreement on what counts as Christian theology, let alone good theology. 'Theology' is the rubric under which we customarily name a particular kind of exercise, but, judged by the canons of academic practice, it is neither a coherent discipline nor even broadly a demarcated field. Surveying the whole theological landscape, with the bird's-eye view of an omniscient and omnipresent eagle, we might attempt to formulate a functioning general criterion for the validity of (Christian) theological statements by identifying a lowest common denominator along some such lines as: 'conformity to the memory of Jesus as liberator'. But, as there is no consensus on the edifying content of that memory or the material content of that liberation, the criterion is toothless, if criteria can be toothless.

I am merely calling it as it is, not as it should or must be.[1] My assignment in this chapter is to say something about the current state of writing on the atonement against its historical background and it can only be usefully said with reference to this backdrop. There are various theological discussions and various theological polemics going on and voices are raised, but there is no Theological Debate, as such, on the atonement, if we take the whole theological scene into account, for debate requires shared criteria and we do not have them. Nevertheless, it remains possible to pick out at least one topic, in connection with the atonement, which features relatively prominently on the contemporary theological scene. Accordingly, I shall do so. However, let us first step back in time.

The Shadow of Gustav Aulén

A volume by Gustav Aulén, published in 1930, has had a surprisingly good run for its money.[2] As Aulén saw it, two views of the atonement had held the field historically. On the one hand, atonement was a satisfaction made to God, a sacrificial self-offering by the Son to the Father, which remitted the debt incurred by humanity and was effective as substitution for that same humanity. On the other hand, atonement was a manifestation of divine love, climactically exemplified in the death of Christ, whose designed effect was to reconcile to God the wayward sinner who believes in and receives forgiving grace. The former is the 'objective' view: something is accomplished on the cross irrespective of our response, although it calls for our response. The latter is the 'subjective' view: there is no intra-divine transaction on the cross; atonement is effected in divine–human reconciliation. On the objective view, we receive by faith a reconciliation achieved; on the subjective view, we achieve reconciliation by faith. Both these theories have their origins in the Middle Ages, in the thought of Anselm (c.1033–1109) and of Abelard (1079–1142) respectively.

However, Aulén believed that there was a neglected third view, one that he found in the New Testament, Church Fathers and Luther. Like that of Anselm, this position sustained the objectivity of the atonement, but it neither bore the rational form of Anselm's theory nor concurred in its substantive notion of satisfaction. On the third view Aulén retrieved, the death of Jesus must be theologically interpreted inseparably from his incarnation, life, resurrection and exaltation, as far as its atoning significance is concerned. In all these things, Jesus Christ is victor over sin, death, the law, the Devil and the wrath of God, so *Christus Victor* names this view. In the patristic age, the work of atonement as understood here was typically set out in pictorial or mythological guise, which occasionally gave rise to lurid imagery and encouraged dismissal of their outlook in the form of rationalist Anselmian reaction, to which Abelard, in rational turn, then reacted. But the reaction was unjustified. If Anselm was wrong to treat the atonement in a rationalist way, Abelard was wrong to treat it in a subjective way.

This was Aulén's position in outline. I said that his treatment has had a surprisingly long run. His simple taxonomy is still significantly helping to order accounts of the atonement.[3] This is rather surprising because, first, Aulén's historical exposition was flawed and, second, alternative taxonomies with equal, if not greater, claim to helpfulness were subsequently paraded. On the first point: it is widely realized that there is an important distinction among schemes which Aulén bundled together under the Anselmian heading. Most significantly, Anselm did not teach a penal atonement; atonement is not viewed by him in terms of the expression of the penal wrath of God on the cross. In fact, he explicitly and calculatedly took a different course. He deliberately spoke of God's way of dealing with humanity, in Christ, as an *alternative* to punishment. Anselm's logic is this: humanity did not owe to God the death of a sinless person. However, Jesus Christ, the sinless one, who is God as well as man, died. By presenting to God on behalf of humanity something that it did not owe, Christ, as both representative of and substitute for sinful humans, cancelled the debt incurred by sin. This is satisfaction. Had there been no satisfaction on behalf of humanity, there would have been punishment. Since there was satisfaction, punishment does not enter into it. In Anselm's categories, Christ makes satisfaction for our sins rather than taking upon himself the punishment for our sins.[4] While remarking on history, we should add that there is an objectivity, in fact, a deep objectivity, in Abelard's view of the atonement. In the death of Jesus Christ, a new age is inaugurated – the age of the Spirit – and the death of Christ is the channel of entry for the Spirit into the world to bring about a new aeon, as objective as the entry of sin into the world through the transgression of Adam.[5]

What about the second point, concerning alternative taxonomies to that of Aulén? At least two others may be mentioned: that of Alan Richardson in *Creeds in the Making,* first published in the same decade as Aulén's work, and the one proposed in the older SCM *Dictionary of Christian Theology,* which Alan Richardson himself later edited.[6] Taking Aulén's work into account, Richardson, in his own volume, distinguished the 'satisfaction' from the 'penal' interpretation of the atonement, ranging alongside them the 'ransom' and 'moral' interpretations. So he came up with four 'theories'. In its article on the 'Atonement', the SCM *Dictionary* also produced four, but these were not quite the same: (a) the 'exemplarist' theory; (b) the 'classical' or 'dramatic'; (c) the 'juridical' (which again joined together the Anselmian and penal views) and (d) the 'sacrificial' theory which, according to the author of the article, was the only one systematically expounded in the New Testament (in the letter to the Hebrews). We are deliberately citing the older literature here but note that, in a recent defence of penal substitution, Stephen Holmes finds at least eight pictures of atonement in the New Testament.[7] In another context, we should need to explore the important distinction between theories and pictures. Our point at the moment is simply to remark on the rather surprising longevity of Aulén's scheme. Obviously, it has been widely felt that Aulén was onto something – that, at the least, thinking about the atonement is helpfully ordered by attending to this scheme, whose attraction presumably lies in its economy and the perceived inadequacy of the two notions which he rejects. Theology has changed a lot since Aulén wrote, and it has oxymoronically morphed into that generic formlessness to which I jauntily alluded at the start of this essay. Yet Aulén remains with us.

If we can identify a watershed in post-Aulénian twentieth-century western theology – a dangerous exercise when we are not long out of that century – presumably it is in the 1960s and early 1970s. Up till then, academic theology on the global scene, led by the West, was largely dominated by Germanophone initiatives. That changed. Latin American liberation theology came into prominence from Spanish and Portuguese-speaking lands in the southern hemisphere and other non-northern or non-western forms of liberation theology also began to feature on the scene. The 'liberation' label has been applied to various theological forms that have proliferated since then. Feminist, womanist, mujerista or Latino-feminist, gay, animal, and theologies which major on environmental or disability issues, for example, may in some respects be interpreted as species of the genus 'liberation theology' without undue reductionism, even if they do not go explicitly under that name. Hegel seems perspicaciously to have got it right as far as theology was concerned: 'World history is the progress of the consciousness of freedom.'[8] Germany and Switzerland have ceased to set the global theological pace for over a generation. But, when all this is said, if we may settle on one theme in relation to the atonement which is alive today, one which *both* emerges out of the morass of theologies in the early third millennium *and* is visibly connected with the Christian tradition, it is, I suppose, the theme of penal substitution. In relation to that question, Anselm, the Reformers and Aulén are alive on the contemporary scene albeit, in the first two cases, often on trial or, rather, indicted, tried, sentenced and under an edict of banishment.

Discussion of Penal Substitution

Discussion of penal substitution today largely pivots on the issues of violence and abuse. Supposing, for a moment, that we interpret penal substitution as meaning that the Father punished the Son for our sins in our place. (Whether or not this formulation does justice to the historical theological substance of the penal view, in what follows I describe the scene from the standpoint of detractors.) On this interpretation, the cross surely appears as the scene of paternal violence. Perhaps the most dramatic and almost certainly the most widely repeated expression of the protest against this view of the atonement is that it constitutes child abuse. Patriarchal male abuse of women has, of course, been a prominent theological and extra-theological subject of discussion for some time and it is in this context that the vocabulary of child abuse in relation to the atonement seems to have originated.[9] A penal substitutionary view of the atonement reflects – worse, undergirds; worse still, promotes – an oppressive and unjust social order, to put the matter with anodyne mildness. The violence which lies at its heart contrasts with the reconciling peace whose announcement and propagation lies at the heart of authentic Christianity. Thus, both the title and the content of a recent, lengthy volume on the atonement: *Stricken by God? Nonviolent Identification and the Victory of Christ*, is quite representative of much that is going on on the contemporary theological scene.[10] It advertises an ongoing 'Nonviolent Atonement Seminar' and, although described as offering a 'wide panorama of perspectives' over the course of its five hundred pages, there is unity in opposition to a penal view of atonement.[11]

In alighting on the question of violence, current debate on the atonement reflects a wider social debate or, at least, exchange. 'New atheism', for example, violently attacks the connection between religion and violence, which it regards as causal from the religious end. The cultural theory of René Girard remains influential and Charles Taylor, in his analysis of *A Secular Age*, is outstanding among those who try to interpret the perceived connections between religion and violence against a deep historical background.[12]

Charged as I am with the remit to be descriptive, let docile tractability mine outward vesture be.[13] That is appropriate enough. The tone in which we theologians sound forth on our subject-matter actually often demonstrates our deep alienation from it. In relation to the cross, you would think that human suffering alone, which, at the minimum, the cross most certainly depicts, would dispose us all to more humility and less stridency in salient respects.

In relation to the current argument over penal substitution, what must be underlined is that the argument is not, in the first instance, an argument over penal substitution. Rather, it is an argument over the nature of God and of sin. That is so in the case of many theologically fundamental arguments. Agreement on the nature of God and of sin may not entail one particular view of the atonement. But rejection of a particular account of God and of sin does entail rejection of a particular account or accounts of atonement. If there is one point at which Calvin might be expected to command a wide consensus in our day, it is where he launches his *Institutes* with the words: 'Nearly all the wisdom we possess, that is to say, true and sound wisdom, consists of two parts: the knowledge of God and of ourselves.'[14] He adds that, while they are 'joined by many bonds, which one precedes and brings forth the other is not easy to discern', a remark whose familiarity makes us liable to forget how deceptively interesting it is in the context of Calvin's theology. If we now turn to the question of penal substitution directly, we shall readily see that the underlying question is about God and sin. This is a truism, but it may be useful to remark on it.

It is par for the course for many advocates of penal substitution to distance themselves from what they insist is a caricature of it and this takes us back to the way in which we formulated penal substitution earlier. It is a formulation from which many advocates of penal substitution distance themselves. It is wrong, they say, to suggest that Father and Son are contrastingly disposed, the one being angry and hectoring, the other benign and complicit. Dispositionally, they are one. The Son does not voluntarily placate a legalistic, heavily frowning Father. 'God', a word often used interchangeably with the word 'Father', in the Christian tradition, initiated the atonement in mercy. In an e-mail which I received just before the conference at which the original version of this chapter was presented, the sender, a long-time believer in penal substitution, protested to me about a sermon in which the preacher had talked of 'God punishing Jesus'. An example of significant differences in the way in which penal substitution is understood by those who subscribe to some form of it is found in a fairly recent defence, much acclaimed in some conservative circles, by Jeffery, Ovey and Sach.[15] They list a number of defenders of penal substitution, three

of whom belong to the twentieth century: Martyn Lloyd-Jones,
James Packer and John Stott.[16] But the three most theologically
weighty twentieth-century defences known to me – those of James
Denney, Emil Brunner and Karl Barth – are absent.[17] What does this
signify? It signifies the fact that 'penal substitution' actually covers
a number of different positions which vary very greatly indeed,
and so we must ask whether the Jeffery, Ovey and Sach volume
is not a defence of merely *one* of its forms.[18] Are we not scanning a
very broad umbrella?

Substitution in Perspective

An investigation of its various forms would take us into greater
detail than an introduction of this kind permits. But the basal
principle of penal substitution was probably as well expressed
by James Denney as by anyone. Jesus Christ 'puts away' God's
condemnation of our sin:

> by bearing it. He removes it from us by taking it upon Himself. And
> He takes it upon Himself, in the sense of the New Testament, by sub-
> mitting to that death in which God's condemnation of sin is expressed.
> In the Bible, to bear sin is not an ambiguous expression. It means to
> underline its responsibility and to receive its consequences: to say that
> Christ *bore* our sins is precisely the same thing as to say that He *died*
> for our sins; it needs no other interpretation, and admits of no other.[19]

Inasmuch as judgement is involved on the cross, there is a penal
element; inasmuch as we deserve a judgement that it is God's
design to spare us on account of the cross, it is substitutionary.
But there lies a presupposition behind this account in any of its
classical forms which alters its whole aspect, as it is often depicted
today. It is that Jesus Christ is very God, not just very man –
homoousios, of one being, with the Father. In a passage frequently
cited in defence of penal substitution, Paul emphasized that 'God
was *in* Christ reconciling the world to Himself' (2 Cor. 5:19 [NAS,
emphasis mine]).[20] Penal substitution may be right or it may be
wrong; what it never has been, in the Christian tradition, is an
interpretation of the cross which depicts God as a divine Father

and Christ as a subordinate, human Son. To take seriously the deity of Christ, something fundamental in the tradition in which penal substitution developed, is to affirm that the Son of God who paid the penalty for human sin is one with the Father. Whether or not its critics are right to oppose penal substitution, the Trinitarianism which undergirds it seems to be forgotten by some opponents of penal violence who appear to treat Jesus as purely human, even if an exceptional human. At the same time, it may be granted that its defenders may sometimes have been guilty of couching penal substitution in terms that logically undermine or obfuscate this presupposition in their exposition, especially in popular presentation and preaching.

As the Trinitarian background makes all the difference to the way in which we understand penal substitution, so does human experience of forgiveness. Defenders of penal substitution in some form have sometimes emphasized the substitutionary dynamics of inter-human forgiveness, quite apart from any religious dimension or any connection with atonement. As Horace Bushnell, often classed as a theological liberal, used to emphasize: substitutionary forces are abundantly in operation in human affairs.[21] An example may be useful. Supposing I suddenly lash out verbally at a colleague (let us call him Boso) with a most hurtful and palpably false allegation. I then retract it and ask for his forgiveness. He graciously gives it and, despite the damage done, receives me back into friendship. But it happens again. And again, over a sustained period of time. Before long, witnesses might reason as follows.

'Now there is something amiss here in Boso's response. While we admire him for his gentle and forgiving nature and cannot hold a candle to him in that respect, there is such a thing as an appropriate personal dignity, beyond what Bishop Joseph Butler used to call "reasonable self-love". Is that dignity rightly preserved and protected by the way in which he consistently responds to Stephen Williams? It is not just a matter of proper and healthy self-respect. There is a wider moral order out there' (here the witnesses all lapse into mouldy old jargon) 'and it is not well served by his repeated forgiveness of Williams. We do not quite know how to formulate this, but Boso surely needs to uphold some principle here for the principle's sake – which is, in fact, for the world's sake, not just for his own sake, for we always have to consider

the wider consequences of what we do or fail to do. We realize
that some people will defend the moral propriety of resentment
on Boso's part. We realize also that, on the other hand, others will
say that resentment is never right and that a forgiving disposition
is what is appropriate.[22] But we all agree that he should not go
as far as to repeatedly take Stephen Williams back into genuine,
unconditional friendship. A proper self-respect and respect for
the public display of right and wrong should mean that he keeps
some distance from Williams. Williams cannot just flout the moral
law like that, a moral law which pertains to relationships and
which is anything but impersonal law. Actually, for his absolutely
outrageous behaviour, Williams would be paying a terribly small
price for his wrongdoing if Boso insisted that actual reconciliation
was impossible unless Williams both categorically desisted from
such behaviour and apologized for it.'

But now, these spectators of the drama learn that Boso has both a
far healthier self-respect than does anybody else, including themselves, and that he has an infinitely deeper passion for what we
are calling 'the moral order'. So how do they explain his conduct?
Well, they might be inclined to conclude that the moral order
is being upheld in a way not visible to us; but they might also
become very dimly aware of a *possibility* in relation to forgiveness
when someone suggests that perhaps the penalty for Williams'
wrongdoing is actually being paid, borne by Boso in a way that
we cannot understand, although we hope that somehow, somewhere, this will be publicly displayed and explained. Boso may
be deliberately taking on himself the consequences of Williams'
wrongdoing. Perhaps a 'deep magic' is at work here – dimensions
abounding which are real, but hard to apprehend, except through
vague, but not vacuous, imagination.[23]

My tale is not far-fetched. It is actually in line with what the
prophet Hosea is trying to get across in the case, not of slander, but
of adultery, when the prophet, representing YHWH to the people,
bears the penalty for another's fault.[24] Of course, there is bound to
be a disanalogy between inter-human experience and any valid
perspective on the atonement. But, if, in human experience, we
often pay the price for another's wrongdoing, what accounts for
the fact that some experience a *visceral* opposition to this dimension, which lies at the heart of penal substitution? Supposing I

believe that God is holy and transcendent, as well as merciful, and that sin is personal dishonour (as it would be even in the case of another human being) as well as a breach of cosmic order (as it seems to be even in the case of another human being). Why, then, will *all* forms of penal substitution be emotionally distasteful? What is the problem? The problem presumably lies with the very conceptions of God and of human sin which undergird a penal substitutionary account in the first place. Guilt is hard to admit, unless I can do so under self-respecting, controlled conditions.

My objective here is not a defence of penal substitution.[25] What I am trying to illustrate is this: the fact that Anselm and the penal view are closely connected in the course of criticism, despite the fact that Anselm's view is non-penal, suggests that it is, indeed, the notions of God and of sin that underlie views of the atonement that cause the problems.[26] It is a truism worth underlining. Anselm's view is conceivably viewed as substitutionary, but it is not penal. He configures the notions of God and sin by emphasizing God's majesty, which embraces both a created honour personally due and a just order divinely created. On this account, there is an impossible impropriety involved in God's straightforwardly forgiving sin with a word of the mouth. What seems to be troubling people here is the way in which Anselm hauls in notions of divine honour and sin's heinousness. An acknowledgement that his view is non-penal will not, I think, much modify the objection to his position on the atonement, for the Anselmian connection between God and sin, expressed in his view of the atonement, remains objectionable.

However, if Anselm's account lacks any suggestion of divine violence, by virtue of its non-penal nature, we have to go beyond our concentration on underlying notions of God and of sin if we are to address the specifically violent element putatively involved in penal views of the atonement. Many of us who lack direct experience of violence and do not love well enough to try to enter into others' experience have no idea at all of the horror of violence. My wife is a trauma counsellor, who has heard things that she would not want to repeat to me even if her professional code permitted it. But I know that violence is unspeakably dark, including that violence which is inflicted by men on women and children because they are women and children. God, according to John, is

the opposite – light (1 John 1:5). As the Bible depicts it, grief over
human violence leads God to the verge of active regret that he had
ever formed humanity (Gen. 6:6). The prophets long for peace,
shalom. Within this vast *inclusio*, the Hebrew Scriptures tell their
tale. Given the presence of divine violence in that tale, we may
be perplexed by the *inclusio*, but, however we interpret matters,
Israel, as part of its testimony, is seeking to convey the extremity
of the moral and emotional distance between God and violence.

Conclusion

In conclusion, I want to lapse into substantive judgement. The
problem of interpreting the Hebrew or Christian Scriptures is not
helped by trivializing violence. This occurs in a prominent contribution to the current debate and one which makes some positive
use of penal substitution. I am thinking of Hans Boersma's qual-
ified defence in his volume on *Violence, Hospitality and the Cross*.
To my mind, Boersma works with an impossibly broad notion of
violence implicit in a programmatic statement: 'All activities that
we undertake in our present historical circumstances are indeed
necessarily accompanied by inhospitality, by a kind of violence.'[27]
Violence is dark, but its darkness is lightened, rather than deep-
ened, when we interpret as violence anything which disturbs our
autonomy, as Boersma apparently does. If we accuse of violence
the parent who vigorously snatches the toddler from the fire into
which he is proposing to put his hand or the parent who insists
that her toddler goes out with her shoes on, rather than in bare
feet on glass-specked sand, or if I accuse of violence a stranger
when he saves me from drowning by grabbing me by the scruff of
the neck, we are trivializing the issue. I do not underestimate the
need to be sensitive to people's constructions of violence. I have
a highly intelligent, virulently anti-Christian, disabled friend who
went ballistic once when I expressed my judgement that she was
mistaken on some issue. It was only when we talked it through,
in tense and terse e-mail exchanges (the only practicable way),
that she explained to me how she associated my sort of argumen-
tative approach with assault of the kind which, I fear, she had
experienced all too often on her body when she was young.[28] No

one who has encountered the abuse of women or children will sit lightly to the criticism of penal substitution as involving divine violence, however wrong-headed they judge that criticism to be.[29]

So what should we say of violence in relation to penal substitution? In the New Testament narratives, God does not command the violence of the cross. It may be foreknown; it may be turned to God's purposes; it may even be the object of that concurrent divine action to which both historian and prophet testify in the Hebrew Scriptures. But, in that case, it follows a pattern with which we are familiar from the Hebrew Scriptures, whereby God harnesses human evil to saving, beneficent purposes, not contingently, it is true, but without being the cause of the forces of violence which scar the moral world. It is possible that, in the economy of salvation, an experience of separation is permitted which enables the Son to identify with the condemnation of a humanity which deserves it at the hand of God. If so, what this meant for God the Father is beyond imagination but, if it is possible to tread on this holy ground, it is surely theologically inconceivable that what the Son experienced is not experienced also by the Father.[30] If bitter accusation be levelled against penal substitution, it should be that of masochism, and not child abuse.[31] It is not an accusation that should be sustained. And, if it is, critics will presumably then accuse penal substitution of promoting a culture of self-harm. It suffices to say that it is possible to maintain belief in a form of penal substitution that does not attribute to God paternal violence on the cross in the way commonly depicted by its critics. If we can secure this point, there may be no Theological Debate, but the occasional theological discussion or polemic may be better shaped.

DOES CHRISTIANITY REALLY NEED A DOCTRINE OF THE ATONEMENT?

Richard Clutterbuck

Nearly thirty-five years ago, in what now seems to have been a last flowering of liberal Anglican theology, Maurice Wiles (then Regius Professor of Divinity at Oxford) wrote an essay on the theme of 'Christianity without Incarnation?'[1] That essay, and those of the other contributors to *The Myth of God Incarnate*, argued that the traditional doctrine of the incarnation was ill-founded in terms of Scripture and relied too heavily on a metaphysical framework that was no longer tenable. We could, suggested Wiles, get along pretty well as Christians without the baggage of this traditional, but increasingly embarrassing, doctrine. Wiles and his colleagues came under heavy fire from a wide range of Christian theologians and their volume now reads like an interesting, but not terribly relevant, footnote to the history of twentieth-century theology. The general judgement has been that Christianity without a doctrine of incarnation is not really Christianity at all, a judgement underlined by the resurgence of Trinitarian theology in recent years.

Now, as it happens, I agree wholeheartedly with Wiles' critics. However, I do think it a worthwhile exercise to ask questions about the necessity and centrality of areas of Christian doctrine. Hence the title of this short piece: 'Does Christianity really need a doctrine of the atonement?'

More specifically, the question I want to raise is this: are the forms of atonement doctrine that have developed in Western Christianity during the last millennium required by the Scriptures and early Christian tradition, or do they distract us from the heart of the Christian gospel? To some this will seem as outrageous as asking whether we can get along without the incarnation. But that, I believe, is not so. Although atonement theology is at the heart of evangelical Christianity and has been prominent throughout Western Christendom, not all Christian traditions and not every Christian epoch has had this emphasis.[2] Perhaps there are alternatives to this way of construing the significance of the death of Jesus. Let me explain why I think this is an important question.

I start with a cultural rather than a strictly theological observation: the passion and death of Jesus began to dominate western culture during the later Middle Ages and it has left as its legacy a pervading religious culture of suffering and death.[3] The fascination with the gruesome violence and intense suffering of the passion of Christ, which is today characterized by Mel Gibson's now infamous film, was expressed in innumerable ways in the late medieval centuries.[4] Paintings of the crucified Jesus, increasingly realistic and harrowing, featured in altar pieces, frescoes and illuminated manuscripts. Carvings of wood and stone illustrating the passion adorned Christian buildings and homes.[5] Passion plays outside the church and liturgical ritual within it both conveyed the dramatic cruelty of the crucifixion, while literary depictions are found in books of meditations, and in poems and hymns. Rood screens made the crucifix the visual focus of church buildings as art increasingly emphasized the human compassion and suffering expressed by the crucified Jesus. *The Dream of the Rood* and Julian of Norwich's *Revelations of Divine Love* are just two of the best-known literary works on the passion from this period, while the *Stabat Mater* – the intensely emotional meditation on the mother of Jesus standing at the foot of the cross – has inspired countless musical settings, right up to the present.[6]

Protestants may be tempted to point out, with just a hint of smugness, that their cross is empty, allowing them to concentrate on the risen, rather than the crucified, Saviour. Yet this is disingenuous, for non-visual devotion still keeps the cross occupied rather than empty. The Bach Passions, by any standards a high point of

Protestant culture, provide intense devotional identification with
the suffering of Jesus on the cross. Take, for instance, the chorale,
O hilf, Christe, which pleads for the believer to be transformed
through looking intently on the crucified and dying Jesus.

We could find similar sentiments in Stainer's *Crucifixion*, one
of the most popular choral works of the late Victorian era, which
often alternated with Maunder's *Olivet to Calvary* in the Passion-
tide repertoire of British Nonconformist choirs. On a more popular
level, the crucifixion is central to many of the hymns of the nine-
teenth-century author, Fanny Crosby,[7] as well as the contemporary
evangelical songs of Stuart Townend.[8] In Protestant culture, too,
the cross is full and Jesus is, as it were, still suspended in suffering.

This cultural fixation on the suffering and death of Christ (and
of course I have referred only to a tiny fraction of this output) has
its counterpart in the theologies of the cross that emerged and, in
a sense, competed during the same period and in later centuries.
While the theology of the earlier centuries of the Middle Ages still
focused mainly on the cross as victory (and still does in such a
late work as *The Dream of the Rood*), later periods saw a flowering
of alternatives. Among these are what have become the usual
suspects in a class on the atonement in any basic course on Christian doctrine: Anselm and the satisfaction of an unpayable debt of
honour; Julian of Norwich and her vision of the crucified's compassionate love; Abelard and Christ's sacrificial example; Luther's
demand for a '*theologia crucis*'; and of course Calvin and Christ
as the innocent punished in our place. This tradition is shared by
Catholic and Protestant alike. Even more recent theology, such as
the popular and influential *The Crucified God* by Jürgen Moltmann,
tends to remain firmly within this culture of suffering and death,
even while critiquing some of its earlier expressions.[9]

It is worth noting that this focus on the suffering of the crucified
has seeped out of the churches into western culture as a whole
and become part of what has sometimes been called 'the myth of
redemptive violence'.[10] It often finds expression in war memorials,
where the frequent inscription, 'Greater love hath no man than
this, that a man lay down his life for his friends', associates the
suffering of the fallen with the death of Christ on the cross. It also
comes through in the critics of war; think of Wilfred Owen's World
War One poem about a shell-shattered wayside crucifix in which

Christ's suffering is transposed to the battlefield.[11] In Ireland, this association between the cross of Christ and the violent spilling of blood for a political cause is deeply embedded in both the Republican and Loyalist traditions. Of course, the abuse of a theological idea need not necessarily count against its proper use, yet Christians have not been entirely innocent of the crime of employing theological ideas for profoundly unchristian ends.

So pervasive is this culture of the suffering and dying Jesus and its accompanying atonement theology that it is tempting to take it for granted and to think that this is the way it has always been, that this is Christianity, plain and simple. Yet there is an argument that this is not so, that the early church approached things differently and that Eastern Christianity has never bought into this way of understanding Christ's role in salvation.

The case for a Christianity without atonement theology is made with some style by Rebecca Ann Parker and Rita Brock in their recent book, *Saving Paradise: How Christianity Traded Love of This World for Crucifixion and Empire.*[12] Their opening sentences are nothing if not arresting: 'It took Jesus a thousand years to die. Images of his corpse did not appear in churches until the tenth century.'[13] Their thesis, which I have to admit is pretty one-sided, suggests that early Christianity was essentially life-affirming and focused on the transformation of this life in the light of the resurrected Jesus. This, they say, is the reason why it is virtually impossible to find any visual representation of the crucifixion from the first millennium but easy to find pictures of new life and of paradise. They ask: 'What led Western Christianity to replace resurrection and life with a crucifixion-centred salvation and to relegate paradise to a distant after-life?'[14] And their answer is this: Christianity's increasing collusion with violence through forced conversions, the Crusades and almost perpetual warfare. Their conclusion, not surprisingly, is that Christianity would be better off without atonement theology; it would be more life-affirming and less collusive with the world's violence. I have chosen to look at Parker and Brock because they represent a radical questioning of the Western tradition. There are, of course, plenty of contemporary critiques of this or that version of atonement theology, in particular about the divine violence they might imply. They are important, and they are dealt with elsewhere in this volume. The question that Parker and Brock present so sharply is this: is the atonement really a divine gift or is it a human construct that masks rather than reveals the salvation offered in Christ?

Now, having posed the question, I am not about to take Parker and Brock's answer at face value. I should at least point out some of the areas where they deserve a robust critique. First, the absence of crucifixion imagery from the first millennium is not quite as complete as they would have us imagine. Even in the West, the doors of the fifth-century church of Santa Sabina in Rome seem to depict the crucified Christ, set between the two thieves,[15] while Irish high crosses from the late first millennium feature aspects of Christ's suffering.[16] And in Eastern Christianity, in the period after the iconoclasm controversy, the plain iconoclast cross was gradually replaced by icons of the crucifixion, showing each of Christ's feet separately nailed to the cross. There is also more than one explanation for the rarity of crucifixion scenes in early Christian art; while there was indeed an emphasis on healing and on the renewed life that Christ brings, there was also the sheer disgust within Roman society at the sight of a body hanging on a cross. Even for Christians that disgust took some time to wear off and probably only did so long after actual crucifixions ceased to be commonplace. Furthermore, Parker and Brock cannot be allowed to get away with their assertion that the dominance of the suffering, crucified Jesus in medieval Europe was entirely reflective of and collusive with an age of violence. Surely it had as much to do with a sense of the compassion of God for a world of pain as it did with an idea of God 'joining in' or underwriting the violence of the world. The pastoral letters of St Anselm and the pastoral compassion of Julian's *Revelations of Divine Love* link the crucifixion, not with a divine legitimization of human violence, but with God's profound and costly desire to bring humanity into deep friendship with the Trinity. Finally, we need to note that Parker and Brock are not much concerned with the Bible as the basis for Christian doctrine. By contrast, those who see themselves working in the mainstream of Christian theology (be it from a Catholic, Orthodox or Protestant perspective) will want to take seriously the place of the passion and death of Christ both in the narrative of the gospels and within the exhortations of the epistles.

Nevertheless, the question I posed at the beginning is a real one, and those of us, myself included, nurtured in the cross-centred culture of Western Christendom, need to broaden the perspective within which we discuss the theology of the cross. I, who have Bach's Passions and several contemporary passion settings on my iPod, who have a collection of crucifixion paintings on my computer and a file full of poetry on the same theme, have concluded that this concentration may not be quite as healthy as I once thought. A theology narrowly focused on the cross is not good Christian theology because it fails to do justice to the full story of salvation history. We need to read the Scriptures, not just through the eyes of the Reformers and their late-medieval predecessors, but also through the eyes of the early Christian theologians and their successors in Eastern Christianity.

Within the limitations of this brief essay, let me suggest a few points where this perspective will lead us.

First, we need to set the cross within the two great pillars of what Christian doctrine affirms of Jesus Christ. These are his incarnation and his resurrection. We can and should affirm that the incarnation, not the crucifixion, is the foundational fact of Christianity and therefore (according to the early Fathers as well as the Eastern tradition) the chief means of our salvation. *Kai ho logos sarx egeneto* ('and the Word became flesh', John 1:14) marks the decisive and incomparable gift of God. The eternal Word comes, not to die, but to live and to give eternal life. That it is the incarnate Word who is crucified on Calvary gives the cross its theological significance, but it is the incarnation itself that is the decisive salvific event.[17] Hence Irenaeus' theology of recapitulation, in which Christ's journey of holy obedience reverses the disaster of the fall, and Gregory of Nazianzus' claim that 'the unassumed is the unhealed'. The christological debates of the first five centuries were essentially debates about salvation. The other side of this is that, although the cross may be a pivotal moment in the story of God's salvation through Jesus Christ, it is not the climax of the story. Just as the cross only has significance because of the incarnation, so it also requires the powerful victory over death signified by the resurrection. It is, after all, the resurrected life of Christ to which Christians aspire, even if this means being united with Christ in his death. Significantly, the Eucharist in Eastern Christianity is neither the sacrifice of the Roman Catholic Mass, nor the memorial of the Protestant Lord's Supper; it is a stepping into the resurrected life of heaven. To quote a contemporary Orthodox theologian: 'the crucifixion must not be subjected to the sacrificial logic of speculation . . . or in any theology that makes of the cross a necessary moment for God, a taking into himself of suffering and death, because Easter unsettles every hermeneutics of death, every attempt to make death a place of meaning.'[18]

Second – and as Stephen Williams helpfully points out in his chapter – whatever happens on the cross must be an act of the triune God; it must in no way set the Father against the Son or the Son against the Father. All the acts of God are the actions of the whole Trinity. This is one reason why I have difficulty with those song lyrics that imply that God the Father turned away from Jesus on the cross.[19] It is also why I wish I could stop people saying 'the body of Christ, broken for you' as they give out the bread at the Eucharist. Both expressions seem to me to do an injustice both to the biblical witness to the unity of the Father and Son and to the more developed doctrine of the Trinity. It is striking that Augustine, who is so often blamed for introducing atonement theology in its juridical sense, is quite sparing in his references to the cross in his preaching. The cross is often cited as the sign of Christ's deep humility and of his sacrificial love, even as an example for Christians to follow. Only occasionally in his sermons does Augustine dwell on the cross as a focus for the Christian understanding of salvation, and even then he is anxious to understand it in the context both of the whole of Christ's life and of the whole work of the Trinity.[20] It is surely no accident that the historic creeds deal much more emphatically with the doctrines of the incarnation and Trinity than they do with the theological significance of Christ's death. Of course, that is partly because these were the two areas then in most dispute, but it is also a reflection of the doctrinal priorities in the patristic church.

Finally, the question with which I began ought, I hope, to make us cautious about one way in which traditional atonement theology is frequently transposed in contemporary thought. This is to see the cross as God's embracing, and identification with, human suffering. Bonhoeffer's cry that 'only a suffering God can help' has been taken all too literally in much modern theology, not least among those who want to see the cross in relation to the evil of human violence and the traumas faced in pastoral ministry. Jürgen Moltmann's *The Crucified God* urged Christian theology to abandon what he called 'classical theism' for a more thoroughly cross-shaped understanding of God. Only in this way, he argues, can the Christian God have any relevance for a world that is so imbued with cruelty and suffering. In this he has been followed by many others, not least in the world of feminist theology[21] and pastoral theology.[22] In one sense this can be seen as an attempt to avoid the pitfalls of much traditional atonement doctrine, with God as the victim rather than the perpetrator of violent punishment. However, it shares many of the same risks as the various forms of Western atonement theology; at worst it produces an anthropomorphic view of God that valorizes human suffering rather than delivers new life.[23] A recent Orthodox contribution to a symposium on the theme of 'non-violent atonement' critiques the Western tradition of juridical atonement and then goes on to develop this positive statement: 'the holy Cross remains "*from ages unto ages*" a symbol of life eternal through Christ's exquisite sacrifice. In no way does it symbolize death nor does it imply an act of atonement for everlasting human guilt. Rather, the Cross and Resurrection represent for all mankind the same potential "sonship" with God that is enjoyed eternally by Christ.'[24] God's gift in Jesus Christ, in other words, is the gift of peace and of a life that encounters violence without being overcome, defeated or changed by it.

Do we really need a doctrine of the atonement? Yes, I believe we do, for the one who was given as 'God with us' was also given up to death for us. But a theology of the death of Christ must always be subservient to a theology of his life. Karl Barth reminded us that God's first word and last word to humanity is always 'yes' and that any divine 'no' has to be seen in that light.[25] Similarly, however important, the atoning death of Jesus is bracketed by his birth and resurrection: it is not the first or last thing we should say about him.

RECONCILIATION BETWEEN BLAME AND LAMENT

Cathriona Russell

That Jesus died for our sins is a shared aspect of Christian faith and one that unites Christians. Scripture tells us how this was achieved, that his death was a payment for sin and that it restored the distorted relationship between God and humanity. Nevertheless, although it is a shared doctrine, there 'has been much disagreement concerning the specific nature of atonement.'[1] In his chapter Prof. Williams traces three traditional models for atonement and reconciliation in the theological tradition. The central mainstream model for both Protestantism and Catholicism is the frequently misunderstood satisfaction theory of Anselm of Canterbury (1033–1109), which later influenced Aquinas and the Reformers alike.[2] A second model is that of Peter Abelard (1079–1142) who interpreted atonement not from the point of view of payment to God but its converse, as a manifestation of divine love. Third, Prof. Williams brings us to a neglected model, one that dominated the work of the early Church Fathers, the ransom model of *Christus Victor*, the victory of Christ over the powers that hold humankind in bondage.

As Danaher recounts, in one version of *Christus Victor* Satan held all human beings captive. God could not use violence to liberate humanity – since humanity had gone over to the Devil freely – so God handed Jesus over to Satan as ransom.[3] Anselm objected to this view because he argued that Satan had no claim over human beings: neither the Devil nor human beings belong to anyone but God, and neither stands outside God's power.[4] Abelard, too, argued that the payment was made not to the Devil but to God. However, he argued that Anselm's position pictured God as vengeful. From the perspective of divine love Abelard suggested that it is not God but human beings who required the death of Jesus in so far as they needed to see the extent of God's love for them.[5] As Prof. Williams suggests, all later theories of atonement are variations on one of these three major approaches, notwithstanding their strengths and weaknesses. Each throws light on the nature of God, human finitude and frailty, and on how we narrate and conceive of evil and suffering in Christian anthropology.

Having examined these models, Williams concedes, as we must, that the dominant interpretation of atonement that later emerged from this plurality – atonement as penal substitution, Christ punished for the sins of humanity – needs much translation and has been under scrutiny since the nineteenth century. It presents a concept of God that implies that his honour and wrath is greater than his love, and seems to disrupt the hope that 'atonement reveals God's presence with us in our sinfulness'.[6] In its connotation, if not in its intention, the word 'atonement' still carries with it the idea of retribution and possibly even revenge, the threat of violence that Prof. Williams referred to. Even its synonym, reconciliation – which is generally understood more positively especially in the context of post-conflict resolution – can still fall short. It can imply no more than a rebalancing of the account.[7] Although balancing the account is an important aspect of justice, neither of these interpretations gives us a picture of the restitution of a flourishing and bountiful relationship with God, something that I suspect was intended, in whatever way they understood the flourishing life, by Anselm and Abelard, and indeed Aquinas and Luther in their turn.

Atonement and reconciliation point us therefore, as Prof. Williams reminds us, beyond penal substitution to the nature of God and of sin. The traditional language of sin in its turn both transmits and conceals the tensions between these different aspects of the doctrine of atonement and reconciliation. It has, Hermann Häring argues, 'constricted Christian anthropology and in modern times has led to a split between philosophy and theology'.[8] In addition, the Augustinian heritage in relation to sin has been eroded in several directions; through a decentralization of Western theology – the doctrine has never been accepted by the theologians of the Eastern churches; through a re-evaluation of what it means to suffer and to cause suffering; and through a reassessment of the cross as a scene of penal violence, particularly in light of the barbarism of the twentieth century. Can there be a non-violent atonement? Are God's love and his wrath to be integrated by turning to the inner relations of the Trinitarian God, despite the attendant danger of making violence a divine attribute? Or do we return to the ancient theodicy that suggests that God will harness evil for the good? These and other questions are raised anew as we re-examine the traditional models.

In order to reinterpret, we need to situate the doctrine in light of contemporary understandings of evil, suffering and sin and in relation to the pressing needs of our time, crucially in conflict resolution, but no less urgently in relation to a sustainable life together on this planet.

Evil as a Challenge for Philosophy and Theology

First, it is necessary to acknowledge that evil is not just a problem for theology but also one for philosophy. If we interpret evil, as Paul Ricoeur does, as the suffering we cause to others and which we ourselves must endure, it is a problem therefore, too, even for the new atheisms that are so quick to make a causal link between violence and the religions.[9] Prof. Williams recalls in his opening the challenge levelled at theology by Richard Dawkins among others, the accusation that the religions drive violent conflict in part because they have no (rational) means to settle their differences. This charge glosses over the reality of evil in human experience. Ricoeur opens his essay, 'Evil, a Challenge to Philosophy and Theology', with this persuasive broadside: 'That both philosophy and theology encounter evil as a *challenge* unlike any other, the greatest thinkers in both these disciplines are willing to admit.'[10]

Christianity did not invent evil and suffering, although it could be said that Augustine has given us an understanding of evil before God (sin) that has undoubtedly governed Latin western anthropology, history, art and literature, which continues to fascinate and repel in perhaps equal measure.[11]

> Augustine, who reflects at length on creation and the fall in paradise, on the human heart and social relationships, and who wrote intensively about God's grace in Christ now ties these individual elements together in a rationally conclusive package . . . Anyone who wants to interpret this positively will praise the theoretical compactness and efficacy of Augustine's theory. Those who have difficult[y] with it will point out that in this theory Augustine is treating a highly complex myth as a rationally compelling statement.[12]

Augustine's view of sin is 'an exaggeration', in that he forced a reconciliation between individual responsibility and the question of the origins of evil in the cosmos. He transposed the cosmic dualism he had rejected in Manichaeism onto the sphere of human action and responsibility without remainder. His aesthetic theodicy highlights the aspect of culpability, of blame, but not that of innocent suffering, of lament.[13]

As a corollary to Ricoeur's argument – that philosophy and anthropology have to face the challenge posed by evil and suffering – we likewise find that the other religions too also know an 'essential sin'.[14] It is true, as Häring argues, that not every religion might agree on the terminology of 'sin', but every religion is able to express the fact that human existence is bound up with evil. Häring concludes that evil is a common human problem; only after that is it a problem for theology. Evil and suffering therefore, as a consequence, pose a problem for all of our anthropologies.

Evil as a Challenge for Christian Anthropology

How we understand the relationship between evil and suffering will profoundly influence our understanding of atonement and reconciliation. Evil as wrongdoing and evil as suffering belong to two different categories according to Ricoeur: that of blame and that of lament. We are to blame, in that we must take responsibility for the suffering we cause, but we also lament because of the suffering which we undergo: 'blame [he says] makes culprits

of us, lament reveals us as victims.'[16] Evil as lament befalls us, we
do not make it happen and it has many causes: 'the adversity of
physical nature, illness, the infirmities of body or mind, or afflic-
tion produced by the death of loved ones, the perspective of our
own mortality, affronts to our dignity.'[17]

Blame and lament are inextricably linked to one another. Despite
the polarity, these two phenomena are intertwined. And the relationship is not straightforward: for example, punishment for evil,
as Ricoeur points out, can itself be a form of suffering; guilt can
entail the feeling of being seduced by overwhelming powers: a
'strange experience of passivity, at the very heart of evildoing,
making us feel ourselves to be victims in the very act that makes
us guilty.'[18] Theologically, we can say that we are both sinful and
sinned against, but that also means that we are faced with the realization that this is not only about individual culpability; we also
have to take responsibility for inherited injustices that are not of
our own making.

How should we relate this analysis of blame and lament to our
discussion of reconciliation and atonement in pastoral practice?
Any teaching on reconciliation should reflect the pre-established
basic structure set down by the biblical testimony. There are two
aspects to that structure according to Ullrich. The message of
reconciliation and the cross spell the end to every sacrificial cult,
every kind of self-justification and every duplicitous arrange-
ment.[19] That is the first aspect. The second is that they also open
up the possibility of a new life in self-surrender, a new justice
and a new relationship between God and humankind and among
humans.[20] Reconciliation changes the state of enmity and establishes peace, and offers the way of hope as a firm guide. This
reframes our pastoral response, not only asking how reconciliation was achieved but also working from a perspective that it is
possible, working from the perspective of what God has already
done in Christ. How should we respond to God's universal offer
of salvation in this now-but-not-yet, in the context of our human
experience of both blame and lament?

The early church, Anselm and Abelard each offer us a response
in their time, a response, not a timeless solution to the question
of sin and suffering. We can no longer talk easily about exchange
formulas or ransom or satisfaction or later of penal substitution

without a great deal of elaboration and translation. Not because evil is not a reality – clearly Ricoeur puts it emphatically back on the map – but because we have different interpretations of suffering from that of classical theology, from that which has gone before, in relation to the impassibility of God, for example. The question is about how to find ways to express the gift of reconciliation, already given by the God who loves us first, in the context of the human condition understood in terms of blame and lament, of individual responsibility, but also in terms of community building.[21]

Reconciliation in Environmental Theology

Jacques Haers SJ suggests that our contemporary theologies of reconciliation offer promise for praxis exactly because they point to the question of how to live well together.[22] Reconciliation reinterpreted in this way has several aspects to it that can provide lessons for the pressing issues of our time, in conflict resolution but also in relation to environmental questions, both of which require more than individual accountability. Reconciliation refers to a process of community building; it has an interpersonal focus and carries with it the implication that we need structural analysis as well as personal responsibility.[23] It overcomes the paralysis that can occur when people 'experience conflicts or oppression as "structural", as realities that involve them but on which their actions have little effect.'[24] Haers suggests that this is true of violent conflict but also of our 'predatory patterns for natural resources and competition with endangered species in their habitats that have come to dominate our relation to the planet'.[25] He argues that 'reconciliation in times of environmental challenges affecting the entire planet calls for more than a personal sense of responsibility. It also demands a readiness to deal with structures of injustice resulting from the variable impact of environmental crises and the predatory nature of our world-views. We also need to question our innate, and at times religiously motivated, tendencies to unilateral anthropocentrism.'[26] We need to include reconciliation with others that are unfamiliar to us as actors and protagonists: our fellow humans not yet born but who nonetheless will depend on the world we

leave them; other creatures; ecological communities; and the plan-
etary system itself.[27]

The challenge for praxis is whether or not we learn from the
past – from the ambiguities of all our structures of violence: war;
social injustice veiled as necessary for economic growth; colonial and neo-colonial exploitation – to collaborate in processes
of community building through common projects, through overcoming conflict and colonial power games.[28] This, Haers suggests,
is what theological perspectives on reconciliation can bring to
these global issues and to the core challenge of engaging in the
common project of a sustainable world.[29]

Conclusion

Our models for atonement both reveal and conceal. That Jesus
reconciles sinful humanity with God is a shared Christian doctrine
whether we read this through the lens of God's wrath in his stead-
fastness against evil or his forgiving love. This is the theological
context that frames the ambiguities in human experience of both
guilt and suffering. As Danaher put it, 'His judgment is that evil is
to be opposed, but his opposition to evil is forgiveness.'[30] This has
echoes of the early church's understanding of *Christus Victor*: God
defeats the Devil (evil personified as a creature, as Satan) through
justice, not violence.[31] It is also captured from different angles in
Anselm's insistence on honour and Abelard's on love. In relation
to environmental challenges in the contemporary context, reconciliation points Christians to the pressing need to engage in the
common project of a sustainable world.

2

THE CROSS AND THE REDEMPTION OF THE COSMOS

Ron Elsdon

Introduction

It is fitting that this subject should feature in a symposium on the cross, taking place in a theological training institute in Ireland. Some members of the audience are training for ordained ministry and this at a time when few congregations are now content to swallow whole what is preached simply because 'the minister says so'. The age when minister and doctor were the only educated people in the local church have long since gone. Many of those sitting in church pews are at least as well educated as their ministers. They have also learned to be sceptical, and there must always be a place for the right kind of scepticism. Sloppy thinking, therefore, has no place in the theological education of either the church's ministers or their congregations.

Nowhere is this issue more urgent than in areas where science and faith overlap, intersect, graze each other tangentially, diverge wildly or collide head-on. It is this latter case which usually pervades the public consciousness. There is, for example, the uneasy feeling that somehow science has 'disproved' the Bible, a case argued forcefully by the new atheists. This misapprehension is variously fed, and sometimes the media are to blame. One well-known radio broadcaster in Northern Ireland, with his own talk show on Radio Ulster, dealt on more than one occasion with issues of science and faith, and he once uttered the terrible phrase '*the* conflict between science and faith' (my italics). There are, though, to be fair, other radio and TV programmes that do explore openly the ways in which science and faith can interact with each other.

Some specific areas continue to need urgent attention. The painful reality is that, for many people (including some ordained ministers), the only issue on the horizon is the need to subscribe to young-earth creationism. While the American origins of this modern movement have been thoroughly documented,[1] it has become increasingly influential in the UK and Ireland in recent years.[2] At a lecture in Belfast in 2010 Dr Garth Earls, then Director of the Northern Ireland Geological Survey, remarked that on the issue of creationism 'Northern Ireland punches above its weight'.

Another less obvious barrier to understanding the relationship between science and faith is to do with *the future of creation within the purposes of God.* There is a common, unstated assumption that our future is purely 'spiritual'. It is summed up in the idea that eternal life is about 'going to heaven when you die', in which 'heaven' constitutes a purely spiritual existence in which we leave behind the physical realm in which our present lives are lived out. In this, it can be argued, our thinking owes more to the influence of Platonism or even Gnosticism on the Christian theology of the early centuries than to the content and meaning of Scripture. The persistence of this kind of thinking may also reflect the failure of many Christian adults to go beyond what they learned as children in Sunday Schools.

In thinking like this, the idea that creation has no future in God's purposes follows quickly. From among the biblically knowledge-able come 'proof texts' such as:

> And, 'In the beginning, Lord, you founded the earth, and the heavens are the work of your hands; they will perish, but you remain; they will all wear out like clothing; like a cloak you will roll them up, and like clothing they will be changed. But you are the same, and your years will never end' (Heb. 1:10–12).[3]

> But the day of the Lord will come like a thief, and then the heavens will pass away with a loud noise, and the elements will be dissolved with fire, and the earth and everything that is done on it will be dis-

closed. Since all these things are to be dissolved in this way, what sort of persons ought you to be in leading lives of holiness and godliness, waiting for and hastening the coming of the day of God, because of which the heavens will be set ablaze and dissolved, and the elements will melt with fire? (2 Pet. 3:10–12).

Assuming its selection is broadly similar to those of other hymn-books, the contents of the Church of Ireland Hymnal suggest that some of the hymns it contains that refer to 'heaven' can easily be read in this way. The section entitled 'The Communion of Saints' is instructive in this regard; so is the section titled 'The Christian Hope' where Hymn 675 ('Peace, Perfect Peace, in This Dark World of Sin?') ends with the verse which connects the end of earthly strife with heavenly peace.[4]

Parallel to this is the notion (or, at least, the *assumption*) that God's eschatological purposes are concerned solely with the salvation of individual human beings. One evangelical mission agency I know well emphasizes the fact that the primary task in mission is evangelism, mainly in order to save people from hell. Acts of compassion and healing have no value in themselves; their only purpose is to lead to openings for gospel preaching. Thus David Gillett writes:

> In basing its spirituality almost exclusively in redemption rather than creation, and in seeing this redemption more in terms of how it is applied and experienced in the individual than in its communal and cosmic significance, certain endemic weaknesses have appeared within evangelical spirituality. There has been, for instance, a recurring suspicion of various forms of art and culture, a reluctance at times, to see creation, ecology and social issues as Christian priorities, and a difficulty in developing theological and spiritual understanding from any base other than the work of God within the individual.[5]

This writer's experience over many years of trying to present a rounded biblical theology of creation has sometimes been of encountering apathy or even hostility. One night at the end of a talk to a hundred members of a university Christian Union, no one could think of a single question to ask me. On another occasion, I attended a conference of five hundred people where I led a seminar attended by a mere handful, and struggled to get a proper discussion going.

But there are other hymns in the Church of Ireland hymnbook which point to a different vision of the place of creation within the purposes of God. For example, Robert Grant's wonderful hymn 'O Worship the King, All Glorious Above' ends with a verse which pictures the whole of redeemed creation singing the praise of God.[6]

Less well known is a twentieth-century hymn by Ian Fraser, whose first and last verses are as follows:

Lord, bring the day to pass / When forest, rock and hill,
The beasts, the birds, the grass, / Will know your finished will:
When we attain our destiny / And nature its lost unity.

Creation groans, travails, / Bound in its future plight,
Until the hour it hails / The new-born of the light,
Who enter on their true estate. / Come, Lord: new heavens and
    earth create.[7]

These words echo clearly Paul's vivid language in Romans 8:18–25 and are arguably the most explicit reference in Church of Ireland worship to a vision in which the whole of creation is included within the scope of God's redemptive purposes. This is not the only reference within Pauline theology to the redemption of creation, nor is this theme unrelated to a wider biblical theology.

There is a clear choice facing churches today, to envision a future which is to be seen in purely spiritual terms, or an alternative future in which creation plays an essential role. One theologian, displaying significant scepticism, puts the choice in these graphic terms:

Is the final aim of God, in his governance of all things, to bring into being at the very end a glorified kingdom of spirits alone who, thus united with God, may contemplate him in perfect bliss, while as a precondition of their ecstasy all the other creatures of nature must be left by God to fall away into eternal oblivion?

    Or is the final aim of God, in his governance of all things, to communicate his life to another in a way which calls forth at the very end new heavens and a new earth in which righteousness dwells, a transfigured cosmos where peace is universally established between all creatures at last, in the midst of which is situated a glorious city of resurrected saints who dwell in justice, blessed with all the resplendent fullness of the earth, and who continually call upon all creatures to join with them in their joyful praise of the one who is all in all?

With the question posed this way, a large majority of modern biblical scholars would self-consciously, or as a matter of course, choose the first option . . . in keeping with their interpretive assumptions which have been so thoroughly shaped by the spiritual motif.[8]

The Witness of the New Testament

Four elements in the Old Testament's theology of creation are relevant to the theme of this chapter. First, sustained controversy surrounding the idea of young-earth creationism has often blinded us to the importance of the theme of the goodness of creation in Genesis 1. All that God makes is 'good' (vv. 4, 10, 12, 18, 21, 25), culminating in the pronouncement 'God saw everything that he had made, and indeed, it was very good' (v. 31). The goodness of creation is one of the themes that can then be followed through Scripture;[9] reading the Bible as *story*, it can be seen as an essential element in the 'plot'. In the Old Testament, the goodness of creation is not an abstract proposition but an essential quality of that part of the created order that the people of Israel were to experience in their occupation of and life in Canaan.[10] This is expressed, for example, in laws for creation care and in the reminder that the earth is the Lord's (e.g. Lev. 25; Ps. 24).

Second, as if on the reverse side of a coin, Genesis 3:17 records a curse on the whole of creation arising from Adam and Eve's disobedience. Again, this curse is not to be thought of as an abstract idea, but would be experienced in Canaan if Israel disregarded the God-given laws under which they were called to live. They were confronted with a choice: their obedience would lead to blessing and a fruitful earth, but disobedience would lead to the curse being realized in the failure of the land to be fruitful (e.g. Deut. 28f.). This latter scenario is then reflected in the quasi-apocalyptic picture of a polluted and scorched earth in Isaiah 24 and elsewhere, flowing directly as a consequence of Israel's disobedience.[11]

Third, the New Testament themes of incarnation and resurrection each reaffirm the goodness of creation in their own way. Rather than speculating on a mechanism by which incarnation might take place, N.T. Wright speaks of the 'appropriateness' of God the creator coming to live on earth as one of his creatures.[12] In the case of the resurrection, both Luke 24 and John 20 describe resurrection appearances in which the risen Jesus clearly has a physical body (in marked distinction to the fear of the disciples who thought they were seeing a ghost; Luke 24:37). Wright this time speaks of 'trans-physicality', because there is clearly something different – less earthbound – about Jesus' body on this side of Easter morning.[13]

Fourth, there are also futuristic pictures of a new kind of order, supremely in Isaiah 65:17–25 ('For I am about to create new heavens and a new earth'):[14]

[17]For I am about to create new heavens and a new earth; the former things shall not be remembered or come to mind.
[18]But be glad and rejoice for ever in what I am creating; for I am about to create Jerusalem as a joy, and its people as a delight.
[19]I will rejoice in Jerusalem, and delight in my people; no more shall the sound of weeping be heard in it, or the cry of distress.
[20]No more shall there be in it an infant that lives but a few days, or an old person who does not live out a lifetime; for one who dies at a hundred years will be considered a youth, and one who falls short of a hundred will be considered accursed.
[21]They shall build houses and inhabit them; they shall plant vineyards and eat their fruit.
[22]They shall not build and another inhabit; they shall not plant and another eat; for like the days of a tree shall the days of my people be, and my chosen shall long enjoy the work of their hands.
[23]They shall not labour in vain, or bear children for calamity; for they shall be offspring blessed by the LORD – and their descendants as well.
[24]Before they call I will answer, while they are yet speaking I will hear.
[25]The wolf and the lamb shall feed together, the lion shall eat straw like the ox; but the serpent – its food shall be dust! They shall not hurt or destroy on all my holy mountain, says the LORD.

This one passage is enough to indicate how the New Testament vision of a redeemed creation is based on the Old, and this applies especially to passages such as Romans 8:18–25, which has already been mentioned. In recent years there has been increasing attention given to the development of an eschatological theology broad enough to include creation itself.[15]

Here we examine three Pauline passages in order to discuss how they describe the redemption of creation itself, and how they describe the link to the redemption of human beings.

Ephesians 1

We come to this passage first, because Colin Gunton has argued that it is here that the New Testament comes nearest to a promise of redemption for the whole universe. He also notes Romans 8, which we shall deal with later, but suggests that in the latter case it is the redemption of human beings which is central:[16]

> [9]he has made known to us the mystery of his will, according to his good pleasure that he set forth in Christ,
> [10]as a plan for the fullness of time, to gather up all things in him, things in heaven and things on earth.

A key issue in exegeting this passage is the meaning of the phrase 'gather up all things' (ἀνακεφαλαιώσασθαι τὰ πάντα). While it is possible to argue that the phrase has some specific reference such as rebellious beings in the spiritual realm, it is important to note that the two categories which contain 'all things' are heaven and earth. This shows that in Paul's understanding nothing is to be excluded: the physical sphere of creation is clearly in view.

As is well known, the term 'gather up all things' (ἀνακεφαλαιώσασθαι τὰ πάντα) became a central pillar of Irenaeus' doctrine of recapitulation. That he used it to wage war against the Gnostics in his multi-volume work *Against the Heresies* shows his positive understanding of creation in the eternal purposes of God. It is not that creation is evil in itself; it has been affected by the results of human sin: 'The summing up of all things in Christ means the unifying of the cosmos or its direction toward a common goal . . . the cosmos had been plunged into disintegration on account of sin and . . . it is God's purpose to restore its original harmony in Christ.'[17]

Although Gunton's judgement, previously noted, seems to suggest a unique emphasis on creation here, what leads up to verses 9–10 sets Paul's assertion in a more specific context. In terms of his argument, what happens to creation itself not only follows from the redemption of sinful human beings ('In him we have redemption through his blood, the forgiveness of our trespasses', v. 7); it is also announced beforehand ('he has made known to us the mystery of his will . . . as a plan for the fullness of time', vv. 9, 10) to people who have already received redemption through Christ's blood (that is, his death on the cross). It is not that the redemption of humans is part of a wider plan; in a real sense Paul's argument is that it is the redemption of the cosmos which is part of a wider divine plan centred on the redemption of humanity.

Both references place the emphasis on the redemption of human beings; the implication is that, in some way unspecified, the cosmos is included in the blessings that flow from Christ's cross. Such a perspective might leave Paul open to the modern charge of anthropocentrism, but that is clearly the way his understanding of the cross is expressed. As will become evident, this is not unique to Ephesians, but expresses his wider thought in general.

Another issue is to do with chronology. We have already received our redemption (v. 7) and were included in Christ when we heard the gospel of our salvation (v. 13). Although in a real sense our redemption is a past event, the redemption of creation lies in the future. It still suffers at the hands of sinful human beings. In Ephesians 1, however, does Paul speak of 'gather[ing] up all things' as a past event? Certainly he uses the aorist infinitive ἀνακεφαλαιώσασθαι but this may be to place too much weight on the significance of the verb tense. This remains true even when much of Paul's use of the term 'mystery' refers to a present reality (3:3–6, 9; 5:32; 6:19; also Col. 1:26, 27; 2:2; 4:3).

Yet this is to make too rigid a distinction between realized and future dimensions in eschatology. The redemption of creation here flows from a past event: the cross. The same is true of people who have trusted in Christ. But as creation still awaits the full realization of its destiny, so do we. Thus Ephesians 4:17 – 6:9 lay down guidelines for Christian conduct, and it is clear that Paul envisages that living with integrity in a sinful world will not be easy (cf. 'My friends, if anyone is detected in a transgression . . .', Gal. 6:1). And in the final section of the letter 'our' struggle against spiritual forces of evil (Eph. 6:10ff.) is not one he wages alone but others wage with him.

Colossians 1

Much of what has been said about Ephesians 1 also applies to Colossians, a very similar epistle in many respects, although the language used of creation here is both different and more detailed:

[15]He is the image of the invisible God, the firstborn of all creation; [16]for in him all things in heaven and on earth were created, things visible and invisible, whether thrones or dominions or rulers or powers – all things have been created through him and for him. [17]He himself is before all things, and in him all things hold together. [18]He is the head of the body, the church; he is the beginning, the firstborn from the dead, so that he might come to have first place in everything. [19]For in him all the fullness of God was pleased to dwell, [20]and through him God was pleased to reconcile to himself all things, whether on earth or in heaven, by making peace through the blood of his cross. [21]And you who were once estranged and hostile in mind, doing evil deeds, [22]he has now reconciled in his fleshly body through death, so as to present you holy and blameless and irreproachable before him – [23]provided that you continue securely established and steadfast in the faith, without shifting from the hope promised by the gospel that you heard, which has been proclaimed to every creature under heaven. I, Paul, became a servant of this gospel.

The flow of the concepts takes us through a somewhat different landscape. Thus Paul starts with an altogether bigger vision of who 'our Lord Jesus Christ' is (v. 3); he then introduces the concept of reconciliation, applying it first to 'all things' (v. 20). It is only then applied to human beings (v. 22), although he has already dealt with this using different theological language (that of rescue and redemption, vv. 13f.).

Here the crucial point of interpretation is again the meaning of the phrase 'all things' that are *reconciled* to God 'through the blood of his cross' (v. 20; καὶ δι' αὐτοῦ ἀποκαταλλάξαι τὰ πάντα εἰς αὐτόν, εἰρηνοποιήσας διὰ τοῦ αἵματος τοῦ σταυροῦ αὐτοῦ, [δι' αὐτοῦ] εἴτε τὰ ἐπὶ τῆς γῆς εἴτε τὰ ἐν τοῖς οὐρανοῖς). Notable is the repetition of τὰ πάντα, created 'by him' (τὰ πάντα δι' αὐτοῦ καὶ εἰς αὐτὸν ἔκτισται, v. 16) and held together 'in him' (τὰ πάντα ἐν αὐτῷ συνέστηκεν, v. 17). R.P. Martin has pointed out that the correspondence is strengthened by the literary device of chiasmus, in which verse 16c is mirrored by verse 20a:

τὰ πάντα . . . δι' αὐτοῦ καὶ . . . καὶ δι' αὐτοῦ . . . τὰ πάντα[18]

He also suggests that the phrase τὰ πάντα is expanded in verse 20 by the final phrase 'whether things on earth or things in heaven' (NIV) (εἴτε τὰ ἐπὶ τῆς γῆς εἴτε τὰ ἐν τοῖς οὐρανοῖς)[19] and that the unusual placing of this final phrase shows it to be Paul's thought, and not part of the original hymn which is often seen as the origin of the passage as a whole. He proposes further that the addition of εἰρηνοποιήσας διὰ τοῦ αἵματος τοῦ σταυροῦ αὐτοῦ transforms radically the meaning of the reconciliation; in its pre-Pauline form Christ might have been seen as Lord by *fiat* rather than through his death.

But what exactly does the reconciliation of 'all things' refer to? It would be tempting to look at this text simply through twenty-first-century eyes and say that *of course* it refers to a marred creation. But it is necessary to ask what Paul meant, given that he lived in a world with its own problems but without any knowledge of global warming, for example. So while he may certainly have meant the world of subhuman creation, there are also commentators who point to the reconciliation of fallen angels ('things in heaven . . .').[20] But although there are one or two possible references to such a concept in the Old Testament, we have already seen how important is the theme of creation – its goodness and the curse that results from human disobedience.

It is also worth remembering that Colossians is not a treatise on environmental issues but on the lordship of Christ, as the hymn in

1:15–20 makes clear. So we should approach the question of *what* is being reconciled from the standpoint of *who* it is who effects this reconciliation, and how it is achieved. Noting again the parallelism between the uses of the phrase 'all things' in verses 16, 17 and 20, and assuming they all refer to the same categories, what is to be reconciled is that which was once created 'by him' (τὰ πάντα δι' αὐτοῦ καὶ εἰς αὐτὸν ἔκτισται [v. 16]) and held together 'in him' (πάντα ἐν αὐτῷ συνέστηκεν [v. 17]). It seems clear that the primary referent is therefore to the physical; creation, rather than cosmic powers and fallen angels – an unseen world similarly coming within the scope of the cross but in a separate section and using a separate vocabulary: 'He disarmed the rulers and authorities and made a public example of them, triumphing over them in it' (Col. 2:15). Here the 'powers and authorities' are not reconciled but *disarmed, defeated and humiliated.* Paul's own language therefore tends here again to suggest that what he has in view in his use of the phrase τὰ πάντα is the world of subhuman creation. This is particularly significant if the background to Colossians is some form of incipient Gnosticism, driving as it does a wedge between God and the material world.[21]

A further point is important. Suspicions are sometimes aroused by the use of Scripture in developing theologies of creation that they leave no room for the *personal* dimension to reconciliation, to which Paul so clearly refers, for example, in 2 Corinthians 5:14ff. In the case of Colossians 1:15–20 it is therefore important to note that Paul follows with a clear statement of the work of Christ on the cross in the reconciliation effected with sinful human beings: 'And you who were once estranged and hostile in mind, doing evil deeds, he has now reconciled in his fleshly body through death, so as to present you holy and blameless and irreproachable before him' (Col. 1:21–22).

Having identified reasons for understanding Paul's references to τὰ πάντα as primarily references to the reconciliation of a material creation, we can now go on to examine a third major Pauline text.

Romans 8:18–25

Much attention has been paid in recent years to this passage in particular by commentators seeking to demonstrate the potential

of New Testament theology to address both ecological issues and
a rounded theology of creation. Its particular significance is that
only here does Paul spell out what is wrong with the cosmos:

> [18]I consider that the sufferings of this present time are not worth com-
> paring with the glory about to be revealed to us.
> [19]For the creation waits with eager longing for the revealing of the
> children of God;
> [20]for the creation was subjected to futility, not of its own will but by
> the will of the one who subjected it, in hope
> [21]that the creation itself will be set free from its bondage to decay and
> will obtain the freedom of the glory of the children of God.
> [22]We know that the whole creation has been groaning in labor pains
> until now;
> [23]and not only the creation, but we ourselves, who have the first fruits
> of the Spirit, groan inwardly while we wait for adoption, the redemp-
> tion of our bodies.
> [24]For in hope we were saved. Now hope that is seen is not hope. For
> who hopes for what is seen?
> [25]But if we hope for what we do not see, we wait for it with patience.

The language is particularly striking – note terms such as 'futility'
(τῇ γὰρ ματαιότητι), 'bondage to decay' (τῆς δουλείας τῆς
φθορᾶς) and 'groaning' (συστενάζει). Dunn, Cranfield and others
note that Paul's use of ματαιότης stems from his use of the noun
in 1:21ff. where the term denotes the vacuousness of thinking that
does not recognize God and, therefore, misunderstands the role
of creation in the scheme of things. Dunn, among others, goes on
to relate this to Old Testament themes, and to the curse on the
earth stated in Genesis 3:17.[22] David Horrell et al. have questioned
this linkage on the grounds that Adam is nowhere mentioned in
Romans and that the language Paul uses does not reflect the LXX
of Genesis 3;[23] but the general conclusion does not seem to rest
on such particularly detailed considerations. It is then possible to
state the relationship between human sinfulness and futility as a
feature of creation in the following terms:

> the sub-human creation has been subjected to the frustration of not
> being able properly to fulfil the purpose of its existence, God having

appointed that without man it should not be made perfect. We may think of the whole magnificent theatre of the universe together with all its splendid properties and all the chorus of sub-human life, created to glorify God but unable to do so fully, so long as man the chief actor in the drama of God's praise fails to contribute his rational part.[24]

It is this kind of understanding of the relationship between human sinfulness and futility in creation that makes sense of a further feature of Romans 8:18–25. Here it is not simply that the atonement leads to the liberation of creation as well as the redemption of human beings. As Paul states it, the former *follows directly from* the latter ('the creation itself will be liberated from its bondage to decay and brought into the glorious freedom of the children of God'; v. 21 [NIV1984]). Tom Wright restates Paul's thesis as follows:

In other words, when God's children, the redeemed human race, are 'glorified', set at last (as was always intended) in obedient authority over the world, then the whole creation will heave a gigantic sigh of relief and become truly what it always had the capacity to become but what, through the failure of humans to govern it with the 'glory' God had in mind, it failed to attain . . . When God redeems the whole creation, redeemed humans will play the key role, resuming the wise, healing sovereignty over the whole world for which God made them in the first place.[25]

Three Particular Issues

So far the New Testament vision of the redemption of creation, and its linkage to the redemption at the cross of sinful human beings, has been addressed in purely theological terms. It is clear, however, that certain contemporary questions arise from this, and at least three of them deserve attention here.

Should churches be involved in creation care?

Reference has already been made to texts such as Hebrews 1:10–12 and 2 Peter 3:10–12. A common argument used by some

Christians states that if the material universe is headed for annihilation (having served its temporary purpose, or being too
corrupt to be saved), then there is no point in stewarding it. Thus
the addition of caring for the integrity of creation as one of the
identifying marks of the church is viewed with suspicion. The
point of the argument in Hebrews 1, however, is not to make
absolute statements about creation, but to establish the superior
status of 'a Son' (v. 2), to whom the readers are implored to listen.
In the case of 2 Peter 3 it is debatable whether the *annihilation*
of creation is in view. What is promised is 'new heavens and a
new earth' (v. 13). The terminology is similar to Ephesians 1 and
Colossians 1, as well as Revelation 21, all of these texts echoing
the prophecy of Isaiah 65:17-25.

Indirectly, therefore, this vision of the future of creation, which we
can also link to Jesus' announcement of 'the kingdom' (e.g. Mark 1:15),
is to inspire Christians to demonstrate their hope in this kingdom by
living according to its promise. If that includes a transformed creation, then there is every incentive to incorporate caring for the integrity of creation into the lifestyles of Christians and churches. This
conclusion pertains irrespective of whether Anthropogenic Global
Warming is real or imagined. Creation care is in Scripture an integral
part of living wisely and joyfully within creation; the eschatological
implication of this is equally clear: to live joyfully within creation is
to take seriously the promise of its future redemption.

Can the scriptural hope of the transformation of all creation be reconciled with cosmological projections of the ultimate death of the universe?

Increasing scientific knowledge of the universe enables projec-
tions as to its apparent ultimate fate. All depends on the battle
between gravity and the speed at which stars and galaxies are
moving away from each other. If gravity wins, expansion will
eventually cease, contraction will set in and the universe ends
in a 'Big Crunch', the reverse of the Big Bang. Given increasing
evidence that expansion prevails over gravity, the universe would
then ultimately wind down to a 'Big Freeze'. Stars eventually
cease to shine, eventually even protons themselves decay, black
holes prevail and their ultimate demise results in the emission

of 'Hawking Radiation'. In a markedly understated judgement, John Polkinghorne surmises: 'On the face of it, the ultimate prospects are bleak.'[26]

There are two possible alternative scenarios here, one physical and the other theological. The first is that carbon-based life will continue to develop in such a way as to adapt itself to the gradual evolution of an increasingly cold physical universe. Various speculative suggestions have been made by eminent physicists and others. Dyson's eternal intelligence hypothesis, for example, proposes that an advanced civilization could survive for an infinite period of time while consuming only a finite amount of energy. Such a civilization would store a finite amount of energy in anticipation. It would then alternate brief periods of activity, in each of which they would use one-half of the remaining available energy, with periods of hibernation; each cycle would then become increasingly lengthy, and each period of activity increasingly short. The cycle would, in theory, be infinitely long.[27]

Polkinghorne judges such scenarios to be ingenious but abstract. He chooses a second scenario: the biblical hope is that the universe continues to be held within the love of God, in whom it therefore finds its eternal destiny. It is important to understand that this is an important issue where theology cannot rest upon scientific confirmation. It is a different type of vision, inspired by a different kind of knowledge that is as authoritative as that of science: 'If there is a true and lasting hope – and it is a deep human intuition that there is such a hope – then it can only rest in the eternal mercy and faithfulness of God.'[28]

Can the biblical data encompass the problem of 'natural evil'?

When Romans 8:22 speaks of creation 'groaning in labour pains' – a phrase clearly anticipatory – it is natural to understand it in terms of a redemption linked to the redemption of humanity from the consequences of its sinfulness. But it is perhaps because of the vividness of the metaphor that a further question arises: can Romans 8:18–25 be legitimately extended to encompass an understanding of the redemption of the cosmos as also including its liberation from what is often called 'natural evil'?

The question becomes pressing since one of the barriers to Christian belief in the modern world is to do with the nature and origin of suffering in the world. Live TV news footage enables us now to see almost immediately the results of natural disasters, examples of which include recent catastrophic floods in Australia and Pakistan, and earthquakes and resultant tsunamis in the Indian Ocean (Boxing Day 2004) and close to the Japanese coast (March 2011). The question then arises: does the biblical understanding of creation, and its redemption in particular, address this issue?

To attempt to explain 'natural evil' as the result of 'the fall' (Gen. 3) is simplistic.[29] Even the term 'natural evil' is in some sense misleading. In previous times scientific explanations of how and why such events occur were not available. Twentieth-century geology, however, has contributed to human knowledge an understanding of the processes leading to such events that can now be incorporated into what is known as *plate tectonics*.[30] Of particular significance is that phenomena such as earthquakes and volcanic eruptions are not random, completely unpredictable events. Although they can lead to widespread death, injury and destruction, they have been bound up for billions of years with the geological evolution of the earth, together with the formation of its oceans, atmosphere, land, soils, ore deposits, and reserves of coal, oil and gas. In other words, they are essential to the processes that produce a fruitful earth and that sustain biological life in all its forms. Modern geological knowledge also enables predictions of such events, although with very limited precision.

This merely throws into even sharper relief the question of the applicability of Romans 8 to such a set of issues. Few commentaries on Romans 8 allude to this possibility; a few leave it open. David Wilkinson suggests that it is not clear what kind(s) of suffering Paul is referring to here but that it could include living in a 'fragile world'.[31] Polkinghorne links Romans 8:20 with the processes of biological evolution.[32] Tom Wright starts from the agency of human sinfulness in frustrating the role of creation in the purposes of God. He then goes on in a slightly speculative fashion:

> Mysteriously, this out-of-jointness seems to become entangled with the transience and decay necessary within the good-but-incomplete

creation, so that what we perhaps misleadingly call 'natural evil' can be seen as, among other things, the advance signs of that final 'shaking' of heaven and earth which the prophets understood to be necessary if God's eventual new world was to be born . . .[33]

Although the book of Job is an extended treatment of the place and purpose of suffering in the world, there is little in Scripture that understands phenomena such as earthquakes as 'natural evil', which needs thus to be explained in terms of its presence in God's world. Richard Bauckham points out that in Job 40, Leviathan can be understood as 'a personification of the destructive forces in nature that threaten the order of God's creation'.[34] However, in Genesis 1 and Psalm 104 this chaos-monster has been tamed. Thus creation is depicted in an ideal or eschatological way.[35] Although one might infer that Paul understands the Old Testament Scripture thus, it is not made explicit in Romans 8.

Another proposal may take us slightly further. Polkinghorne admits that his discussion is somewhat speculative when he points out that a large body of scientific knowledge is consonant with 'creation-through-process' in which 'God in his wisdom bestows on a universe allowed to exist over against him and permitted to make itself through the realisation of its own fruitful potentiality.'[36]

Richard Bauckham and Trevor Hart argue that if Romans 8 sees God as taking into his eternal kingdom the whole of creation, this should not be understood *synchronically*; that is, creation as it is at the end of time. It should rather be understood *diachronically*; that is, it refers to 'the whole temporal course of creation's history'.[37] If we take the latter choice, it will include the whole *geological* course of history, in some way incorporating billions of years of plate tectonic activity, with all its fruitfulness and destructiveness together. Thus all the destructive results of plate tectonic activity are taken up, along with its constructive aspects, into the transformed creation that Romans 8 testifies to.

A scientific analogy may assist. In a 2011 TV programme in the 'Wonders of the Universe' series, Professor Brian Cox explained the implications of the fact that light travels at a finite speed. This means that the stars visible in the night sky are not the stars as they presently exist but *as they existed when the light that is now registered by our eyes was first emitted*. The night sky, therefore, is not a three-dimensional portrait of the universe but is actually *four-dimensional*. This becomes even more significant when one views the stars, not through the naked eye or an optical telescope, but in the form of Hubble Ultra Deep Field (HUDF) images. Here, the points of light (galaxies as well as stars) are so far away that the light which we *now* see was emitted many billions of years ago. Indeed, it is possible to claim that HUDF photographs show us the whole history of the universe in a single glance.[38]

Envisaging this is an exercise of imagination as much as of inquiry. Bauckham and Hart suggest that the role of apocalyptic texts is not only to refer beyond this world to another that must be taken seriously as promised reality. They also make the reader realize that 'our expectations of the new creation must not be constrained by our experience of this world'.[39] It then becomes possible even in a shadowy way to understand how, in the final purposes of God, creation is not annihilated but radically transformed and renewed. The exercise of imagination is an activity which is not easy. Perhaps it is appropriate on this island then to let C.S. Lewis have the last word:

> The things that began to happen after that were so great and beautiful that I cannot write them. And for us this is the end of all the stories, and we can most truly say that they all lived happily ever after. But for them it was only the beginning of the real story. All their life in this world and all their adventures in Narnia had only been the cover and the title page: now at last they were beginning Chapter One of the Great Story which no one on earth has read: which goes on for ever: in which every chapter is better than the one before.[40]

3

The Cross and God's Embrace of Suffering

Richard Bauckham

Introduction: Envisaging Undeserved Suffering

On 11 March 2011, a massive earthquake and tsunami devastated northwest Japan, killing about 28,000 people and making hundreds of thousands homeless. As a physical phenomenon the earthquake was the most severe in modern Japanese history, though it was not actually the most catastrophic (more than 100,000 people died in the Tokyo earthquake of 1923). Of natural disasters on this scale, it has been the most fully recorded – both by scientific monitoring and by photography and film, including the extraordinary footage filmed on mobile phones as the great wave of the tsunami approached at great speed. But the pictures that perhaps especially brought home the scale of the disaster were those of the aftermath: miles and miles of brown mud where flourishing towns had stood, the wreckage of buildings and possessions scattered here and there but dwarfed by the expanses of newly created wasteland. In the past few years I have visited both Hiroshima and Nagasaki, and these pictures of the ruin the tsunami left in its wake reminded me of nothing more than the pictures of the wasteland that was Hiroshima and Nagasaki after a very different kind of disaster. Many people have commented how peculiarly sad it would be if Japan, the only country that has so far suffered both the annihilating power and the long-term effects of atomic bombs, were also to suffer on a large scale the effects of radiation from the Fukushima Daiichi nuclear power plant. The effects have been limited, but it is still not clear how serious the situation there is.

It is striking that it was the same kind of natural disaster – a massive earthquake followed by a huge tsunami – that stands symbolically at the beginning of the modern discussion of theodicy in Europe: the 1755 Lisbon earthquake, which may have been of similar magnitude to the 11 March earthquake in Japan, and caused the death of up to 50,000 people in Portugal, Spain and North Africa. This tsunami made an impact as far away as the west coast of Ireland. The catastrophe served, among many Enlightenment thinkers, notably Voltaire, to refute the optimistic theodicy of Leibnitz, who famously said that all is for the best in the best of all possible worlds. All was certainly not for the best.

It was as a natural disaster for which humans could not be held responsible that the Lisbon earthquake made its point against blandly optimistic theodicies. In the twentieth century, discussion of the so-called problem of suffering was influenced more by the appalling scale of human evil seen in the Holocaust, in Stalin's massacres, in the bombing of Hiroshima and Nagasaki, in Cambodia and Rwanda, and in other horrors of modern history. In the twenty-first century, beginning with the Boxing Day tsunami of 2004, natural catastrophe has so far loomed larger than human evil. The problem of suffering as an argument against belief in God was raised in the western media after the Boxing Day tsunami, though not, it seems, by the victims of the catastrophe, many of whom were sustained and enabled to hope by their religious faith. But an important aspect of the impact made by earthquakes and tsunamis is the point they make, not so much against theodicy as against the more humanistic modern western faith in technology. Like climate change, they are a brutal reminder that we have not, in fact, mastered the forces of nature and bent them to our wills and desires – nor are we likely to do so.

It is true that natural disasters are often exacerbated or even caused by human activity, as in the case of the effects of climate change. The Boxing Day tsunami would not have affected coastal areas such as those of Thailand so badly had the vegetation that formed a natural protection not been cleared away to make room for tourism. But in the case of the 11 March earthquake and tsunami, as far as I can see, if we leave the nuclear factor out of account, there was nothing that could have been done to ameliorate the impact (unless, of course, Japanese people stopped living in areas likely to be affected by earthquakes and tsunamis, but this is hardly a practical suggestion). The Japanese build in such a way as to minimize danger from earthquakes; they have good early warning systems; people expect earthquakes and are well prepared. But in the face of such massive forces of nature, Japanese organization and technical expertise were even more helpless than the fishing boats in Katsushika Hokusai's famous picture of *The Wave off Kanagawa*. (Though the wave is probably not a tsunami, this painting certainly expresses awe at the power of the ocean.)

The governor of Tokyo, Shintaro Ishihara, called the tsunami divine judgement visited upon Japan as punishment for 'the egoism, which has attached itself like rust to the mentality of the Japanese people over a long period of time', though in the face of public outrage he quickly retracted this statement and apologized. It is true that the Old Testament prophets not uncommonly saw natural disaster as God's judgement on human sin, but perhaps one has to be a prophet to do so. Certainly no one has the right to suppose that Japan deserves a tsunami any more than their own country does. There is a category of undeserved suffering, a category that is not to be rejected on the grounds that no one is innocent of sin (except very small children, many of us would want to add). Perhaps we all deserve tsunamis, but they do not seem to be allocated fairly, any more than the effects of global warming will be (indeed, have already been).

Does undeserved suffering belong within the scope of atonement theology? I take that question to mean: does it belong within God's great project of putting the world to rights through the life, death, resurrection and future coming of Jesus?

The Scope of Atonement

The Christian doctrine of atonement presupposes that there is something deeply, not just superficially, wrong with the human condition. The diagnosis has broadly three aspects:

1. There is moral evil, which means not simply the evil we do and bear responsibility for, but the fact that there is something deeply wrong with *us*, individually and socially, something that needs more than good advice and education to cure.

2. There is meaningless suffering, tragedy, and what the book of Ecclesiastes calls vanity or emptiness. This does not seem just to be something wrong with us as moral agents (though much undeserved suffering is caused by human acts), but something deeply wrong with how things are in this world.

3. There is death, which is not just a biological necessity, though it is that, but something deeply unsatisfactory that threatens the value of human persons.

But, at the deepest root of these three elements in a Christian diagnosis of what we need liberating from, there is a common factor. The deepest dimension of all three facets of what is wrong is the lack of God. In the evil we cannot help contributing to, in the meaningless tragedy of life, and in the inconsolableness of death, what we miss is the love at the heart of reality. When we do evil we turn our back on that love; when we experience evil that love seems to turn its back on us. Either we have forsaken God or God has forsaken us. Death may come to us either as God's verdict on our failure or as God's abandonment of us, leaving us to perish. When we go to the depths of what is wrong with human life, in every case what we find is alienation from God, who is the love at the heart of all reality and the life that sustains all reality. This alienation from God is what much of our culture most of the time succeeds in hiding from us, while the new atheism makes a virtue of it.

If the diagnosis is right, then what we need more than anything, and in every part of our lives, is to find God. In a Christian doctrine of atonement this is only possible if God finds us – that is, if God finds us where we are in the depths of our alienation from God. That happens on the cross, where in Jesus' dying cry of agony and godforsakenness he himself plumbs the depths of the human plight – so that the love of God can reach those who are in those depths. We shall return to this shortly.

In the Western tradition of atonement theology the focus has been on guilt and our need of forgiveness and on evil as a power of compulsion to sin from which we need liberation. In the Greek Fathers and the Eastern tradition the focus has been more on mortality and our need of eternal life, which is participation in the eternal livingness of God. The meaningless tragedy in which God seems to leave people to suffer for no apparent reason has not figured very much in the theological tradition before the modern period. The sense that in the cross those who suffer, whether or not by their own fault, find God with them in suffering, healing their abandonment, has probably been much more a feature of Christian spirituality than of formal theology.

However, does this understanding of the cross have any basis in the New Testament? Is not the cross in the New Testament overwhelmingly understood in relation to sin and death, not undeserved suffering – except in the sense that Jesus, who did not deserve suffering on his own account, submitted to it for the sake of those who did and do?

The Passion of Jesus and the Psalms of Lament

One feature of the passion narratives in the Gospels is worthy of our attention in this connection. All four of them make many and unmistakable allusions to (and even quotations from) the Psalms of Lament. These are the psalms in which the psalmists cry out to God from the midst of suffering, not only seeking deliverance but frequently also questioning why God has abandoned the psalmists, leaving them to suffer. In these psalms of lament there are only rare references to sin that could be understood as the cause of God's inaction. Most protest against apparently undeserved suffering.[1] They are not only psalms of lament but also psalms of complaint and protest.

In Mark's narrative (followed by Matthew) the connection with such psalms is the more visible and significant because here Jesus' dying words, cited in Jesus' native Aramaic, are the opening words of Psalm 22: 'My God, my God, why have you forsaken me?' These words express both the intimacy of Jesus' relation to his Father (in the double 'My God') and the reality of his abandonment (which is

not just a feeling). I do not think that these allusions to the psalms
are a case simply of fulfilment of messianic prophecy (though that
is especially important in John), as though the psalms are being
read as prophecies of what the Messiah as an individual is to
suffer. For one thing, Jewish Christians would have been well used
to the praying of these psalms as giving voice to the experience of
whoever found them relevant to their case. But nor is Jesus just
one righteous person who, just like others, voices his anguish in
the words of the psalms. Mark certainly means more than that, as
the many allusions to the psalms of lament in his passion narrative show. In Mark's narrative the psalms are being understood
in a messianic way, but in the sense of an inclusive, not exclusive,
messianism. By that I mean that Jesus in his passion is identified
with all who had or could pray these psalms for themselves, all
who suffer the meaningless abandonment from which they cry to
God. Jesus identifies with them as his messianic destiny to suffer as
they did on their behalf. He does not need, on his own account, an
answer to the question 'Why?', but he makes the question his own,
speaking not in the Hebrew of the psalm but in his own Aramaic,
in an act of loving solidarity with all who question why God has
left them to suffer.[2]

The Cross and the Story of Jesus

To understand more adequately this loving solidarity of Jesus
with all who suffer we need to avoid isolating the cross, as theories of atonement have too often done, from the total story of
Jesus – both before and after his death. In the first place, Jesus'
death can only be understood as God's loving solidarity with all
who suffer if we read it in the light of the incarnation (and all the
Gospels, in my view, recognize the divine identity of Jesus). The
incarnation is God's radical self-identification with humanity, the
act in which God enters human history as himself a human and
identifies not merely with humanity in the ideal or the abstract,
but with humanity as it concretely is, in its sinful and suffering
condition. Jesus begins to make that loving identification with
humanity in an intentional and public way when he submits to
baptism by John the Baptist. He comes for baptism, not because

he needs to repent and receive forgiveness on his own account, but as an act of messianic solidarity with his people Israel. This is the outset of a ministry of bringing God's love into people's lives by a practice of loving identification. Jesus understands people's selves and situations empathetically, with the sort of love that is not mere benevolence from a distance but which engages with people where they are and thereby makes a transformative difference. In the Gospel narratives his loving identification is with all sorts of people: women and men, children, poor people, wealthy people, sick people, disabled people, outcasts, the dregs of society, the people who ran society, the religious and the irreligious, the people who thought they were righteous, the people who knew they were sinners. He treated all these people differently because they were indeed all different. But especially he identified in understanding compassion with the people who knew the depths in one way or another: the mad, the despairing, the chronically sick, the utterly destitute, the outcasts, the notorious sinners – all the people who knew too well their forsakenness by God or who were often enough reminded by others that they had turned their backs on God. To the people who knew the depths Jesus enacted God's loving identification with them, bringing forgiveness, healing, new hope, and life out of death.

The cry of godforsakenness from the cross is the final, climactic point of Jesus' loving identification with all. He enters the human situation at its negative extreme. He does so not as just one more human being, ending up by force of circumstance where so many others do, but by choice, in obedience to his Father's will, in order to bring God's love for all the forsaken precisely into that extremity of abandonment by God. If God is to be found there, then there is no dimension of the human plight in which he cannot be found.

It may be important to stress that the cross, understood in this way in the context of the biblical story, is not merely an example or illustration of God's loving identification with all people in every aspect of the human plight. Jesus *enacts* God's love. His cross is God's definitive act of solidarity with all who suffer. It is as the crucified one, who really entered their darkness then and there and still bears the marks of it, that Jesus is, as the Japanese Catholic novelist Shusaku Endo puts it, 'the eternal companion' of those who suffer.[3]

Does It Help?

If Jesus' loving identification with those who suffer, as I have expounded it, is presented as a response (though certainly not a solution) to the problem of undeserved suffering, one could ask the question: how does that help? What good is it to those who suffer to realize that Jesus is in the same boat with them? It certainly does not abolish the suffering. But it can, as Jürgen Moltmann puts it, remove 'the suffering in suffering'.[4] The 'suffering in suffering' is the abandonment, the sense of being left to suffer, the lack of love. It is not difficult to appreciate, on a human level, that someone close to a person who suffers, someone who loves them with understanding empathy, who enters to some degree into the situation of the one who suffers because they choose to do so out of love, can help the person who suffers bear their suffering, can take some of the load from them. But deep in the heart of suffering is the sense of being abandoned by love itself, by the love at the heart of reality, by God. Even those who have experienced abandonment by all human companions can find strength and encouragement in the companionship of the crucified Christ.

It seems peculiarly appropriate to cite Shusaku Endo at the present time. In some of his novels and in his *Life of Jesus*, Endo tried to develop an appropriately Japanese form of Christian faith, some aspects of which in its western versions he found uncomfortable, like an ill-fitting suit of clothes, in a Japanese context.[5] One of his characters, Otsu, who learned his Christian theology in Europe but found it alien to his Japanese way of thinking, explains why he nevertheless remains a follower of Jesus: 'I haven't been able to adapt myself to the thinking and the theology of Europe, but when I suffer all alone, I can feel the smiling presence of [Jesus], who knows all my trials.'[6]

Endo is very conscious that the love of Jesus as he represents it, as a suffering with people that cannot make a material difference to the conditions that cause their suffering, appears weak and ineffectual in worldly terms, and sees this as the reason for the eventual rejection of Jesus by those who had enthusiastically hailed him as Messiah. It is a rather bleak theology that offers no reason to hope for the alleviation of suffering by removing its causes. Both liberation theologians and charismatic Christians, for different reasons, would especially find him too close to a passive acquiescence in suffering, to the sort of fatalism that saps any attempt to improve things. Perhaps this is related to what the western commentators, reporting the aftermath of the tsunami, have been calling Japanese stoicism. But if you live in a country in which earthquakes are frequent, you may be more aware than many of us westerners are of the unavoidability of some kinds of suffering and the need to cope with them.

There is a difficult path to be trodden (difficult at least in theory) between protest against suffering and some kind of acceptance of such suffering as just having to be borne. It is a luxury of the modern West, perhaps, to be able to put all the emphasis on protest and activism. But if one thinks, for example, of the suffering of those who endure oppression in an unjust system, one can see how a sense of the solidarity of Jesus Christ with them in their sufferings can enable them to resist the dehumanizing effects of their suffering, to resist the deprivation of identity and dignity that their oppressors impose, to escape despair and to embrace hope. This is impressively evidenced in the spirituals of American black slaves.

However, it was not in the cross of Christ alone that those black slaves found solace and strength, but also in his resurrection and his future coming, which gave them hope for liberation from slavery. This is the other side of understanding the cross within the story of Jesus, which did not end with his death. Just as Jesus died in loving solidarity with all who suffer, so he rose from death still in solidarity with them, as God's promise of a new future for them. Hope may be difficult in suffering but it is also most alive in suffering, and the resurrection of Jesus enables that lively and active hope in those who know his loving solidarity with them.

The Im/passibility of God

To speak of the cross as God's suffering solidarity with all who suffer raises the dogmatic question: is not God, by nature, immune from suffering? So we cannot leave the subject without some consideration of the orthodox tradition of Christology and its implications for the doctrine of God.

In the incarnation of God in Jesus Christ, the eternal Son, the Second Person of the Trinity, becomes the subject of all the activity and experience of Jesus. The fully human reality of Jesus' human experience is essential to real incarnation. That is Chalcedonian Christology. We should be quite clear that it requires both that we attribute every aspect of the human suffering of Jesus to the eternal Son and also that we recognize that such suffering, precisely human suffering in all its very human reality, entailing the frailty and vulnerability of human physicality, human emotions and thinking, can be experienced by God only in incarnation. God in his eternal being cannot be thirsty or fear death or suffer the mockery of tormentors, but in Jesus he really does suffer precisely those things.

Yet if incarnation, with all that it entails by way of human suffering and other human experience, is possible for God, then it cannot be that God is absolutely impassible (unable to suffer) in the way that some, at least, of the theological tradition seems to imply. The fathers really struggled to maintain both the reality of the incarnation and the impassibility of God that seemed to them necessary for God to be God. God the Son 'suffered impassibly', said Cyril of Alexandria, and meant perhaps something like this: the eternal Son acknowledges the sufferings of his human nature as his own, but does not experience them as suffering. The flaw in this is that unless *someone* suffers there is no suffering. At most one might speak of damage. And Cyril, unlike the Antiochene theologians, was quite clear that there is only one acting subject in Christ – the divine Son.

If we insist, as I think orthodox Christology must, that God really suffers in incarnation, might we go on to attribute some kind of suffering to God outside incarnation? One reason for doing so arises when we put the cross in a Trinitarian context, as we certainly need to do but as I have not so far done. In Romans 8:32 Paul looks, as it were, upon the crucified Jesus dying in abandonment by God, not from our perspective, but from God the Father's perspective. God, he says, 'did not spare his own Son, but gave him up for us all' (NIV). There is real pain in those words. As Moltmann puts it, 'not only does God the Son suffer abandonment by his Father, but the Father suffers the death of his Son when he leaves him to die'.[7] The two forms of suffering are different, but what could 'did not spare his own Son' mean at all if it involved no pain? The analogy with what a human father would feel for his beloved son loses any meaning if we are to think of the Father acting dispassionately, unaffected by his loss of the Son. We would also be rather close to that degenerate kind of atonement doctrine that divides the Son who loves us from the Father who does not.

Is God then passible, as many theologians of the twentieth and twenty-first centuries would say, dissenting from the theological tradition? By way of responding briefly to this question, I will make three important points.

First, the doctrine of divine impassibility is a denial not merely that God can suffer but that God can be in any way affected by his creation. The relation between God and the world is understood as a purely one-way relationship in which God affects the world but is in no way affected by it. God's love, on this view, is not a relational involvement with others but a purely active benevolence. He can be neither adversely nor positively affected by the world. Even the incarnation must be conceived as an activity of God in the world that makes no difference to God. This is a view of God that most Christians throughout most of Christian history would, it seems to me, simply not recognize as the God they know in Christian prayer and practice, let alone as the God of the Bible.

Second, if we affirm divine passibility we must be very careful in specifying the sort of suffering that is possible for God. It is the voluntary suffering of love. God is not subject to suffering against his will, as we are. God does not suffer out of weakness, as we do. He suffers out of the fullness of his love for us. He suffers the suffering entailed by the relationship of love into which he has voluntarily opted by creating and relating to his creation. The fathers, when they discussed impassibility, usually worked with a simple contrast between humans who suffer unwillingly out of weakness and God who is not subject to anything. They failed to recognize this particular sort of suffering – the voluntary suffering of love – that both humans and God can undertake purely for love.

Third, all our talk of God is analogical. We can only speak of God by analogy with created, especially human, things. To say that God loves is to say that there is something sufficiently like human love in the divine reality to make the word meaningful, but there is always also a difference. God does not love just like us, but we cannot specify the difference. To say that God undertakes the voluntary suffering of love is to say that God does something sufficiently like what humans do when we say that of them for the language to be meaningful. It truly tells us something about God, but there has to be also an unspecifiable difference, or God would not be God. It does not help to say that the difference is that in our case we suffer but in God's case he does not. That amounts to discarding analogy and claiming we know the difference. The appropriate path is to say that God suffers, while remembering that this, like all our talk of God, is analogical.

SPIRITUAL EXERCISE: ENGAGING LAMENT[1]

Often we read Scripture too quickly. In this exercise, we invite you to slow down and to bring the whole of yourself, including your emotions, to the biblical text. Allow God to speak to you through these passages. If you are reading this book with a group, one member might guide the reflection to allow others a more focused experience of silence. The exercise may be repeated with any of the passages listed.

Prayer

> Listening God,
> I offer this time to you.
> Speak to me through your word
> and calm my fears about what I might encounter in it.
> Still my heart that I might hear your voice. Amen.

Entering the Silence[2]

Become aware of yourself resting in the presence of God.

Reflect on the day or the past few days. Ask yourself:
- What has been going on in my life?
- Where did I sense God's presence in those events?
- How have I responded?

Scripture Reading

Read one of the following passages aloud:

> *Psalm 22:1–21; Psalm 74:1–10; Psalm 88:9–18;*
> *Job 9:14–20; Isaiah 53:2–6*

Questions for Meditation

- What are your initial feelings after reading this text?
- Can you identify with any of the complaints the lamenter expresses? Does it resonate or jar with your reflections on where you have sensed God's presence?
- What theological problems does the passage raise for you?
- What does this passage allow you to do in honesty before God?
- What prayer would you like to express to God from where you are in your faith journey?
- Imagine that you are speaking the words of the passage in the presence of the crucified Jesus. What does he say to you?

Concluding Prayer

Crucified Lord,
thank you for meeting me in this silence.
Help me to entrust to you the things that cause me fear and pain.
As you have identified with me in your cross,
strengthen me to enter the pain of others and stand with them.
Amen.

SUGGESTIONS FOR THE USE OF INTEGRATIVE SILENCE

Reflection: Where are you currently in your thinking on the atonement? Did you recognize your own position in any of those described by Williams? Were there questions raised in any of the chapters that you would like to further explore?

Intercessory prayer: Engage in intercessory prayer for aspects of the cosmos awaiting full redemption and/or for situations of suffering in the world.

Meditation: Reflect on Salvador Dali's *Christ of St John of the Cross* (image available online). What does it imply about the relationship between the crucified Christ and the world?

Artistic expression: Chagall's *White Crucifixion* (image available online) depicts Jesus as a suffering Jew among other images of Jewish suffering in Chagall's time. How would you depict Jesus suffering in today's context? What images of contemporary suffering (your own or that of the world) would you want to place in the context of the cross? Draw, paint or imagine your artistic response.

Liturgical composition: Compose a collect or closing prayer that could be used to allow congregations to express anger, frustration or grief to God in the face of human suffering.

SECTION 2

BROKEN RELATIONSHIPS IN A FRACTURED WORLD

And it does appear evident that if theology is the thinking life of faith under the Gospel, it will be passionately concerned with the world and with the motifs of that Gospel.[1]

4

THE CROSS AND THE RECONCILIATION OF ENEMIES

David Tombs

What role can the cross play in the reconciliation of enemies? It is a daunting privilege to be invited to reflect on this question in the light of the last ten years I have spent working on a Conflict Resolution and Reconciliation programme in Belfast.[1] During these years I have learned a good deal about the subtle – and sometimes not so subtle – ways in which religion can contribute either to violence and conflict, or to peacebuilding and reconciliation, or, as is very often the case, how it might be ambivalent and may contribute in opposite directions simultaneously.[2]

Northern Ireland is a good example of the complexity of the relationship between religion and political violence, and the often unexpected ways in which well-intentioned faith can support violence. In the work of the programme we frequently draw on the research completed by Joseph Liechty and Cecelia Clegg in their book *Moving Beyond Sectarianism: Religion, Conflict and Reconciliation in Northern Ireland* (2001).[3] One of the important insights in the book is that it is often the unintended consequences of religion which can have a destructive impact, and these are all the more damaging because they are usually harder to identify.

One of my hopes in this chapter is to broaden our discussion out, so that the cross and its place in a Christian understanding of reconciliation and atonement is not seen as only relevant to personal relationships between individuals, but also applicable at a wider social and political level. In this I hope to consider how a theology of the cross might help to shape a moral imagination that contributes towards conflict transformation.[4]

The first section of the chapter draws on the work of Liechty and Clegg in Northern Ireland to think about religion's complex role in conflict and reconciliation. It identifies two areas of insight which we find especially useful in the programme: first, the need to consider religion's consequences and not just religion's intentions; second, the systemic nature of sectarianism and a pyramid model for understanding participation in sectarianism. Taken together, these two areas of insight provide a wider and more nuanced perspective for addressing questions of religion and violence than might otherwise be the case.

In the second part, I will draw on this wider perspective to suggest how the cross might be seen as a challenge to remember the underlying humanity of those with whom we might find ourselves in conflict. Remembering that those we see as our enemies share a common humanity with us can be a vital check on the escalation of conflict. It also acts as a safeguard against abuses in conflict, and can ultimately serve as a theological and ethical basis in support of initiatives for peace and reconciliation.

Religions, Conflict and Reconciliation

Religion's intentions and religion's consequences

One of the valuable insights in the book *Moving Beyond Sectarianism* by Joseph Liechty and Cecelia Clegg is that it is helpful to think of consequences and not just intentions when considering the dynamics of sectarianism.[6]

This approach is readily applicable to a consideration of religion and politics beyond sectarianism, and especially to understanding the influence of religion on violence. There is religious support for conflict and violence which is overt, explicit and intentional, but there is also religious support for conflict and violence which can be a consequence even when it is not an intention.

The most obvious examples of the intentional end of this spectrum are the religious sanctions of holy wars – whether crusades or jihads or their parallels in other traditions. The violence presents itself as worthy of support for explicitly religious reasons, and the 'religious cause' is presented as the primary motivation in the conflict. Intentional religious contributions are likely to provide the most dramatic examples of religion's role in wars and violence. It is these examples which are most likely to be picked up in popular and media discussions of religion and violence. Therefore a particularly rich area for consideration is how different understandings of the cross – from symbol of crusade to symbol of sacrifice – might shape attitudes to enemies. However, at least as important and much more likely to be neglected are the areas where religious support for political violence is less direct. The political cause does not make a direct claim to holiness or an explicitly religious justification, but differences over religious identities nonetheless have important consequences. In these instances, the religious cause is not claimed as the primary cause of the conflict; on the contrary any religious element is likely to be seen as unimportant or totally irrelevant. However, a more critical analysis can quickly highlight ways in which religion still exerts a strong influence on how the conflict and its associated violence are shaped and understood in any specific case. Above all, the religious dimension can help us understand why the primary causes assume particular significance and how they can become the subject of intense hostility. Unwrapping and unpacking these different dynamics to understand what is really going on can take a lot more time than seems to be the case when religious support for violence is intentional. It is therefore much less commonly addressed in popular and media discussions of religion and violence.

The belief that religion is unimportant to these conflicts and their violence is not limited to analysts and commentators outside the religious traditions. It is readily found among believers within the traditions themselves. At its strongest, it extends to an attempt to detach religion fully from politics; often a strategy which is based on the unrealistic claim that 'the spiritual' and 'the worldly' should not mix. The result of this is usually to disown responsibility for whatever is happening in the political sphere, and not make any attempt to address it for the good, or address ways in which religion might be a determinative factor in destructive actions.

This end of the spectrum of the impact of religion is perhaps the most neglected and in many ways the most easily missed. Its counter-intentional support for violence is likely to be hidden, and therefore harder to identify. Those who are responsible for violence at this end of the spectrum do not set out to promote violence; on the contrary they often see themselves as offering a message of peace and opposition to violence. Yet the consequences of what they do, and how they do it, nonetheless contribute to violence, albeit in indirect ways. Often this aspect of religious influence is most significant in shaping attitudes and beliefs about political violence which help sustain violent conflict in the long term. For example, repeating a religious message of 'Peace, Peace', when it is detached from a wider political involvement, is a limited role and potentially self-defeating strategy for religious leaders. It is not sufficient to ensure that religions are doing all that they can for peace, and it can distract from ways in which religions operate in practice to sustain the divisions and potential enmities on which conflict and violence are grounded. It is not enough just to talk of peace if religions are also creating conditions which make peace more difficult rather than more likely. The talk of peace becomes worse than useless; it becomes a masking mechanism which allows the real problems to escape detection and thereby makes a constructive response more difficult.

The Conflict Pyramid and its relationships of affinity

Alongside an awareness of both intentions and consequences, a second area of insight discussed by Liechty and Clegg is the pyramid of sectarianism in Northern Ireland.[6] One of the most helpful insights of the book is that sectarianism in Northern Ireland operates as a system and that because of its systemic nature everyone is involved in some way. The pyramid illustrates how everyone can be involved and yet their form of participation varies.[7]

The sectarianism pyramid is made up of different layers: Psychotic Killers; Paramilitary Groups; Politicians, Community and Religious Leaders; Ordinary Citizens. Each level marks a shift away from direct sectarian violence. However, each level supports the levels above it, and therefore carries a level of responsibility

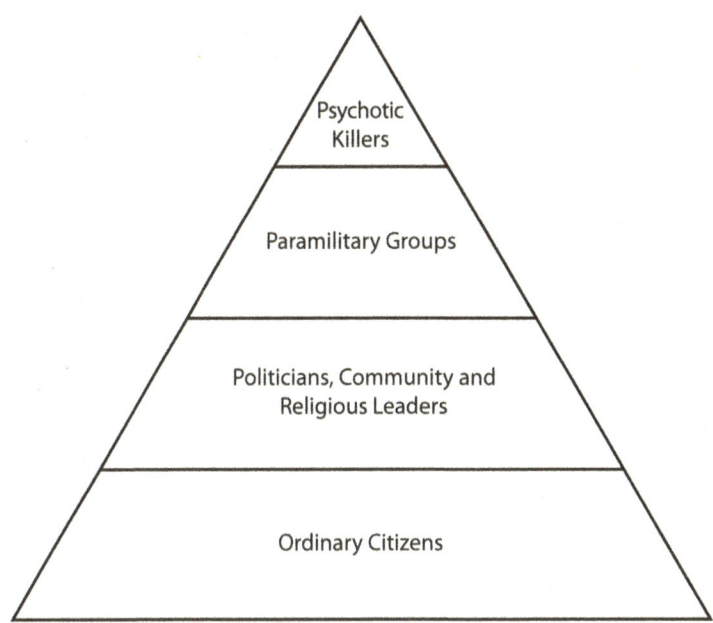

even for the actions of the 'mad dogs'. The pyramid does not imply that everyone has the same responsibility, but it does indicate that involvement takes different forms and that everyone carries some level of responsibility.

As with the spectrum of religion's influences, Liechty and Clegg present the pyramid with reference specifically to sectarianism, but it is equally adaptable to other issues. If adapted to address religious responsibility for conflict and enmity more generally, then the top layer might be seen as a layer of religious violence, which rests on enmity, which in turn rests on religious opposition, and is sustained by religious separation and division arising from perceptions of other religions as 'other' and different.

This is not to prejudge the existence of genuine differences that exist between religious traditions, or to suggest that difference is in itself a problem. A great deal depends on how differences are understood and what significance is given to them, in particular the ways in which differences might be constructed as complementary or as oppositional. This relates to wider questions, especially in relation to the boundaries and bonds of identity to which

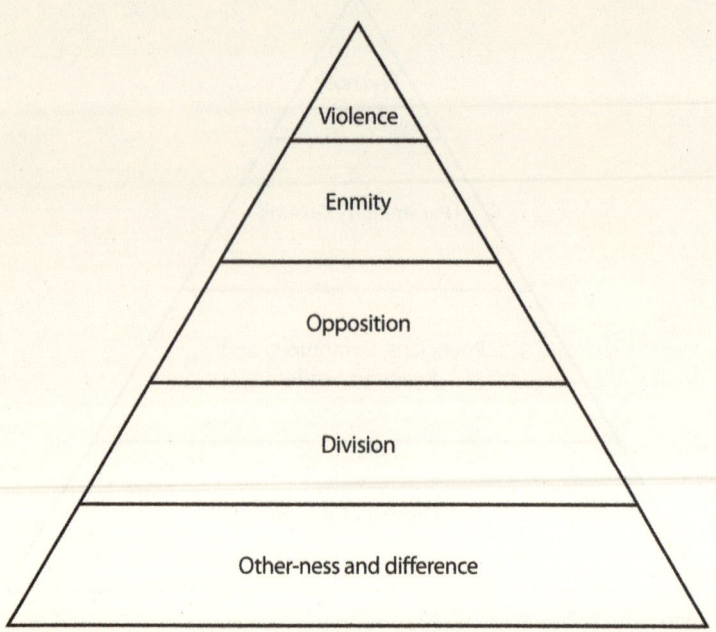

religious differences relate. Are the boundaries of identity seen as open and permeable, or as closed and impermeable? Are the bonds of community seen as an ongoing relationship which is open to change, or as a static fact which is intransigent? When identities emphasize an oppositional character and harden the boundaries against others they make it more likely that contact with others will lead to conflict, and that this conflict will be channelled into violence.

It should be noted that Liechty and Clegg are not suggesting that the relationship between levels is fully causal or entirely inevitable. It takes more than separation or division or difference to generate opposition; likewise, it takes more than opposition to generate enmity, or enmity to generate violence. The relationships between layers of the pyramid are best understood as relationships of 'affinity'. This is to say that the likely movement will be from one to the other. In most social environments, the default dynamic when conflict arises is likely to be in an upward direction; it has an inherent tendency to escalate because each action prompts a stronger reaction.

For anyone interested in conflict resolution or conflict transformation it is important to remember that it does not have to be this way. It is possible to stimulate and guide a de-escalation or transformation of conflict. Many conflict resolution analysts and practitioners will point to conflict as a normal process and to the potential in conflict – as long as it is addressed in a constructive way – for positive change and desirable outcomes. Conflict can prompt outcomes which all parties embrace, and which can be the basis for renewed and strengthened relationships. It is not that conflict is inherently destructive, or locked to outcomes of negative enmity, but that these negative outcomes will often be the result if a positive attempt is not made to address conflict constructively. Conflict readily gives rise to enmity if it is not dealt with proactively, effectively and with moral imagination.

The Cross and Moral Imagination

How might Christian theology bring positive insights from the cross to address the challenges of conflict, violence and enmity discussed above?

The cross can serve as a powerful resource for renewing the moral imagination in a society that has been distorted by enmity and violence. However, for this renewal to be at its most effective it should go beyond a conventional emphasis on the cross as a spiritual solution to sin. There is a danger that the spiritual significance of the cross can be emphasized in ways that detach it from lived experience. The spiritual significance of the cross should be found in relation to real life and not on a separate spiritual plane. Likewise, it should not be limited only to what Christian believers claim their intentions to be – no matter how important these are – but should also examine what unintended consequences there may be. For example, in debates around the salvific significance of the cross, it is necessary to address the criticism of those who argue that an unintended consequence of many models of atonement is to valorize violence in one way or another.[8] If this valorization of violence has a harmful impact on social behaviour and social values, it needs to be considered as part of the indirect or counter-intentional consequences of

Christian influence, no matter how much this goes against the original intentions.

Walter Wink's insights on the 'myth of redemptive violence' shed light on how readily wider society embraces the belief in violence as a redemptive force. If Wink is correct on this wider cultural context, then it may help to explain why uncritical assumptions about the relationship between violence and salvation go largely unnoticed in theological models of atonement.[9] Likewise, René Girard has explored the violent dynamics of rivalry, scapegoating and violence as dynamics in societies past and present. For Girard, the violence of scapegoating is a universal process, which provides a temporary resolution to the violence which has built up in a society.[10] The works of Wink, Girard, feminist critics, and others, have encouraged some theologians to focus more systematically on the problem of violence in the Christian doctrine of atonement, and to offer 'non-violent' readings of the cross.[11]

The next section looks at how the cross might open up a new avenue for moral imagination, by looking at the common tendency in violent conflicts to dehumanize the enemy.

The cross and our perception of the Other

A common feature in situations of violent conflict is that the people one is in conflict with are seen as different to oneself, and rendered as 'the Other'. This is reflected in the 'division and separation' at the bottom of the Conflict Pyramid. Small differences tend to be magnified and/or additional significance is given to incidental differences. This typically both reflects and reinforces the original reason for conflict. It helps to harden the identities of the parties to the conflict, so that the other party takes on a distinctive and fixed identity of difference.

Differences are often constructed in oppositional ways whereby one's own positive qualities are a mirror image for the negative qualities of the other. As the enemy's otherness becomes stronger, two things can happen.

First, the otherness of the enemy becomes a reason to impute malevolence to their actions, and this malevolence in turn serves as a self-justification for one's own actions. The otherness helps to explain the wrongness of what others do to you, and helps to excuse any wrongdoing you may yourself be involved in, since you see your own wrongdoing as provoked by their actions. The blame for the conflict becomes increasingly entrenched and asymmetrical, with a much greater burden placed on them, and therefore a much greater moral justification for one's actions as the 'innocent' party.

Second, the otherness of the enemy becomes an explanation for the original conflict. The sense of the conflict as 'over something' may recede and the sense that it is 'against someone' is likely to increase. The original cause of conflict can become less important, and might even be forgotten, as the conflict is now able to fuel itself on attitudes of hostility and enmity which become self-sustaining even when detached from the original spark.

Difference and otherness easily lead to hostility and enmity. In violent conflicts between groups and nations, a vicious circle quickly develops, reinforcing animosity towards the other. These negative dynamics of conflict often encourage a steady dehumanization of the enemy. This can happen in different ways – but what they all have in common is that the enemy (or alleged enemy) is rendered as not just different and 'other' but as less than fully human.

Dehumanization is at its most extreme in situations of genocide and ethnic conflict, where it is expedient to portray victims in ways that mask the enormity of one's own crimes against them. So the Nazis presented the Jews as rats and the Hutus described Tutsis as cockroaches. Both examples pictured human beings as much less than human, and in both cases the creatures were so stigmatized that their extermination was intended to be a matter of indifference or even desirable.

Referring to opponents in culturally dismissive ways in other contexts gives less extreme examples, but the underlying effects of derogatory racial or cultural epithets can also have dehumanizing effects. The overall impact is to make others not just different but considered less worthy of human respect and humane treatment. Examples of this can seem quite mild when viewed in isolation, but they tend to encourage and support much more extensive and serious ways in which people can be dehumanized. For example, the derisory term 'rag heads', used by coalition troops in the war in Iraq, helped to create the culture in which it was acceptable to insult and demean prisoners. The insulting and demeaning of prisoners contributed to the climate in which it was seen as acceptable to strip prisoners naked as a common practice, and this in turn created an environment in which all manner of demeaning abuse was acceptable.

One of the most important checks on a downward spiral of violence and abuse in conflict is therefore a sense of the humanity of one's enemy and the shared humanity that one has in common with them. It is because the sense of shared humanity can be an effective check on violence that those who are most committed to violence will intentionally seek to dehumanize their prospective victims.

It is with this in mind that I now turn to the third section, and reflect on how thinking about the cross might serve to guide moral imagination in this direction.

The Cross as Memory of Dehumanization

Crucifixion in the ancient world was a dehumanizing ordeal. It slowly stripped away all vestiges of the victim's honour and dignity in a painful public spectacle of shame.

For Christians who are focused on the atoning significance of the cross it is easy to pass over the actual experience of crucifixion with only a vague sense of what was really involved. While crucifixion practices varied with local circumstances, it was invariably a brutal, protracted and shameful form of death. At its most elaborate it made public torture into a perverse theatrical display.

The German scholar Martin Hengel has done much to make us more aware of what crucifixion entailed.[12] There is a general consensus that victims of crucifixion were tied or nailed to a wooden cross or sometimes to a tree. It is likely that wooden crosses were used for more formal executions when part of the punishment was for the victim to carry their own crossbeam (*patibulum*) to the point of public execution. For *ad hoc* punishments, which were closer to a state lynching, any available tree might be used. Victims were usually either tied or nailed at their wrists and ankles. The nails had to go through the wrist area (rather than the hands); otherwise the hands were likely to tear, especially if the nails had to support the body's weight.

Before crucifixion it was usual for victims to be stripped and flogged. As Mel Gibson's film *The Passion of the Christ* showed, this could involve horrific brutality, reducing the victim to something less than human in the eyes of many onlookers. Following this, on the cross, victims suffered the further physical pain of over-stretching, self-exhaustion and slow suffocation.

Added to this was the humiliation of public display; the shame for Jews was further heightened by the belief that 'anyone hung on a tree is under God's curse' (Deut. 21:23), a curse that Paul refers to in relation to Jesus' crucifixion in Gal. 3:13.

The different forms of Roman capital punishment reflected the social divisions of the day.[13] A Roman citizen condemned to death could – if otherwise respectable – expect simple decapitation. By contrast, slaves and non-Romans were more likely to be subjected to *tormentum*, the aggravated forms of capital punishment: cruci-fixion; burning; and *damnatio ad bestias* in the amphitheatre. All of these aggravated punishments were intended to do more than simply kill the victim; the intention was to debase the victim utterly in the process of death. *Damnatio ad bestias* was perhaps the most literal way of 'dehumanizing' a person, but crucifixion was in many ways even more degrading.

In some cases, crucifixion could even be combined with *damnatio ad bestias*. For example, the bandit-leader Laureolus – who had been executed by crucifixion – provided the role model for later shows in the amphitheatre in which victims were both crucified and attacked by a bear while defenceless on the cross.[14] Tacitus (*Ann.* 15.44.4) records that Nero's persecution of Christians in Rome included covering some victims in animal skins to be torn apart by dogs, while others were fastened on crosses and burned at night.

To heighten the public shame the Romans crucified their victims naked, a practice which should be named as sexual abuse but rarely is. This is partly because Christian art invariably hides this aspect of the reality. Roman crucifixions can be seen as elabo-rate rituals of dehumanization yet the specifically dehumanizing aspects of crucifixion have received very little attention in discus-sion. Ironically, I suspect part of the reason for this is that there is a rather different process of dehumanization at play within the Christian community. This dehumanization of Christ serves to preserve his dignity but insulates him from real experiences and removes him from actual history. What happened to Christ is typically sanitized of the shame and humiliation of crucifixion. In fact for the first four centuries Christian artists did not depict the crucifixion. It was only after crucifixion had been abolished as a punishment by Constantine that Christian artists started to depict the figure of Christ on the cross.[15]

The painful truth of crucifixion leaves a lot of disturbing questions, some of which I am trying to explore in other areas of my work. I am not suggesting that facing up to the realities of crucifixion means that the churches should rush to present only the most degraded and dehumanized images of Christ on the cross. However, nor does it mean that they should be completely excluded from consideration.

A clearer sense of crucifixion as a ritual of dehumanization can make a significant contribution to Christian concern for conflict transformation and the reconciliation of enemies. Christ on the cross is a vivid reminder of the destructive forces of violent conflict and an urgent summons to oppose them. The cross represents the forces of human evil at work and holds up their awful result.[16]

The Easter story– in which crucifixion is linked with resurrection – sets the dehumanization of Good Friday in a wider narrative, linking it to the new hope and new life of Easter Sunday. In this wider narrative, God does not abandon the victim, no matter how shamefully he is abused, but raises Christ anew. This memory of the cross can challenge Christians to recognize the humanity of all, and resist our urges to see our enemies as less than human. Instead of stigmatizing our enemies more and more strongly as 'other' and less than human, the cross calls on us to reach out in understanding and to reverse the urge to stigmatize enemies – to see instead that, whatever our disagreements may be, our enemies share a common humanity with us, and in this they carry the image of Christ, and point to God's presence among us.

5

THE CROSS AND THE RECONCILIATION OF GENDER

Elaine Storkey

The cross of Christ has been pivotal in Christian theology from the very beginning. Christian theologians from many different traditions have focused on the meaning and implications of the cross in relation to reconciliation. Yet an interest in how the cross might break down barriers between men and women was, for many centuries, extremely slim, if not non-existent. Typically, theologians focused exclusively upon the reconciliation of sinful humanity to a holy God, where 'humanity' comprised men and women, usually subsumed under the single category, 'Man'. Although some writers did enter into the power of the cross to bring together people who were at enmity with each other, there was very little sustained enquiry about the implications of this, or any attempt to follow it through in the area of gender. Feminist theology changed all that.

The Impact of Feminist Theology

This chapter focuses on the debate about atonement within feminist theology and the issues it presents to us. The seminal question was posed by feminist theologian Rosemary Radford Ruether: 'Can a male Christ save women?' It sounds like an innocent question – the sort a child might raise.[1] But it was far from innocent, presenting a fundamental challenge to what had long been taken for granted by Christian theologians – that because God sent his only Son that all who believe in him will not perish but have eternal life, Christ's death on the cross was effective for all humanity. Ruether did not question the orthodoxy of this idea, but its coherence. She asked whether as a concept it made any sense – whether Christ's death on the cross could possibly have universal efficacy even for 'all who believe'. For as a male saviour how could Christ save women? What she was doing, of course, was to take the argument familiar in the Catholic Church and reverse the subject. On the issue of women priests the magisterium maintained, and still maintains, an 'impossibilist' position.[2] Women could not be priests. A priest was an icon of Christ; a priest, representing Christ, was a mediator between God and man. To be Christ's representative, they held that you had to be Christ's *representation* – in other words, to share his key characteristics. This long-held idea was made official in the 1976 Vatican declaration that 'there must be a physical resemblance between a priest and Christ'.[3] However, as Ruether pointed out, it appeared that this resemblance was limited to his gender: 'Since this strange new version of the imitation of Christ does not exclude a Negro, a Chinese or a Dutchman from representing a first-century Jew, or a wealthy prelate from representing a carpenter's son, or sinners from representing the saviour, we must assume this imitation of Christ has now been reduced to one essential element, namely, male sex.'[4]

If priests had to reflect Christ's gendered identity, women could clearly not be priests or icons of the Saviour. And they therefore could not represent Christ at the Eucharist or other sacraments. So it made sense to Radford Ruether simply to reverse the question. If gender was so key in the relationship between Christ and human beings, how then could Christ represent women in atonement?[5] If maleness is seen as essential to Christ in his humanity, how is it non-essential in his divinity? 'Incarnation solely into the male sex does not include women so women are not redeemed.'[6] The question recurs in several forms in early feminist theological writings.[7] The dilemma remained; for Korean theologian Rita Nakashima Brock, therefore, the question 'Can Christ redeem women?' led inevitably to another question: 'Can women redeem Christ?'[8]

The issue for the church had been how the *particular* (in this case women) could possibly represent both *universal* humanity and the *universal* Saviour: the one who died for all on the cross. In her simple question, Ruether unmasked the concepts of both 'humanity' and 'Saviour', and showed that, in the way the church referred to them, they were not universal, but gendered; and both privileged the male. Humanity, indeed, was Male and men have had predominance over women throughout the whole of Christian history. Christ was a man – and women could not represent him. And if a female priest cannot represent Christ, how can a male Christ save women? The discussion refocused away from trying to map a relationship between *particular* and *universal*, to the conviction that, however much they masqueraded as universal concepts, those relating to gender were all particularized ones.

This whole process of enquiry was one which was to become familiar to feminist theology. It was to subject accepted Christian doctrine to deconstruction: probing the assumptions beneath firmly held statements, the location from which it was being written, the attitudes which then held sway, and the systems of power which influenced the formation of Christian orthodoxy. The result was the relativization of what had previously been accorded as universal creedal statements. In seeing them in the context of the past, it had to be acknowledged that, throughout human history, Christians and the church had privileged the masculine, and women had been, at best, subsumed linguistically within the male gender. At worst, they had been silenced, in the practice of the church as well as in its creeds, councils, language and theology, and the male has continued to be the norm.

For most reflecting areas of the church, once this process has deconstructed so many of its key concepts and cherished doctrines, it is impossible to return to the previous state of innocence. The net result of this is that the gender issue has not been just 'another concern' to be added onto the list of issues within ethics and anthropology; it has changed Christian reflection and discourse in a groundbreaking way. The early feminist writers faced the implications of this. Some, like Phyllis Trible, welcomed the process as a deepening of our understanding of biblical revelation: 'As the Bible interprets itself to complement or to contradict, to confirm or to challenge, so likewise we construe these traditions for our time, recognizing an affinity between then and now. In other words, hermeneutics encompasses explication, understanding, and application from past to present.'[9]

Over the following decades within the church, self-consciousness about language has changed and women now expect to be addressed inclusively in the context of their faith. Except among those who are determined to reject the debate, 'woman' can no longer be absorbed into 'Man', or 'sister' into 'brother'. But there have been other shifts too. The question of women's gendered personhood and identity has itself become a complex one. 'Woman' can no longer be a unified or essentialist term, for there is no universal woman. Women are clearly from many locations; they speak with different voices. Feminist theologians have explored the differences and diversities in women's context and experience in dialogue, literary, philosophical and psychological studies and at increasingly sophisticated levels.

Varieties of Feminist Responses to the Biblical Text

Helen Sterk notes that feminist criticism of traditional masculine God-language grew out of women's struggle with dominance, even abuse, often legitimated by the subtext of the religious language of headship or submission.[10] Yet, although this may have been the seedbed for feminist theology, and although most feminist theologians at some stage point to some experiences of gender oppression, it became evident from the beginning that they did not speak with a single, united voice.

What separated the differing articulations of feminist theology was more than their divergent emphases or leanings. From early on, they deviated from each other in their hermeneutics, their processes of theological enquiry and their relationships with text and tradition. These differences come out sharply in what feminist theologians accept as authoritative and authentic. In those early heady days, questions revolved around the strength of patriarchal hermeneutics and whether it was possible to retrieve an authentic biblical text which could be regarded as divine revelation; whether we get our understanding of atonement, of Christology, of the Holy Spirit, of the cross from the text or whether we need to go elsewhere. If the books of the Bible were written in male-dominated cultures, how much of the patriarchy of those cultures had infiltrated the biblical text? There were those scholars like Phyllis Trible, who recognized the force of the question, but did not want to give up on biblical authority. In her study of the Hebrew Scriptures, Trible's embrace of feminist hermeneutics led her to attempt to 'recover old treasures and discover new ones in the household of faith'.[11] She suggested in an article in the *American Journal of Religion* in 1973 that much of the biblical text could, in fact, be 'depatriarchalized' and liberated to speak more powerfully to women.[12] In a footnote in *Beyond God the Father*, however, Mary Daly gave her own wry verdict on this endeavour: 'It might be interesting to speculate upon the probable length of a "depatriarchalized Bible". Perhaps there would be enough salvageable material to comprise an interesting pamphlet.'[13]

For women like Letty Russell, there was a constant tension. Conceding that much of the Bible has patriarchal underpinning, she insisted that biblical authority remained important: 'I myself have no intention of giving up the Bible as the basis of my theology . . . The Bible has authority in my life because it makes sense of my experience and speaks to me about the meaning and purpose of my humanity in Jesus Christ.'[14] Yet others challenged what kind of authority it could have, when it takes us into horrifying narratives of rape, violation, abuse of women and incest? How can even feminist hermeneutics help us with passages like Judges 19 which recounts the savage gang-rape of a concubine, and the self-preoccupation of her husband who sees himself as the victim? For, while these stories are not recounted with any kind of approval, nor are they condemned by the narrator, in the way we would wish. Phyllis Trible does not duck this problem, nor does she eliminate these passages from her own scrutiny. Referring to them as *Texts of Terror*, she insists that these are stories that must be told *in memoriam* of the women who underwent such violation.[15]

Similarly, Virginia Mollenkott, then writing from within the Evangelical Women's Caucus, wanted to separate the patriarchal culture of the Bible and the deeper meaning of the biblical text:

Because patriarchy is the cultural background of the Scriptures, it is absolutely basic to any feminist reading of the Bible that one cannot

absolutize the culture in which the Bible was written. We cannot assume that because the Bible was written against the backdrop of a
patriarchal social structure, patriarchy is the will of God for all people
in all times and in all places.[16]

In fact, where patriarchy has predominated it has distorted the
application of a biblical vision. 'There can be no serious question that Christianity as an organized religion has in many ways
departed from the teachings of its own Scriptures. And nowhere
has it departed more radically than by building up tremendous
power structures.'[17]

Different varieties of theological feminism were thus evident
from its beginning, and have grown in number as the decades have
moved on. It is interesting how the Protestant and Catholic traditions left their legacy in early feminist theology. Feminist theologians from a Protestant tradition – particularly those nurtured in
evangelical and Reformed schools – hung on to the Scriptures and
defended them as much as they could. At the most 'orthodox' end
of the spectrum, biblical feminists like Catherine Clark Kroeger
insisted that their quarrel was not with the text, nor with the
theology of the cross, nor even with the 'maleness' of Christ, but
with the church's use of text, theology and practice which has
protected and reinforced the male *status quo*.[18] Their argument is
that there has been *insufficient* biblical orthodoxy, for the church
has been narrow in its confines and restricted in its scope. Above
all, it has failed to understand the challenging nature of Christ's
servanthood and sacrifice, and has failed to apply it in the ways
we have conducted our gendered relationships.

Feminist theologians from a Catholic background were less
enamoured of the text, and saw less need to accord it authoritative status. For all that has made it authoritative, they insisted,
has been the pronouncements of councils of men. They claim that
a 'controlling group marginalizes and suppresses other branches
of the community . . . the winning group declares itself the privileged line of true (orthodox) interpretation. Thus a canon of
Scripture is established.'[19] But now, this 'hermeneutics of consent'
needed to be challenged with what Elisabeth Schüssler Fiorenza
called a 'hermeneutics of suspicion'. Canonical authority had to be
replaced with a 'canon within the canon' (Radford Ruether). We

cannot continue to play the old games of acceptance and continuation. Feminist theology claims that hermeneutics 'which defines itself as "the actualising continuation of the Christian history of interpretation" does not suffice, since it does not sufficiently take into account that tradition is a source not only of truth but also of untruth, repression, and domination'.[20]

In other words, we cannot pretend that some of the things that women have struggled with throughout our gendered history are not actually there in the biblical text. They are reinforced rather than challenged by Christian tradition. So we need a different starting point, argue Schüssler Fiorenza and Ruether. For Schüssler Fiorenza, then, authenticity is found elsewhere, in the ecclesia of women, and from there it can be conferred to the biblical text: 'The locus of divine revelation and grace is therefore not simply the Bible or the tradition of a patriarchal church but the "church of women" . . . the experience of women struggling for liberation . . . from patriarchal oppression.'[21]

Over the decades since Ruether first raised her startling question, feminist theologians have thus found themselves in internal disagreements, as well as with the theological assumptions they together were critiquing. Some withdrew from the fray, wounded by attempts at sisterhood which seemed to have ended in struggle. Today, philosophically, feminist theology slides along a spectrum from Biblical feminism, liberation feminism, eco-feminism, goddess feminism, lesbian spirituality through to many different strands of postmodern and post-Christian feminism. The debate has become increasingly nuanced as the theological enquiry has both broadened and matured.

The question of the status of the Scriptures has remained a key one for the debate between those feminists who wish to remain part of the church. It is from the Bible, especially the New Testament, that we get our Christology and its essential focus on the cross. Many feminists have argued that, of all Christian doctrines, Christology has been most often turned against women. Not only have christological arguments been used to reinforce an exclusively male image of God, and thus to legitimate men's superiority over women, but the image of Christ on the cross has contributed to women's acceptance of abuses of power, as it has often been interpreted as a model of passive submission to unjust suffering.

A Christ-Saviour is thus dismissed by many feminist theologians, including Daphne Hampson, Carter-Heyward and Grace Jantsen, as being a hero figure which prevents human beings, especially male human beings, from accepting responsibility for their own behaviour. There is a strong repulsion among them towards our 'need' for a hero figure held up throughout history as the One who solves our problems and becomes a scapegoat. That is why some feminists have argued for the total rejection of any traditional doctrine of the cross. For them it has become the symbol of a necrophilic religion centring upon a dead male. As womanist Delores Williams said in a Re-imagining conference in Minnesota in the early 1990s: 'We don't need folks hanging on a cross with blood dripping and weird stuff.'[22]

Sin and Gender

Salvation through the cross raises the issue of what we need to be saved from. Within feminist theology, sin is often seen as gender specific. The sins which are assumed by much Christian soteriology are regarded by feminists as 'male' sins: pride, will to power, dominance, egocentricity, denial, and refusal to mutuality. Daphne Hampson argues that the very concept of sin in Christian theology has been shaped by male psychology. She describes it as separateness, opposition, fear of relationship, and angst, which she defines as 'anxiety [without an] . . . object'.[23] By contrast, female sin, as suggested fifty years ago by Valerie Saiving, might be more properly regarded as self-negation, passivity or under-development of the self.[24] Anne Wilson Schaef says sin is being out of touch with our internal process and is self-distortion. And by contrast, living in tune with God means being in tune with what one already is.[25] What is important for Grace Jantzen is that we challenge the 'patriarchal dimensions of the concept of salvation'. Sin is mis-stated. In fact it is an imposition of a male framework on women. For her, we need to recognize the 'luxuriant self-sufficiency implied in the idea of flourishing'. The natural condition of humanity is good: we need only to be allowed to develop naturally.[26] The fact that we have been sold a different message is largely because the selling of that message has largely been left in the hands of men.

You can see the progression here. It begins with a challenge to the non-gendered nature of sin, to locating sin in traditional Christianity as a product of patriarchy, to redefining sin so that it is relevant to women, to its effective abolition as a meaningful concept within women's experience. By the end of the story, sin has been eliminated from authentic women's lives as 'a kind of false consciousness'. If women do need to repent, it is for their lack of flourishing and mutuality, negligence in developing our natural selves, and our unwillingness for openness. And to overcome this, we need to develop the persons we are and look at the divinity within us. We do not look for a saviour (especially not a male saviour) who will plead our case to (a male) God.

The 'How' of Atonement

If salvation and atonement are largely about coming to terms with sin, and sin is such a problematic concept within feminist theology, what happens to the concept of how Christ atoned? For many feminist theologians the cross is seen, not as a place of reconciliation between God and humanity, or even between men and women, but as a symbol used to glorify death and romanticize suffering. For the cross involves ideas of sin, of sacrifice, guilt and suffering, which many feel reflect the negative experiences of women.[27] It justifies brutality (of which women are often victims) and romanticizes it. It is caught up with the Babylonian myth of redemptive violence, the notion that violence heals, might is right. The focus on the heroic but redemptive, violent death of Christ has been much criticized, not least in its portrayal in the film *The Passion of the Christ*. Not only does this focus often lead to an obsession with the details of brutality and barbarity, but it fails to ask the key question: to what extent is violence ever redemptive?

For Radford Ruether, 'Christ's cross is used to inculcate a sense of masochistic guilt, unworthiness and passivity in Christians. To accept and endure evil is regarded as redemptive. Liberation Christians say that God does not desire anyone's sufferings, least of all Jesus'.[28] The way forward for her and other liberation feminists is to assert that the power of atonement lies in human life and human action, not in any historic act of brutality or violent death.

Christ's power is in its spiritual potential within us, to release people into a new future. 'Spirit Christology does not separate out a past, perfect historical Jesus from the ongoing Spirit. Rather it sees Christ as a power that continues to be revealed in persons, both male and female, in the present. Christ is located in a new humanity that discloses the future potential of human life. The reality of Christ is not completed in the past.'[29]

Fundamental Philosophical and Theological Problems

Replacing the particular, historic Christ with the Christ we become in our own context does not solve the difficulties, however. Problems remain for feminist theologians and others who are trying to find a way to bring redemption into the area of gender. In disposing of a God who redeems us, we ourselves are now both redeemed and redeemers. More especially we are redeemed and redeemers if we are women. Mary Grey spells this out when she says that the very lives of women become 'part of the divine dynamic for the transformation of the world' reaching out to all oppressed and marginalized groups.[30] We are here to bring healing. Women ourselves can be salvific. Redemption lies in the healing of relationships and the creation of non-dominative, non-discriminatory patterns of behaviour. Since sexism has been at the basis of these ills throughout history, so overcoming sexism, by women's power of mutual love, the new world order can be ushered in.

This eco-feminist dream of beauty and transformation is one that moves away from what has been seen as the doctrinal divisiveness which has peppered Christian history.

Mary Grey believes that when the ideology of a particularized male Christ with all the concomitant problems is gently erased away, and we are left with a loving, imaginative God, expressed in the open community of women, we stand some chance of halting the brutalization of the world. When the pain is healed, marginal groups incorporated, and the Spirit outpoured in the mutuality and power of being God's women, then this is itself redemptive. It will bring the church into a new future of wholeness.

Assessing the Process

What feminist theology does is to uncover the layers of women's experiences throughout history and insist that these are taken seriously in any theological expression of the Christian faith. In doing that, they have left us in no doubt that the reconciliation of the genders is a far more complex issue than breaking down differences between men and women, or learning to communicate better across the different gender-cultures. It is more than the task of addressing issues of justice and injustice or women's frustration at their inequality or men's alleged inadequacy at intimacy. It is a matter of redoing Christian theology in such a way that nothing is left unchallenged, and much of what was regarded as orthodoxy is abandoned.

Yet there are considerable problems with this process. In a very real sense the journey out of orthodoxy into what we might call 'subjective flourishing' is a journey which leaves us in a similar place from where we started, but with no real solution. When human flourishing does not happen, when women do not produce the redemptive community, when mutuality has not grown, and love has not resulted in non-discriminatory relationships, what then? Where then do we go? The belief that women can be relied upon to bring whatever salvation is needed into the gendered situation is a forlorn hope. For although sin might be gender specific, it is also ubiquitous and needs to be acknowledged as such. It also criss-crosses over gender demarcations. Men as much as women suffer from the sin of passivity, non-mutuality and denial. Male pride might certainly be alive and well, but there are also many men who are poor at developing self-awareness and at recognizing the injustice they themselves face. Similarly, women, as much as men, struggle with envy, selfishness, greed, mean-spiritedness, lack of love and a desire to wound. And even though the sins structured in our society unmistakably reflect the power of patriarchy, there is more to sin than sexism.

What is more, it is quite possible to take seriously the feminist critique of the patriarchal structure of church history, power and relationships, without the need to abandon orthodox theology. The cross can be allowed to speak into our human gendered situation, not by glorifying violence, justifying scapegoating or romanticizing suffering. It does not require us to relativize sin and identify it as only gender specific. The cross speaks into our situation precisely because it says that sin is real, experiential and damaging to us all. Sin fools us into complacency. Sin distorts truth into half-truths and lies. Sin destroys our peace and our relationships. Sin is alienating, destructive, distortive, delusory, addictive, structural and generational, and, if we stand any chance of human flourishing, we need to have it dealt with. Even if it were not an offence to God, human sin puts women and men often at enmity with each other and they need power outside themselves and their context if they are to move on. The doctrine of the cross reminds us powerfully that neither gender can be the saviour of the other. We cannot help ourselves. We need to be able to access something of the power which created the universe and gives life to all, if we are to break the bonds that hold us and keep us in a self-protective existence.

Men and women need to be reconciled in the same way that Jews and Gentiles needed to be reconciled, or slaves and free people (Gal. 3:28). It is no accident that in each of those pairs of relationship the power is not equal. Power is held by Jews, not Gentiles; free people, not slaves; men, not women. What feminist theology helps us to see much more clearly is that before reconciliation can take place in any area there has to be repentance of the misuse of power. In gender relations there has to be repentance of male injustice towards women and especially of male violence towards women which is institutionalized in many cultures in many ways. Whether it is rape as a weapon of war, female genital mutilation, the taking of child brides which is very little more than child abuse, selective abortion of girl babies, domestic violence, and so on. Unless we admit that this is part of the global relationship of men and women, then we cannot begin to leave these issues behind. But there has also to be repentance for unlove, manipulation, disrespect, hardness of heart, unforgiveness and the sins of bitterness. And women are as prone to these as men.

Christ's self-emptying, as depicted in Philippians, is neither a symbol of martyrdom nor a glorification of subordination. It is the voluntary giving-up of power by the God who created all things. It is only in the voluntary laying-down of power that Christ can pick up the sins and wrongdoings of those who are powerless to lift themselves out of the mess they are in. The re-labelling of Christ as a somehow unwilling victim, of a self-righteous vengeful God who exhibits the worst characteristics of masculinity, is a profound distortion of the theology of the cross. In both the gospels and the epistles, Jesus is never the victim in that sense. Jesus abandons his own right to power in order to lift the burdens from others. Many to whom we attribute power are also in bondage, and the power becomes a smokescreen for inadequacy and cruelty. In emptying himself (not in having his identity taken away by others) Jesus is also giving an invitation to all who have power to reflect on the source of their power and recognize its use and abuse. He gives them the opportunity to remove its grip, and to receive greater power, the power of forgiveness and love from God, which ushers in the indwelling and fulfilment of the Holy Spirit.

The picture Paul paints in Ephesians of Christ's outstretched arms is a picture of the strength of reconciliation which is at the very heart of the cross. Christ's arms, stretched out in two direc-tions, gather the two enemies together; those who are far off and those who are near are drawn away from their own hostility into one body – the body which is Christ's own. The picture is dynamic, not passive; powerful, not pathetic; enlivening, not defeated. This graphic picture of peacemaking and reconciliation is applied by Paul to the division between Jew and Gentile. It is strong enough to break down racial and ethnic divisions that have persevered through history. But it goes even beyond that to men and women, for all divisions that lead to strife, bloodshed or violence, can be brought together in Christ. When enemies are brought into one body, they are enemies no longer, but members together in Christ.

Feminist theology has grown from within a church which has not shown or lived out the reconciliation which God offers to humanity through Christ's death on the cross. It has reacted to a church power-structure that has turned a blind eye to injustice, to patriarchy and to inequality. It has grown out of frustration at the collusion with the misuse of power and the erection of controlling hierarchies. At the heart of that church are women and men who need to face the truth about their situation and move into repent-ance and the liberating power of the gospel. For the central message of the cross is not one of violence, suffering, victimization, passivity or defeat. It is simply that God's love in Christ has overcome the deepest hatred that the human heart can find. And death to sin can bring, for women and men, hope, resurrection and the beginning of new life.

GROUP ACTIVITY: LETTER WRITING[1]

Give members of your group the following options and some time to complete the creative-writing activity. These letters are for the group's discussion (and not for posting), but group members should be encouraged to write freely, knowing they will be invited to share only what they are comfortable sharing in the discussion group.

Write to one of the following figures:

1. Someone who, to your mind, represents feminist activism – what would you like to say to this person in light of the cross?
2. Someone you see as restricting full gender inclusion in the church's ministry – what would you like to say to this person in light of the cross?
3. St Paul – what would you like to say to him?
4. Eve – what would you like to say to her?

Alternatively, write a letter expressing a minority report – what do you feel needs to be added to the conversation we are having?

Discussion Questions

1. What emotions did you feel as you wrote the letter?
2. What did you say that you might not have anticipated?
3. How is this letter different from the one you might have written if you had not reflected on the cross?

4. What is the good news of the cross for the person/issue you were addressing?
5. What have you learned from the contributions of the other members of this discussion group?

6

THE CROSS AND OUR ASPIRATION FOR A COMMON DOCTRINE OF REDEMPTION: A DIALOGUE

Con Casey and Stephen N. Williams

What follows is the transcript of an interview of Dr Con Casey and Prof. Stephen Williams by the editors at Trinity College Dublin on 16 December 2013.

McGlinchey: What common themes are there in Catholic and Protestant atonement theology and how might they be developed in ways that are beneficial to both traditions?

Williams: When you ask about common themes, it sounds as though we are starting from different traditions, Catholic and Protestant, and looking for community; whereas we begin with a community of thought. Protestantism has seen itself in its main phases as very much attached to the tradition. So, when I think of common themes, I am thinking really of the whole background in patristic and medieval thought. In all of that shared history, I think if I had to pick one thing out, it might be the significance of thinking about the *Christus Victor* theme. Should I elaborate on that?

Heffelfinger: Please.

Williams: In reaction against the excessively rational way of looking at the atonement, there has been a tradition which, certainly in Protestant circles, has gone under the name *Christus Victor*: Jesus Christ wins a victory over sin, death, the wrath of God, and the Devil. It highlights the greatness of the victory and the mystery of atonement at the same time. It seems to me an important theme because, when Protestants have narrowly concentrated on one way of understanding the atonement, whichever theme they have chosen, what has sometimes been lost is a sense of evil, the dimension of evil. I am so aware of that in our time, as Catholics and Protestants should all be. It seems to me that, if we think hard about the sheer evil in our world, and how the cross is juxtaposed to it, then Catholics and Protestants commonly might well want to recover this great theme of the victory of the cross over the forces of death and evil, quite apart from any other more detailed adumbrations of the atonement.

McGlinchey: So would you say that theme is basically a non-controversial one that both traditions could equally own?

Williams: I would, because it is rooted in the fathers. It may recede a bit with Anselm and on from Anselm, but I do not think it goes away entirely. I would see *Christus Victor* as something common because you can appeal back to its patristic roots. Obviously, the fathers sometimes would have a very crude formulation of the theme and we would want to get rid of some of those crudities. Certainly, they had some very curious ways of thinking about ransom and the Devil, but the general idea of the cross as the victory over evil is something we might well recover.

McGlinchey: Do you sense that there might be ways that the *Christus Victor* theme could be developed that have not been spoken yet, but which could be quite helpful in terms of bringing the two traditions together?

Williams: Paul Ricoeur wrote a book many years ago on the symbolism of evil and he talks there about evil as defilement. Certainly people in contemporary life actually have a lot of experience with defilement, although they think of religion as an alien factor when it deals with such things as cleansing. Nevertheless, people have the sense of being tainted, for example by childhood experiences, which needs to be addressed by something like cleansing. If we think about defilement in relation to evil, and about how the cross, even if you cannot spell out the theory, does something which cleans up a person, I think that is an important way of developing that aspect of Christ as victor over everything that defiles. That would be one thought.

McGlinchey: Con, does that resonate with you, and are there other common themes?

Casey: I found that very interesting and very perceptive. The *Christus Victor* tradition is very noted in the Catholic literature as well, and Stephen is right in saying that the strong patristic roots make one feel at home in a theological discourse of that kind. Stephen is also very right in speaking about the ability of the Christ as Victor theme to shine a light into the evils of the dark places of the world today. One figure that has gotten lost somewhere along the way is the Devil. I think both traditions, Catholic and Protestant, could well meditate on what is meant by something like the Devil. I think that possibly they will come to see that there is an evil that is attributable to humanity that has a depth that needs to be recovered and that both traditions want to speak about.

McGlinchey: So would you see evil as perhaps a personal agency? Is that what you are hinting at?

Casey: I think it is actually very difficult to simplify one's narrative of evil. I think of evil as a kind of system of infidelity to created and graced humanity that is pervasive. You keep correcting it in one direction and it reappears in another direction. I think that the theme that we articulate as original sin is manifest historically in systemic infidelity that keeps occurring in one culture after another. The *Christus Victor* model says that system does not fill up the whole of reality, and the violence of that system does not have the last word. So, I think that Catholic and Protestant traditions are very fortunate that there are two voices at the same conversation with resources to make that conversation fruitful. The *Christus Victor* model is one such resource. But it is great that there is more than one voice, because we are exploring a deep mystery and there needs to be constant opening up of the depths of the mystery from different voices.

McGlinchey: Stephen, you talked about *Christus Victor* having roots in the patristic and medieval traditions. Is there a sense in which it also has roots in Luther?

Williams: Yes, Luther is many-sided. I think it is wrong to try to capture him for one tradition in atonement thinking rather than another. In Luther you would have elements of penal ways of understanding the atonement, and *Christus Victor* as well. I think there is something comprehensive there. Luther is often thought about as Pauline in his ways of thinking, but arguably he is Johannine with a strong sense of light and darkness.

Heffelfinger: Would either of you like to say more about this question?

Casey: Stephen started us off helpfully, but if I was to start it I would say the common theme in Catholic and Protestant atonement theology is the common awareness that the origin of atonement lies in God's gift. This is entirely the story of gift, and there again, what I find exhilarating about the fact that there are two voices at the table is that the gift can be expressed differently from within the two traditions to their mutual benefit. That is only saying: are there common themes? Stephen says *Christus Victor*, and I say the origin in gift, and therefore we have not one theme but two.

Williams: I would agree with that entirely. Both Catholic and Protestant theology are theologies of grace.

McGlinchey: How might the category of theological aesthetics contribute to a re-imagination of atonement theology in an ecumenical context?

Casey: I have come to think that the field of art and literature is actually a companion field to philosophical theology. I have just finished a course entitled 'The Making of Catholic Theology: The Modern Period', meaning 1900 to today, and it concluded with two sessions, not given by myself, on architecture and on art. I was doing it experimentally to see, would it be theology? There was no doubt that you could see the way that church architecture in the Catholic tradition changed dramatically after Vatican II: looking for a clear line in which the lector, the altar and the presider would be three separate but united spaces. You could suddenly see what we were trying to say were the major themes of Catholic theology in the period. I am going on next year to do a section on the meaning of Catholic theology in the Reformation and Counter-Reformation, which I hope to teach not all myself, but hopefully to get someone from a Protestant tradition to teach as well. My aesthetic there is going to be Caravaggio, because Caravaggio was actually a deeply religious painter who understood that among the street people and the unruly people grace was at work, and he paints their bodies beautifully. Again, I think some of the themes of Reformation theology can actually be illustrated through art. Of course there is also film. In that sense, in a day and age when image reigns, theology benefits from theological aesthetics as never before.

McGlinchey: Stephen, your thoughts on this question?

Williams: I personally am very interested in theology and literature. When I think of great twentieth-century literature with strong theological themes, I think of Catholic writers such as G.K. Chesterton and Walker Percy. I am fond of both of them and when I think of theological aesthetics in literature, Chesterton comes to mind. But of course it is a wide-ranging phrase, and if I can widen it out a bit, I suppose that it is easier for Catholics, based on their tradition, to incorporate aesthetic insights into their theology than it is for Protestants. Very often, we have reacted to some extent to the visual. The sometimes restrictive word basis of Protestant theology has meant that the aesthetic has been stripped away from much of it. One way to recapture it within Protestantism is to employ the medieval trio of Beauty, Truth and Goodness and to think, not first and foremost about beauty in its own right, but about the quality of Truth and Goodness, which is Beauty. Beauty is a test of Truth and Goodness, and once we begin to think of Truth and Goodness as beautiful, we might become more broad in our aesthetics than we are.

Heffelfinger: I hear, lurking within that statement, that you might wish to say something about the truth or goodness that we can claim as beauty in the cross. Would you like to say something about how we might think about the cross within those categories?

Williams: Protestants, and not necessarily only Protestants, often set up the whole way of thinking in relation to the cross by saying that there is truth here, in as much as it is a revelation of the nature of human sin and the need for it to be dealt with; there is a goodness here, in as much as God in mercy does something about sin and does it justly. So all those things are met – truth, goodness and justice are exemplified – but I think Protestants very often spell this out in a theological scheme that becomes quite legalistic and little beauty attaches to it. So, God's goodness and truth are described in terms of the fulfillment of certain categories, and it is as though they are abstract ideas that are met in the cross. It is Chesterton who, in one of his Father Brown stories, describes the Paris chief of police as the type of French Humanist freethinker who could make 'mercy even colder than justice' – great line.[1] In relation to the cross, I would like us to think more in Protestantism about the beauty of God's person and of his way of dealing with people. Let us think of a personal God, and of personal relationships into which he enters with humans, rather than thinking in excessively abstract categories. I think we might do that by meditating on the truth that everyday life actually has a lot of beauty about it. Things are not simply and coldly fulfilled in doctrine and morality. They are actually full of beautiful content, and let us think about the cross in those terms.

Heffelfinger: Con, did you want to come back on that at all?

Casey: What I was thinking here, as Stephen was talking, was that probably the best book in theology I have read in the last ten years is by an Orthodox theologian called David Bentley Hart called

Beauty and Infinity. It is a simply profound study of redemption using the category of beauty as one of his lead concepts. So, most certainly there is a way in here and he has found it. I think for that reason it is a very good question to be asking in this context.

McGlinchey: How would an ecumenically sensitive reading of Hebrews give both Catholicism and Protestantism shared categories/concepts for a theology of the atonement?

Williams: I am tempted to say this is more Con's problem than mine, because Protestants have traditionally distinguished their position from Catholics in relation to the *hapax* (once-for-allness) of the sacrifice, and in remarking that I am not presupposing anything about what the Catholic doctrine is, past or present. I think Protestants are saying, just leave Hebrews as it is. However, I think an ecumenically sensitive reading of Hebrews on the part of Protestants would develop in this way: I do not think it would give up at all the sense of the once-for-allness of the sacrifice, but there is a tendency in Protestantism to play down the role of the present priesthood of Christ in his ongoing intercessory ministry. I would be interested to know if this is true in Catholicism as well. It may well be that it is central to Catholicism on the basis of the way they think about priesthood. Certainly, in terms of Christ as an individual, Hebrews portrays him in his intercessory ministry, which means it is something ongoing, and that should deliver us from any memorialism. In as much as there is a memorialism in much Protestant thought that concentrates on the past of the cross and the present memory, reflecting upon the ongoing high priesthood of Christ in Hebrews would be ecumenically significant. I confess that I would want Catholics to relinquish any uncertainty about the once-for-allness of the sacrifice, I confess that, but certainly the ministry, the priesthood of Christ, is ongoing. You know in 1 John it says that Christ is the propitiation of our sins: 'he *is*'. We think very often about the cross in terms of 'it was' – but 'he *is*', and the author of Hebrews, whether or not he employs the category of propitiation, has a great sense of the ongoing ministry of Christ. If, as Protestants, we grasp that more fully, it would give greater content to the presence of Christ in the eucharistic celebration as well as in other areas of life.

Casey: I think it would be good for us Catholics to listen very carefully to what Stephen is saying. I remember at a very early stage in seminary education being introduced to Hebrews and *hapax* (once-for-allness) as absolutely central to Catholic understanding and then weaving a eucharistic theology on the basis of all of that. But the fact of the matter is that in this crucial thing, as distinct from our conversation about grace, we have not listened well. I think a lot of that has to do with eucharistic theology rather than Hebrews. We have not listened well to each other. When Catholics and Protestants have listened well to each other there has almost always been mutual theological enrichment. I can certainly say that as a Catholic. But I think that there are areas, including eucharistic theology and including the once-for-all nature of the cross, where we have not listened well to each other. I think Stephen was doing good listening to the Catholic eucharistic concerns there. In reverse, the Catholics would do well to listen sensitively to the extraordinarily trenchant Protestant insistence that this was once for all and for all, not just once for all, but for all. That would be one of my concerns here; that we have made great progress in understanding the passions of our ancestors in the faith, but perhaps not on this issue in a way that we might. One of the most influential views in Catholic literature is to see cross and resurrection as prayer and answer to prayer, and the prayer being present in the answer, if you like. Cross and resurrection are two sides of the same communication between Jesus and his Father, and to enter into it you have to enter into the two-sidedness. That is what leads us to say that the eucharistic event has the cross in it. I think that is the frame within which we can get back to that point.

Williams: While an ecumenically sensitive reading of Hebrews relates to the Eucharist, it also relates to the discussion we have been having about theological aesthetics. I have been long struck by a sentence I read many years ago by Protestant theologian and New Testament scholar James Denney. He remarked that when he read Hebrews he found something a bit different there from the rest of the New Testament because Hebrews talked in terms of what is fitting rather than what is necessary. Denney said it is more like moral aesthetics than moral necessity. It is fitting that God should do this through Christ, and therefore I think that

Hebrews actually opens up the possibility of thinking again in terms of theological aesthetics in a way which both traditions could do well to heed. Denney was not saying there was no sense of necessity attached to the cross, but he was concentrating interestingly on the distinctiveness of Hebrews there.

McGlinchey: Would you say that at the Reformation there was a sense in which Catholic theologians lost the sense of the once-for-allness of the cross?

Casey: Counter-Reformation Catholic theology is certainly polemical and it is determined by wanting to protect certain insights and is vastly concerned with protecting certain insights around the real presence at the Eucharist. That becomes, as it were, the badge of Catholicism and it still is. But in Counter-Reformation theologies it becomes defended in categories like transubstantiation, which then become categories that have their own imagery that flows out of them. I am not so sure that they lost their awareness of the uniqueness of the event of Christ as that rather they used theories of a theological kind in a polemical context which very easily mislead. Certainly, I think one of the worst things is that they misled the people with whom they were having the polemics. I mean they were not clearly listening to the question at all. They were clearly concerned with saying: we want to say this about the Eucharist, and we want to celebrate the Eucharist like this, and it is clearly central to the faith, and anyone who does not say that is clearly unfaithful, and so on and so forth. I do not think they lost it, but they clouded it over with these kinds of polemical theological understandings which were not helpful.

McGlinchey: Stephen, can I ask you the same question? Do you think that, because a lot of Reformation theology was actually driven by polemics, there was not sufficient listening to what the Catholic Church was saying about the once-for-allness of the event?

Williams: I find it quite hard to answer because we have to ask what exactly the Catholic Church was saying, and as Con, of course, can say much more eloquently than I can, one thing that

is characteristic of confessions or statements is that they restrict
thereafter what can easily be said. What was being said before
the Reformation might have been wider and deeper than what
was said particularly at Trent. But the situation was complicated,
Paddy, by the fact that Protestants disagree among themselves.
So, for Zwingli, for example, Luther is much closer to Catholicism than he is to good old Swiss Protestantism. Was there enough
listening? I think it is very hard to generalize. The Reformers did
know the time in which they lived quite well, of course. They
knew Catholicism. The first-generation Reformers would have
come from Catholic backgrounds, and the leading Reformers
were always very learned men. That sounds like a very Protestant
response, but I think they did do justice to what was around in
their time, but subsequently, perhaps Protestantism has been too
reluctant to see how Catholics arrived at their position. We now
need to take seriously Catholicism here.

McGlinchey: In light of your dialogue how might we respond to
popular criticism of traditional atonement theology?

Casey: There is a very familiar line of criticism of the narrative of
the cross and the narrative of the cross being the source of new
life because precisely it is a punishment. If you went back alone
to art you could perhaps show some of the late-medieval pictures
of the cross in which you have an image of the Father holding the
cross with tears coursing down his cheeks, never mind any of the
many other narratives. The one that I prefer comes from Domin-
ican theologian Herbert McCabe, who says the Father's mission
to Jesus was not the mission to be crucified, but the mission to
be fully human and responsive to the Father's gift of graced life,
and to be crucified is what this world did to such a figure. There
is not a great deal of the 'God punishing Jesus' narrative in the
New Testament. There is some of it, but not a great deal of it, and
there is a far richer narrative, and it is disingenuous to ignore the
far richer narrative.

Williams: Yes, I would affirm all of what Con says, as far as it
goes, but would want to go a bit further, and would want to say
in this area there is a huge amount of irresponsibility abroad and

a lot of misconceptions. Defenders of the so-called penal substitutionary view of the atonement have said it is an insult to God to call it child abuse; to give the counter in this kind of discussion I find it is an insult to children as well. That there is a popular preaching on the lines that Steve Chalke has in mind, that I do not doubt. There is such a preaching. Having said that, there is a lot of misrepresentation. Steve Chalke, for example, talks about God – the exact sentence eludes me, but he uses the word 'suddenly' – God suddenly strikes the Son or something like that. But there is nothing sudden about it.[2] I have never heard any of the defenders of penal substitution talk about suddenness. On the contrary, they talk about a long period of preparation throughout history. So it is not sudden. However obnoxious penal substitution may be, it is not God suddenly breaking out. It is something very different. Two things lie in the background of penal substitution, which itself as a concept has to be unpacked. One is that the responsible church definitions which have affirmed it have been committed to the unity of the Father and the Son, to Trinitarian doctrine. Classically, the Father and the Son are *homoousios*, of one being, so there is no question of the one punishing another who is different – the Father is disposed one way and the Son in another; the Father has a sense of justice and is going to take it out on the Son. I think one of the things that is behind the difficulties people have is a forgetfulness that we are talking about the Son incarnate within Christian theology. We are never dealing with a purely human Jesus. If it is a purely human Jesus with a purely divine Father, one can see all the difficulties. But it has never been set up like that. Second, if I simply take Calvin as an example, it is categorical. It is not implicit in his writing; it is explicit: God does not get angry, and he is not angry with the Son. That is the fountainhead of Reformed, or at least Calvinistic, theology. A lot of things are going wrong here in the way the whole thing is set up. It seems to me on a positive note – the reason I want to go a bit beyond Con here, although he might not agree with this, is that it seems to me that in human life people are always taking the penalty for the wrongdoing of others. What is it that is happening in forgiveness when there has been a wrong done except that you are taking the penalty for someone else's sin? The problem is that we feel too proud to think that God might need to forgive us in such a way. But, if I forgive someone in such a way that I do not dismiss them from friendship, I do not take it out on them, and so forth, there is a sense in which I take that on myself. It is deeply existential. I think once we get into this from an existential point of view, it begins to look very different from a cold-blooded and mistaken idea of a Father taking it out on a Son. In that form it is pretty obnoxious, but that is not the form in which it is classically laid out.

Heffelfinger: Can I ask you both, in light of your comments: what can a Protestant and Catholic voice together say in the public setting about this issue? If there is misunderstanding of the doctrine on some level, what can the two of you together say to the wider world about the atonement?

Casey: There is a great deal of truth if you look on it as Jesus taking our sinfulness upon himself and suffering the consequences for it, a great deal of truth in that. But when you begin to say that it is the Father who is the cause of those consequences from which he suffers, you have made quite a gap open up between the oneness of the Father and Jesus. Yes, Jesus is on the cross because of our sinfulness, because of twisted humanity, and the violence that we have written into history and in particular the way in which the people of Israel who were gifted with the words of God have failed to be faithful to their own vocation. It is as a consequence of all of this that when the one Jesus who comes to bring their vocation to its fulfilment lives it truly, they turn on him. But that is not to say that the consequences that lead to Jesus being on the cross are directly what the Father wills. The Father wills that Jesus would fulfil the vocation that was given to Israel. The one who sought to fulfil that vocation suffered the consequences of those who were systemically engaged in infidelity to it. The consequences lead to the cross. But I go back to the statement, then, that the crucifixion was not something that the Father willed. What the Father willed was that Jesus would fulfil the vocation of Israel and he ends on the cross because that is the kind of world in which his vocation has to be lived through. That is the kind of world, if you want to put us into it, that we have made. It is because of us and the kind of world we have made that Jesus ends on the cross.

McGlinchey: Con, would you say that is a majority view of the atonement within Catholicism, or is that a particular perspective?

Casey: Good question; almost nothing you could say is the dominant view of any of these traditions. There will always be people who have variants, and that is true in Catholicism as well. I would say that the great movement of Catholic thinking in the last century has been going in that direction, trying to articulate the mystery of sin, suffering and crucifixion in a direction like that, and very definitely trying to avoid the kind of cruel and angry God that is involved in the other narrative. I guess all our traditions are always subject to a kind of vicious simplification, a self-serving simplification. Some of the preaching that Catholic preachers have used has really been serving fear and power rather than the gospel. I think we will always be subject to that temptation, but I would still say a very widely broad effort of Catholic communication of the gospel has been one that has been very aware of the dangers of that particular distortion.

McGlinchey: Stephen, did you want to comment on that question?

Williams: If I may, and I would also like to take Katie's question that launched this phase of the discussion. We are tackling a huge subject here and we would really need to make a number of distinctions, which we do not need to go into in depth. I would see things a little differently from Con here, by the sound of it, in that, given the deep background of Israel, including the sacrificial system and all its significance, I would not want to give the impression that the death of Christ is a kind of contingency, which happened to be the end of his days unfortunately, rather than being something that had a much deeper root in what God designed. If there is a stream of Catholic theology, which there is of course, that is more happy than you appear to be with penalty and judgement, then I would say two things about what Protestants and Catholics can say together. First, what I said earlier, we all affirm the unity of the Father and the Son, the classic Nicene formulation, *homoousion*. Second, we together want to say – and this is related to *homoousion*, but puts a sharp point on it – we would all want to say that one of the most important texts in the New Testament which bears on this is the Johannine text in which Jesus says, 'Whoever has seen me has seen the Father' (John 14:9). Far from Father and Son being different kinds of natures or characters, the one who has seen the Christ has seen the Father. As Irenaeus says, the Father is the invisible of the Son and the Son is the visible of the Father.[3] That deep patristic way of looking at everything begins to alter the whole picture. You still might not like the idea of penal substitution, but it just begins to look different, that is all.

Heffelfinger: Is it fair to say that the two of you would agree that the church needs to do a bit more public teaching and explanation of some of the classic doctrines that undergird the atonement, such as the doctrine of the Trinity and the doctrine of the incarnation; that perhaps, by losing sight of those in the public square, we have allowed misinterpretation of the doctrine of the atonement?

Williams: I suspect that Con would affirm with me, even if his theology of the atonement and mine differ a little, that you have got to see this whole question in the context in which it was thought through in the early church and subsequently, which was a sense of the deep unity of Father and Son. If you do not start there, you are going to go terribly astray thinking about the atonement or anything else. We would agree about that, would we not, Con, even if afterwards we have slightly different emphases?

Casey: Indeed, I think that is entirely correct and I think you are right too, Katie, that in our attempts in the public square to say who we are, and what the gospel is, we do not think deeply enough about the great understandings, the Trinitarian understanding, and I think in bringing it to the fore in this conversation in the way he has done, Stephen is really doing it a great service. Unless we begin from that context and with those texts, we are bound to find ourselves stretched in the public forum and in the doing of theology itself as well, so I think that was a great development from Stephen on that critical issue there.

McGlinchey: I am conscious that we have had key events in the past like the ARCIC (Anglican–Roman Catholic International

Commission) agreement on the Eucharist; we have had the book *Baptism, Eucharist and Ministry* where there was, again, quite a measure of agreement that in some way or another the Eucharist was a making present of the reality of Calvary. Do you think that issue has been resolved, or is there an extent to which the concept of eucharistic sacrifice is still a barrier to Roman Catholic–Protestant rapprochement in terms of atonement theology? Also, what misconceptions might be at work in this area, where maybe there is distance still?

Williams: You talked about *Baptism, Eucharist and Ministry* and ARCIC, but actually, Con, you and I have had our own discussions in the past in this area in public. Con has certainly helped me a lot on this question of what is understood in eucharistic sacrifice. To what extent is it a barrier? Well, I think that Protestants have to do two things here. We have to learn from Catholics exactly what is taught and held here. This includes the position taken in relation to transubstantiation. The kind of thing I have learned from Con and others is the precise meaning of transubstantiation, and what is meant by substance. Protestants very often do not grasp it. From the Protestant end, what we have to do is to emphasize something which many Catholics think we have lost, and we have very often, which is the real presence of Christ. Even Zwingli has some sense of that because, arguably for Zwingli, when he talked about memory he had a strong sense of memory as something that makes present. Still, there are things in Zwingli which move us even more towards the real presence than that does, but leaving Zwingli aside, in Calvinism there is a very strong sense of the real presence and it is a spiritual presence. Jesus Christ is thought of in Calvin as having ascended into heaven to the right hand of the Father. In the Lord's Supper, which I suppose is one of our favourite ways of talking about the Eucharist, we are by faith joined to be with Christ there in heaven. So, pictorially speaking, Christ is not present down here with us but in heaven, and through the Holy Spirit we are joined with him there. Therefore, there is a powerful sense of real presence. Calvin actually speaks about mystery in connection with the Lord's Supper, I think, more than he does in any other connection. He says: my words cannot attain to my thoughts on this theme and my thoughts cannot attain to the reality. Anyone who reads Calvin himself on the Eucharist, after thinking they know what Protestants say, is in for a great surprise.

McGlinchey: So how is that worked out in the understanding of what happens to the bread and wine?

Williams: The Lutheran position is often described as 'consubstantiation'. Rather than the substance of bread and wine being changed, the substance remains the same; Christ is present in, with and under. Consubstantiation is a bit misleading because it sounds quite theoretical. What Luther wanted to say was: we do not have a theory on this point; we believe it, that is as much as we can say. Leave it; do not go near that point. Present in what way? In the fullness of his person: divinely and humanly. Is his divinity everywhere? Yes. Is his humanity everywhere? Well, it must be; it is joined to his divinity. Is his humanity therefore present in the bread and wine? Yes. In what way? We do not know; leave it there.

McGlinchey: Con, how would you respond to someone who might say that if Catholic doctrine is saying the one unique sacrifice is being made present each time the Eucharist is shared, what you really have is a repetition of the sacrifice?

Casey: That is the nub of the network of misunderstandings around the whole matter. The absolute key to Catholic – we tend to say 'eucharistic' – theology is real presence. The reason why you would say that it is a sacrifice is because of who is really present. The one who is really present is present because he was thus praying on the cross. So it is that Jesus, as it were, carries the weapons of his sacrifice with him in his presence. Therefore, one speaks of the sacrifice being present. So, in this area, not unlike the Lutherans, you are treading into such a deep mystery that if you get too confident in your way of speaking about it, you tend to reify it, and that did tend to happen in Catholic theology in this area. One of the discoveries of the ecumenical dialogue to this point is that there is a great deal of shared understanding of the mystery of the Lord's Supper, and that the great polemical misunderstandings that arose out of the Reformation and Counter-Reformation arose because of the great passion of our ancestors in the faith with regard to this mystery. It was not that they were bad men pursuing unfaithful Christian theology. The problem is that we have to get beyond what has become a deaf polemic through the centuries. I think it is one of the wonders of our time that we are doing just that, as in the documents you recommend. In Ireland, I would say the Presbyterian–Catholic dialogue has produced very profound rediscoveries of our tradition. We would have thought that the Calvinist tradition simply bypassed a real presence in the Lord's Supper, only to discover that this was a profound misunderstanding. I think perhaps the Presbyterian, Reformed and Lutheran traditions would have thought Catholics are into transubstantiation, as if the bread were changed into another substance, and that is a very crude version of what they are trying to get at in transubstantiation. I think there are liturgical differences that perhaps we still need to understand. That would be for myself. There are still liturgical differences that I need to understand. For us, the eucharistic bread is the bread of heaven and it cannot be treated like ordinary bread. That is then feeding right back into our sense that we were in the real presence of Christ in this meal and that leads us then into tabernacles, and so on. But actually, the 'bread of heaven' is one of our favourite phrases for it, which is an echo of your way of sensing the real presence. I think we have learned a lot in ecumenical dialogue. We have not actually worshipped together enough yet. I will leave it at that.

Heffelfinger: Do you mind if I bring things to a close at this point? It has been a really illuminating conversation. At the very beginning, Con, you said several times how grateful you were that there were both Catholic voices and Protestant voices talking about the atonement, and that you thought that really illuminated things. The working title for this conversation was 'Can We Aspire to a Common Doctrine of the Atonement?' and I want to push that back at you and ask: 'ought' we to be aiming for a common doctrine of the atonement? In your mind, is the multi-vocal nature of this conversation a good in itself that we ought to affirm? Or do you think there are ways we ought to be pushing beyond it towards unity?

Casey: I think undoubtedly both/and. I do think it is our responsibility to seek unity together on issues that have divided us and poisoned our relationship. On the other hand, I do not think any of us benefits from a too one-paced understanding of these mysteries. We will always be surprised by meeting someone who is travelling with us with different thoughts; and I think theologies and traditions, when they cease to be also arguments about the good of those traditions, are much less alive. So, I want there to be Protestants but I also want there to be Orthodox. We do not need to seek a unity that is a failure to acknowledge that without diversity we cannot flourish.

Williams: I will go back, I think, to what I said earlier and agree entirely with everything Con said there. It is not so much that we should start by asking whether we should aspire to a common doctrine. It is actually that we have one. We actually start together, and if you were to make a statement of some of the main general presuppositions and elements of atonement doctrine, you could say 1, 2, 3, 4, 5, both Catholics and Protestants affirm those. So, I do think we start there as a matter of fact. The complicating factor in some ways, though some might say it is actually an enriching factor, is diversity within both traditions, so that some Protestants and Catholics will think more like each other, and some Catholics more like other Catholics, and some Protestants more like other Protestants. If there is one general area where we still need to think our way through to maximum unity, it is probably the Eucharist. I am with you, by the way, on the Orthodox. There is Protestant–Orthodox dialogue going on more and more of which I am aware. In this day and age we can talk about differences, but the place where the line can be drawn is not Catholic–Protestant. Catholic–Protestant disagreements are there and they can be worked on, or they can be lived with. But really, in terms of the times in which we live, we are looking at a very different and significant division between people who will stand for certain things in society and people who will not stand for certain things in society. That is where the real battle is. Catholics and Protestants together will have a certain courage and integrity as opposed to Catholics and Protestants that lack that integrity in terms of living as faithful disciples.

McGlinchey: Thank you both for giving us such a lot of time and such good answers.

7

THE CROSS AND EUCHARISTIC SACRIFICE: A PERSONAL REFLECTION ON AN ECUMENICAL STRUGGLE

Patrick G. McGlinchey

Introduction

The aim of this chapter is to develop the dialogue begun in the previous chapter between Dr Casey and Prof. Williams. The cross and the Eucharist are uniquely related in Catholicism, and ecumenical rapprochement on the atonement cannot bypass the questions raised by this relationship. Perhaps chief among these is whether the Catholic concept of eucharistic sacrifice can be justified theologically. This was more than an ivory-tower question for me as I wrestled with this issue quite intensely during my transition from Catholicism to evangelicalism as an undergraduate. Living and worshipping in a strongly Protestant milieu in troubles-torn Northern Ireland, I had heard echoes of the Reformation critique of eucharistic sacrifice and was aware that for some the celebration of the Mass was deeply objectionable. Calvin himself encapsulates historical Protestant concern over the Mass in the *Institutes of the Christian Religion* when he asserts:

> I am aware how deeply this plague [i.e. the Mass] has struck its roots; under what a semblance of good it conceals its true character, bearing

the name of Christ before it, and making many believe that under the single name of Mass is comprehended the whole sum of faith. But when it shall have been most clearly proved by the word of God, that this mass, however glossed and splendid, offers the greatest insult to Christ, suppresses and buries his cross, consigns his death to oblivion, takes away the benefit which it was designed to convey, enervates and dissipates the sacrament, by which the remembrance of his death was retained, will its roots be so deep that this most powerful axe, the word of God, will not cut it down and destroy it? Will any semblance be so specious that this light will not expose the lurking evil?[1]

Calvin's employment of such derogatory language is indicative of Protestant antagonism to the notion that the Mass is somehow a repetition of the unique sacrifice of Calvary.[2] However, what was to become clear to me, over a period of time, was that Catholic theology itself did not portray the Eucharist as a straightforward repetition of Christ's sacrifice. It was a 're-presentation' or 'making present' of an event which occurred once and for all in history. The ecumenical cogency of such an interpretation was underlined by two significant inter-church documents which emerged in the 1970s and 1980s: the Agreed Statement on Eucharistic Doctrine drawn up by the Anglican–Roman Catholic International Commission (ARCIC) in 1971 and the World Council of Churches (WCC) publication *Baptism, Eucharist and Ministry* in 1982.[3] Both these documents, in their own way, endorse the possibility of a past event being actualized in the present within the context of worship.

Notwithstanding the positive reception of eucharistic sacrifice on the part of the Anglican members of ARCIC, evangelical Anglican response to the Agreed Statement at the time was less than enthusiastic.[4] Moreover, even today there is a sense in which the ecumenical consensus displayed within the ARCIC and WCC documents has neither penetrated nor persuaded the evangelical world at large.[5] Thus the idea of eucharistic sacrifice still stands for many as an obstacle to a common doctrine of redemption.[6] My goal in this chapter is not to challenge the Protestant rejection of eucharistic sacrifice *per se*, but to approach the question as honestly and objectively as I can in order to explore potential ways forward. This process will involve outlining the major theological difficulties attached to eucharistic sacrifice and asking to what degree nuanced Catholic formulations of the notion might assuage Protestant fears. I will draw two primary spokespersons into the discussion: Joseph Ratzinger (Pope Emeritus Benedict XVI) and Leonardo De Chirico, who is one of the most informed evangelicals currently writing about Catholicism. The aim is to assess how far we have progressed towards genuine rapprochement and to make suggestions about steps which might further reduce the theological distance between the two traditions. Such convergence will be to the mutual benefit of both traditions as Dr Casey and Prof. Williams' dialogue indicated.

Difficulties Surrounding Eucharistic Sacrifice

De Chirico's work echoes my own discovery as an undergraduate that the Mass was understood as the actualization of the Calvary event, as opposed to its repetition. He acknowledges that 'the popular evangelical critique of Roman Catholic Eucharistic teaching is simply wrong when [it] attributes to Catholicism the view [that] . . . the eucharist is a mere *repetition* of the cross.'[7] However, this admission does not function as the prelude to a more positive assessment of the Catholic doctrine. De Chirico insists that the way Catholicism configures the Eucharist's relationship to the once-only sacrifice of Calvary is deeply problematic and an impediment to constructive ecumenical dialogue.[8] His concerns are not easily dismissed as knee-jerk Protestant prejudice as they arise from his doctoral research in Roman Catholicism undertaken at King's College, London, and published in the prestigious *Religions and Discourse* series by Peter Lang.[9]

At the centre of De Chirico's critique of Catholicism is a particular understanding of how the concept of time has impacted Catholic theology. Drawing on exegetical insights from John Stott's *Evangelical Truth*, De Chirico suggests that the message of the gospel is adequately summed up by two biblical adverbs associated with time: *hapax* (meaning 'once and for all') and *mallon* ('for evermore').[10] These terms reference the work of the Trinity in the world and delineate two different kinds of divine activity in the economy of salvation. The first, *hapax*, speaks of an action of God which is unrepeatable and utterly final in its soteriological impact. The second term, *mallon*, describes an action that is ongoing and not limited by time (i.e. God's continuing outworking of salvation in history). He suggests that these time-related biblical concepts serve theology well when the boundaries between the two are properly maintained. However, it is his contention that significant difficulties will emerge when the distinction between *hapax* and *mallon* is blurred and this blurring impinges on the church's grasp of the gospel.

> The demarcation which differentiates *hapax* from *mallon* may be subtle but it must be maintained in order to avoid any distortion of the fundamental structure of the faith. If the two are confused, problems arise. If uniqueness is attributed to that which is progressive or, alternatively, if what is definitive becomes by nature continuous, this brings about a distortion in the constitution of faith which alters its fundamental characteristics. With regard to both Christology and the gospel itself, even a minimal violation would become devastating, producing effects of enormous consequence.[11]

It is just such warping of faith's structure that De Chirico claims to witness within the Roman Catholic Church in its characterization of how God works within time. He contends that the Catholic assumption of a fundamental, if not undifferentiated, continuity between Christ's incarnation and 'the extension of that incarnation in the life of the church'[12] has effectively breached the boundary between *hapax* and *mallon*.[13] Properties appropriate only to Christ's ministry have been extended to the church's ministry, causing a distortion to the fundamental framework of faith. According to De Chirico, this breach at the level of incarnation (the role of Christ and the church becoming inappropriately co-mingled in the aftermath of the ascension) precipitated a series of further incursions which impacted, among other things, the understanding of the Eucharist.

De Chirico traces the continuing impact of this understanding of time to the most recent authoritative teaching on the Eucharist, which is found in the *Catechism of the Catholic Church*.[14] His commentary makes it clear that he believes the distortion to the structure of faith caused by the blurring of time distinctions is evident within the *Catechism*. He notes that scant attention is paid to atonement theology in contrast to the space allocated to the Eucharist.[15] 'Here is the crucial point in Catholic magisterial teaching: the *Catechism* is far more interested in presenting the Eucharistic re-presentation and the sacramental actualisation of the atonement than in presenting its once and for all historical occurrence and salvific achievement.'[16]

Almost as troubling to De Chirico as the perceived downplaying of atonement theology in favour of a greater emphasis on the cross' relationship to the Eucharist is the *Catechism's* teaching about the church's participation in Christ's sacrifice, outlined in the following statement: 'The cross is the unique sacrifice of Christ, the "one mediator between God and men." But because in his incarnate divine person he has in some way united himself to every man, "the possibility of being made partners, in a way known to God, in the paschal mystery" is offered to all men.'[17] According to De Chirico, 'the uniqueness, sufficiency, completeness and finality of the cross would not contemplate any sort of addition, supplementation or contribution on our part as individuals or as a church'.[18] This objection to the *Catechism* indicates that for him human participation in the sacrifice of Christ necessarily entails a dilution or subversion of Christ's unique work.

Thus, whether through the church's perceived attempt to insert itself into the salvific act via participation, or its embrace of a worldview that obscures Christ's work and elevates its own sacramental significance, it is clear that De Chirico is deeply dissatisfied with the theology of eucharistic sacrifice. Moreover, he reads the *Catechism's* emphasis on the Eucharist's capacity to make the act of redemption present as a subtle power play that undermines the independent efficacy of the cross.[19] His closing words in his most recent article on the theme acknowledge the flair of Roman Catholicism while at the same time lamenting what he regards as the negative impact of its theological *modus operandi*:

> Here is the Roman Catholic genius of 'complexio oppositorum' (convergence of opposites), an epistemological art which is at the same time both fascinating and disconcerting. The removing of boundaries between *hapax* and *mallon* means the removal of demarcation lines between event and process, between definitive and progressive aspects

of Divine action, between Christ and the church. To undermine the configuration of time is a dangerous game. A *hapax* that is violated gives rise to disruptive rifts in the very fabric of the Christian faith. An extended *mallon* produces 'add-ons' that are Scripturally unsustainable in the economy of faith.[20]

De Chirico's closing reference to the scriptural unsustainability of the church's claims, on the basis of its blurring of time distinctions, highlights what some would regard as a lacuna in his treatment of Catholic eucharistic thought. The acceptance of eucharistic sacrifice in the 1971 ARCIC report and the 1982 WCC report *Baptism, Eucharist and Ministry* was premised largely on the acknowledgement that this was a legitimate reading of the biblical material. The Israelite community's engagement with Passover and its concept of memory were thought to facilitate precisely the kind of view of the Eucharist that has been associated with contemporary Catholicism. Indeed, Christ's invitation to do this 'in remembrance [*anamnesis*] of me' (Luke 22:19) would invite a thorough study of the biblical roots of this word in order to ascertain whether the Catholic understanding of it possessed any cogency. De Chirico has thus far not embarked on such a study and this leaves his conclusions to some degree untested.[21] While there may be an absolute distinction between *hapax* and *mallon*, as he asserts, the possibility must at least be explored that the Bible posits a context in which a *hapax* moment of ultimate soteriological significance may be re-presented for the spiritual nourishment of the believer.

Catholic Engagement with Eucharistic Sacrifice

The ecumenical thaw in the wake of Vatican II has given rise to significant dialogues between the Catholic Church and other theological traditions. This new way of relating has had both its highs and its lows over the past forty-five years. Those in favour of ecumenical rapprochement will emphasize significant historical moments, which have marked a sea-change in the relationship between Catholicism and other Christian denominations. Perhaps one of the most striking examples of such a moment was the *Joint Declaration on the Doctrine of Justification* made in the name of the Roman Catholic Church and the Lutheran World Federation in 1999. The key statement of the agreement reveals the vast extent of ecumenical progress made: 'By grace alone, in faith in Christ's saving work and not because of any merit on our own part, we are accepted by God and receive the Holy Spirit, who renews our hearts while equipping us and calling us to do good works.'[22]

What is less known, in terms of the background to this agreement, is the huge 'behind the scenes' role that Cardinal Joseph Ratzinger played in ensuring that such an historical breakthrough took place. Tracey Rowland reveals that the dialogue between the Lutherans and Catholics was in danger of stalling and that it was only significant concessions made by Ratzinger which allowed agreement to be reached.[23] This intervention takes on greater significance when it is realized that Ratzinger was not part of the Catholic delegation but acted as an independent agent in the situation. It was thus at a private meeting with the Lutheran leaders in his brother Georg's home in Regensburg that the vital concessions were made. His investment in the agreement highlights the deep and sincere ecumenical vision that seems to undergird his engagement with other traditions.[24]

Having applauded Ratzinger's ecumenical vision, it is ironic that one of the ecumenical low points in Catholic–Protestant relationships over recent decades was the release of *Dominus Iesus* by the Congregation for the Doctrine of the Faith (CDF). The person whose signature was on that document, and the one who was identified as its author, was the same Joseph Ratzinger. The statement in *Dominus Iesus* which caused most confusion and consternation was one in which those denominations who were deemed to lack a valid episcope were characterized as being ecclesial communities, and not full churches in the proper sense.[25] Ratzinger's critics saw this as a betrayal of ecumenism while others saw it as a simple re-statement of the formal Catholic position in a document that was less concerned with ecclesiology than with countering the rise of relativism.[26] Given Ratzinger's strong support of the *Joint Declaration on Justification*, which occurred at approximately the same time as the drafting of *Dominus Iesus*, it seems more likely that his contribution to the document was simply in compliance with his role as Prefect of the CDF.

A more accurate window into Ratzinger's ecumenical intentions is his article 'Luther and the Unity of the Churches'.[27] Here he expresses the hope that modern exegetes might unravel some of the theological knots pertaining to long-standing doctrinal controversies and help the denominations genuinely transcend old differences. Crucially, he highlights the Eucharist as one area where he has hope for a way forward.[28]

This long preamble has been done partly to establish Ratzinger's ecumenical credentials and partly to demonstrate that his own theological motivation has been to reach genuine consensus with Protestants. As he now emerges as a legitimate dialogue partner on the theme of eucharistic sacrifice (hopefully, dear reader!), it is important to bear four things in mind about such a dialogue. First, it is clear from Ratzinger's previous writings and his interactions with Protestants that there is no expectation of capitulation on their part. The purpose of dialogue is to create a genuine way forward for *both* traditions. Second, it would seem that ecumenical progress (if it is achieved) will be premised on each side gaining a new perspective on an old idea or theme. His hope is that fresh insights will emerge which will break the ecumenical deadlock and offer a new way of advancing the discussion. Third, the role of Scripture will be vital in the process as Scripture itself provides the raw materials from which ecumenical solutions may emerge. Fourth, Ratzinger has already begun the dialogue on eucharistic sacrifice and made the biblical text the quarry for his own specific ecumenical proposal. Our challenge is to meet him on his chosen ground and explore whether new insights can help us transcend old differences.

Ratzinger and eucharistic sacrifice

Joseph Ratzinger was among the first post-Vatican II Catholic theologians to engage with the ecumenical problem of eucharistic sacrifice. Like his colleague John Jay Hughes who set out upon the same task, he begins with a consideration of the magisterial Reformers whose stance vis-à-vis this issue has set the trend for Protestantism.[29] Both scholars demonstrate sympathy for Luther et al. on account of the manner in which eucharistic sacrifice was articulated and defended by the church of the time. Ratzinger situates Luther's hostile response to the church's teaching in his

concern to protect the doctrine of justification by faith. He demonstrates that the Reformer was convinced of two mutually exclusive
ways in which human beings can relate to God – the path of faith
or the path of law – and how that perspective caused him to
distrust the Mass since it apparently involved humanity's *offering*
of a sacrifice for its own salvation. The following articulation of
Luther's stance highlights the degree to which Ratzinger has
sought to understand the Reformation position from the inside:

> [T]he orientation of faith is directly opposed to that of the law. It is the
> acceptance of God's gracious gift, not the offering of gifts. Christian
> worship, by its very nature, can only involve receiving not giving. It
> is man's thankful acceptance of God's unique salvific action in Jesus
> Christ, which was performed once yet satisfies for all time. Thus the
> very essence of Christian worship is distorted and completely per-
> verted if the offering of gifts replaces the action of giving thanks. For
> then the Law is replacing grace once again, the sufficiency of Christ's
> saving action is being denied, and man is trying to save himself by his
> own efforts and deeds. That is why Luther regards the sacrifice of the
> Mass as a rejection of grace, as a revolt by man, as a relapse from faith
> into the Law – a relapse so sharply criticised by Paul.[30]

What is more significant than Ratzinger's sympathetic depiction
of Luther's stance is his validation of much of what Luther says.
He acknowledges the theological weight behind Luther's argument and concedes that even if we should set his views aside we
would find similar ideas present in the New Testament itself.[31]
Thus the questions raised by Reformation reflection on the Eucharist must be faced head on and not side-stepped.[32] An essential
step in this process is seeing that Luther's analysis, though polem-
ically driven, contains positive conclusions which will benefit the
church in its engagement with the Eucharist.[33] The first of these
is the understanding that 'Christ's salvific activity is the sacrifice
which is offered once and is sufficient for all time'.[34] Ratzinger
understands this idea as being the major theme of Hebrews as
well as the core of Luther's theology. Next, he ratifies another
non-negotiable Reformation conviction. Because Christ's death
marks the end of cultic worship in which human beings offer their
own gifts to God, Christian worship must now be understood as

essentially thanksgiving (*eucharistia*) for Christ's salvific action on the cross.[35] That these ideas are articulated and endorsed as Luther's own suggests that we should read them in ways which are not at variance with the Reformer's original intention.

At this stage in Ratzinger's proposal, he advances a thesis which is daring and unexpected. Having accepted Luther's strictures on how we must interpret Christ's action on the cross and its implications for our definition of worship, he suggests that there still lie within Luther's theology 'two valid take-off points . . . for understanding the Eucharist as a sacrifice in a way that is . . . fully in accord with the New Testament concept of faith.'[36] The first of these 'take-off points' – and the one we will focus upon in this brief section – concerns what one might legitimately expect to encounter in worship.[37]

Ratzinger states, 'If the Mass is the offering of Christ's gift to his faithful, must it not involve the presence of this gift in some way, the presence of Christ's salvific activity?'[38]

It is clear from the second clause that the 'offering' referred to in the first clause cannot be read as meaning anything like eucharistic sacrifice. How can he ask *whether* that 'offering' should contain 'the presence of Christ's saving activity' if the term used already presumes that it does? Rather, taking seriously the fact that we are considering a 'valid take-off point' from *Luther's theology*, the word 'offering' employed here is more likely to mean 'the proclamation of the message of grace'. In this light, therefore, Ratzinger is suggesting that if the Eucharist proclaims God's saving action, it makes sense that, in some way, that saving activity will be present to the believer, hence his reference to what we might legitimately expect to encounter in worship.

How does Luther's theology offer a valid take-off point for this kind of conclusion? The answer lies in Luther's marked emphasis on what the faith does 'for me'.[39] Ratzinger interprets Luther as viewing God's salvific action as not relating to past history but to the present lived experience of the individual. This claim is given significant force with a citation from Luther: 'If it is not imparted to me, then as far as I am concerned, it is as if it had not happened . . . the blood-shedding is only real when it is poured out for me.'[40] While these sentiments cannot be used as evidence for Luther's openness to the idea of a 're-presentation' of the once-only sacrifice, they offer a potential starting point for such an idea. When Luther speaks of the salvific event needing to become a present reality for the individual, then Ratzinger, the Catholic theologian, cannot help but see the potential for this occurring in the sacramental re-presentation of Calvary.

This notion of 're-presentation' or *anamnesis* is central to Ratzinger's whole proposal. Indeed, it is the most potentially fruitful idea available to Catholic theology in its bid to make the notion of eucharistic sacrifice accessible and believable. Of course, Ratzinger's employment of the term is not based on mere pragmatism. He is convinced by the work of scholars such as the French Calvinist theologian Max Thurian that Jesus' command to 'do this in remembrance of me' (Luke 22:19; 1 Cor. 11:24–26) has deep roots in Old Testament theology and the particular concept of memory identified with the term *anamnesis*.[41] He contends that *anamnesis* was central to Old Testament cultic worship and that it entailed bringing to mind and making present the great events of deliverance. 'When Israel celebrated her memorial remembrance of salvation history, she embraced it as a present reality; she stepped within this history and participated in its concrete reality', claims Ratzinger.[42] The obvious inference is that the Eucharist should be engaged in such a manner so as to avail of the benefits achieved by Christ's sacrifice. We shall have opportunity to engage briefly with how this understanding of memory has been received by some biblical commentators in the evangelical tradition in the closing section of the chapter. It may suffice for now to note that much turns on this idea. Arguably an event can be entered into again without its uniqueness and unrepeatability being compromised. If the claim extends beyond that to suggest that the priest has the ability to summon Christ on to the altar in order to offer an unbloody sacrifice on a more or less continual basis, then the argument falls foul of the strictures of Hebrews. John Jay Hughes, in another nuanced Catholic treatment of eucharistic sacrifice, is aware of these dangers and highlights the problems for Catholic theology when such ideas are promoted:

> The difficulty with this way of conceiving the eucharistic sacrifice is that it makes it very difficult to answer the objection first raised in the Reformation, and maintained by Reformation Christians today, that

the mass so conceived is in fact a new sacrifice, dependent on Calvary it may be, but nevertheless separate. This seems to be in clear contradiction to the Epistle to the Hebrews, which teaches unequivocally that Calvary can never be repeated or added to.[43]

In terms of argumentation, it must be acknowledged that *anamnesis* functions as the major, if not the only, rational justification for eucharistic sacrifice in Ratzinger. Everything else he writes about the subject is dependent upon this particular way of understanding the concept of memory in Scripture. This line of approach echoes other Catholic treatments which deem the concept of *anamnesis* sufficient to warrant acceptance of eucharistic sacrifice. In this respect, there is little more that can be said about the manner in which Catholics promote it, aside from pointing directly to the exegetical arguments. However, there are two other aspects of Ratzinger's treatment of the idea which deserve reiteration in advance of the closing section of this chapter. First, he provides a model for how theologians ought to engage with a thorny issue such as this. In his interaction with Luther he was able to enter imaginatively into the Reformer's mindset and acquire an informed understanding of his concerns. Moreover, he demonstrates a rigorously honest ecumenism which is willing to face the hard questions. As he put it himself, 'Burying questions does not further theology's progress, nor does it help the faithful to reach the fullness of life.'[44] Anyone concerned with theological controversies would benefit from emulating such an approach. Second, he poses a pastoral question which lies at the heart of this debate and which arguably indicates a way forward. He asks: if the Eucharist portrays God's saving action, should it not also involve the presence of that saving activity? In other words, 'Is there not a need to experience the benefits of the cross in the here and now of our own experience?'

Drawing Things Together

In a book which is committed to an eirenic approach to the atonement, it is relevant to ask why we should include such a contentious theme. Part of the answer to that question is location.

We teach on an island with a troubled political and theological history, and some of the religious debate has been crystallized in this issue of eucharistic sacrifice. The Eucharist lies at the very heart of Roman Catholic worship and it has also been a subject of immense suspicion by Protestants on account of its alleged subversion of the cross. Our goal is not to exacerbate those divisions but to explore ways in which they can be overcome. Our conviction is that 'atonement is gift' and our hope is that the celebration and proclamation of that gift in the Eucharist would become less a symbol of contention and 'otherness' and more a symbol of shared faith and love. This outcome will be more likely if the issues of contention are addressed sensitively and openly. We are also acutely aware that the Eucharist has a direct bearing on the theme of the book. In this publication we explore the horizontal impact of the cross, believing that it offers tremendous riches to both the church and the world. Arguably the Eucharist is a major channel by which God's riches reach the church and therefore it is worthy of exploration on its own terms. The fact that debate about eucharistic sacrifice has raised more acutely the manner in which these salvational benefits are transmitted highlights the need for this theme to be incorporated into the discussion in one form or other.

An essential element of my methodology in this final section of the chapter will be modelling out a theological honesty which does not balk at the hard questions. The goal is to see progress made on this contentious issue but this will not be achieved by playing down some of the current difficulties. Leonardo De Chirico's analysis of Roman Catholicism's dynamics reveals that one highly articulate strand of conservative Protestantism takes cognizance of Catholicism's employment of *anamnesis* in its depiction of the Eucharist but does not see this as an answer to the ecumenical problem. Rather than being a mediating concept which serves to bring the traditions closer, eucharistic sacrifice based on the idea of *anamnesis* is identified as part of a theological superstructure which skews the proper relationship between Christ and the church and arrogates powers and privileges belonging to Christ for the church. This challenge has echoes of the Reformation about it and it is difficult to imagine how the Catholic Church should respond to so bold and fundamental a criticism. However, it would be surely valuable for evangelical scholars of De Chirico's cast of mind to engage further in honest dialogue with Catholic thinkers over this contentious issue. Tough honesty of the kind advocated by Ratzinger would give De Chirico et al. an opportunity to further test this theory against the insights of those within the Catholic tradition. It would also give an opportunity for the kind of close listening that would enable Catholic scholars to comprehend more deeply the kind of principled objections to Catholicism that still remain within Protestantism.

Alongside De Chirico's fundamental objection to the way Catholic theology configures Christ's relationship to the church, he raises supplementary points of criticism to corroborate his underlying thesis. It may be helpful to enumerate these and briefly respond to them.

1. The disproportionate amount of space given to the Eucharist over the atonement in the *Catechism* is evidence that the cross has been subsumed in the Eucharist.

There is certainly a disparity in the amount of word space allocated to the two themes in the *Catechism* and this would indicate that the discussion of the Eucharist has incorporated much of what the Catholic Church would want to say about the cross. It is a moot point whether this is incontrovertible evidence that the cross has been swallowed up in the Eucharist. However, two observations about the manner in which official Catholic theology prioritizes the Eucharist in its treatment of the atonement suggest themselves. First, the New Testament account of the atonement does not seem to focus on the Eucharist to the same extent that contemporary Catholic theology does. St Paul locates the power and impact of the atonement in the verbal proclamation of the cross, and exhortatory teaching about the Christian life often appeals to the cross independent of its relationship to the Eucharist (1 Cor. 1:18; cf. Rom. 5:1, 8; Heb. 9:23–28). It is arguably the case that Catholic magisterial teaching on atonement should better reflect the balance of New Testament teaching on cross and Eucharist. Second, if the above claim is acceptable, the current implosion of Catholicism within its European heartlands points to the need for a rebalancing of its atonement theology. A strong focus on eucharistic sacrifice may make more sense in a milieu where the majority of those associated with the church seek to proactively draw strength from the church's sacramental life. In a period of increasing secularization where this is not the case, there may be missional purchase in simply presenting the soteriological benefits of an unmediated Christ who can be encountered amid the throes of doubt and uncertainty. Pope Francis I's Easter homily in 2013 is a model for this kind of approach and, arguably, this offers a way forward when an increasing number of Catholics need to be fundamentally evangelized before they can be appropriately initiated into the benefits of the Eucharist.[45] Neither of these observations should be heard as hostile criticisms of the Church.

2. The *Catechism's* emphasis on the Eucharist's capacity to make the act of redemption present undermines the independent efficacy of the cross.

De Chirico's language in his treatment of this theme is very strong and unequivocal. He asserts that, according to Catholic theology, '[the work of the cross] is unable to actualize its own efficacy without the active participation of the church in making it present'.[46] This is a difficult position to uphold in that, as much as the *Catechism* stresses the Eucharist's capacity to make 'the sacrifice offered once for all on the cross [remain] ever present',[47] there seems to be no corresponding claim that without the Eucharist the cross is devoid of any soteriological significance. The *Catechism* is arguably not geared towards the kind of soteriological and ecclesiological assertiveness that De Chirico detects lying underneath the surface of its eucharistic claims. The New Testament does not conceive of a situation wherein the Eucharist will not be a consistent part of the church's life. Given this close and essential link between the two, it would not be unnatural to use language such as that which De Chirico cites from the *Catechism*, if what is in mind is the continual impartation of the cross's reality by means of the eucharistic memorial. There is no necessity to interpret the words as a move to power which effectively subverts the New Testament's *tetelestai* ('It is finished') language. Indeed, as the earlier summary of Ratzinger's position intimated, he was content to affirm the sufficiency of the once-only sacrifice in terms which reiterated Luther's concerns and those of the writer to the Hebrews. As the Church's former chief doctrinal enforcer who commissioned the *Catechism* project and had ultimate oversight for it, there are at least reasonable grounds for assuming that he will not have done a *volte-face* on this matter and given his approval to a view which was against the logic of his own position.

3. The Church's claim to participate in the sacrifice of Christ necessarily dilutes and subverts the work of redemption.

The first point to observe in relation to De Chirico's argument is that the *Catechism* itself explicitly refrains from speculating on what participation in Christ's sacrifice might mean. The suggestion is simply that, *'in a way known to God'*, it may be possible for human beings to be 'partners in the paschal mystery'.[48] Given this imprecision in the *Catechism*, De Chirico is arguably making a hostage to fortune when he asserts unequivocally that any and every potential means of human participation in Christ's sacrifice automatically diminishes the work of the cross. To demonstrate that such a scenario is not necessarily so, I would commend the work of Presbyterian theologian Alasdair Heron, who has offered us an explanation for why eucharistic sacrifice (if the concept is accepted) allows us to speak of human participation in Christ's self-offering. This use of Heron is not an affirmation of eucharistic sacrifice, *per se*, but merely a means of showing that once the concept is granted, it is possible to envisage participating in Christ's sacrifice in such a way that his redeeming action is not compromised. Heron asserts:

> He and he alone offers and is the sacrifice by which our reconciliation is achieved. Yet his self-offering is not *only* a sacrifice of expiation and propitiation; it is at the same time the sanctifying and offering of our sinful human nature to God. His sacrifice was made for us; he himself is our offering to the Father; we have no other to bring, but he is the sacrifice who puts himself into our empty hands. To offer Christ is to present him as our sacrifice because he has made himself so; and in the power of that offering to offer ourselves 'a living sacrifice'. It is not to add on to what he is and has done, nor is it to repeat it.[49]

This brief engagement with De Chirico's model leads us to our final consideration: the theory of *anamnesis* (understood as the making present of a past reality in worship) and its impact on our discussion. The possibility that this may be Paul's Hebraic interpretation of what is happening in the Supper is still the strongest single argument in favour of the Catholic idea of eucharistic sacrifice. Decades after the ARCIC report and the publication of *Baptism, Eucharist and Ministry* there is still a virtual consensus in favour of this understanding of remembrance within the mainstream academy.[50] While this consensus does not settle the issue in any absolute way, it stands as a challenge to evangelicals who wish to simply dismiss the idea out of hand. Contemporary evangelical scholarship seems also to be increasingly aware that the conventional minimalist interpretation placed on the idea of remembrance does not do full justice to the concept that Paul articulates in his Lord's Supper discourse. Thiselton speaks of *anamnesis* as not denoting 'the exclusively subjective mental or psychological process of recollection characteristic of Cartesian or modern thought'.[51] His alternative rendering of the concept is a complex combination of biblical and philosophical thought which is too involved to easily break down. One insight that he is happy to endorse, drawing upon Bentzen, is that in some way the narrative remembrance of the Lord's Supper enables members of the congregation to 'become contemporary with the fundamental fact of salvation'.[52] Bruce, writing at an earlier stage, speaks of biblical remembrance being more than a 'mental exercise' and 'involving a realization of what is remembered'.[53] While these statements are not endorsements of the Catholic view *per se*, there seems to be a greater sense among some of the ablest of evangelical scholars that the Eucharist, as understood by Paul, conveys the reality of what Christ has done to the believer in his or her own situation.[54] Perhaps this may be a good starting point for further dialogue between evangelicalism and Catholicism.

Summing Up

This discussion has highlighted De Chirico's critique of Roman Catholic eucharistic theology. It has urged that there are good biblical and missional reasons for the Catholic Church to more closely reflect the New Testament balance between cross and Eucharist in its own official teaching about the atonement. Such a change in emphasis would help allay Protestant fears. De Chirico's claims that the Church's eucharistic teaching has undone the independent efficacy of the cross and that any concept of participation in Christ's sacrifice automatically undermines the salvific uniqueness of the cross has been challenged. I have shown that these conclusions are not clear from the evidence he cites. Ratzinger's acknowledgement of Luther's Reformation concerns lends weight to the notion that key figures in Roman Catholicism understand and accept the limits that the Book of Hebrews places on speculation about the cross. *Anamnesis* continues to be the major issue in the whole discussion, and evangelicals should not summarily dismiss the long-term academic consensus that Paul was influenced by a Hebraic notion of remembrance which involved making a past event real in worship. Significant evangelical biblical scholars are identifying a greater realism in Paul's Lord's Supper discourse and I suggest that this change in perspective is a good starting point for future ecumenical dialogue between Catholics and evangelicals.

SUGGESTIONS FOR THE USE OF INTEGRATIVE SILENCE

Reflection: What would it look like in your context for there to be increased understanding between Roman Catholics and Protestants about atonement and Eucharist? What possibilities would that open up for shared worship? Draw, journal, or reflect on the implications.

Self-examination: In what areas of your life is there a need for reconciliation? What feelings surround those issues for you? If you were to imagine a conversation between yourself and Jesus on the cross about those issues, what would you want to say to him? What would you imagine he might say to you?

Liturgical composition: Compose a prayer of confession or intercession focused on the reconciliation of relationships. You might choose to focus on reconciliation of enemies, genders or faith communities.

Biblical study: Read Colossians 1:15–23 reflecting on this text's claims about the extent and nature of atonement accomplished in the cross.

SECTION 3

RE-IMAGINING THE SELF IN THE LIGHT OF THE CROSS

Theology is that discipline in which the deepest longings and highest hopes of the great majority of human beings find their most articulate expression.[1]

8

THE CROSS AND OUR CAPTIVITY TO SHAME

Robin Stockitt

Introduction

All theological enquiry emerges from a habitat. That habitat is the environment in which ideas germinate, take root and eventually blossom. The habitat from which these ideas have emerged has been my reflection on many years' experience as a teacher, an ordained minister, a husband and a father. Over the course of these years I have searched for resonances between my Christian faith and the people I have encountered. I have met many people who experience something more profound, and perhaps more intangible, than the rather straightforward sin–guilt–forgiveness paradigm of traditional Christian orthodoxy. It is far more difficult to define but afflicts us all in a pervasive way. It is the nagging feeling that maybe we are not quite good enough, that we are insignificant, that we have not made our mark on the world. In more severe cases it expresses itself in the driving need to perform, to compete against others for the right to exist. Or it is manifested in the desire to hide, to withdraw, to retreat into some safer world where no one can hurt or destroy. This malaise sometimes erupts in violence done to others for no sufficient reason, or it smoulders beneath the surface, eating away at our self-esteem and our bodies. For some people it is camouflaged by an excess of pious spirituality; for others by a weary resignation. We go to extraordinary lengths to run away from this disease of the soul, by denying it is there, by refusing to stop, by filling every corner of our lives with busyness, hoping that the dread feeling will simply drift away and disappear.

What is the name of this experience?

It is called shame.

It may also masquerade under a variety of different pseudonyms: mocking, ridicule, humiliation, unworthiness, contempt, disgrace, exclusion, condemnation, to name but a few. I intend, however, to collect this cluster of names together under one heading, the title of shame. If this shame is so pervasive, so universally evident, then surely we require a theology to understand it and to address it? To my knowledge very little theological exploration has yet been done on this theme.

What does shame look like? What is its design, structure and purpose? How does it function in both ordering and distorting our world? These are questions that demand to be heard and point us in the direction of the foundational creation texts in the book of Genesis which articulate a view of what it means to be human. Our search therefore is for a biblical anthropology, in which shame and its natural counterpart – honour – have a pre-eminent place.

Right from the outset we are given indications that God functions relationally both within himself and towards the world he has just brought into being. In the second chapter of Genesis the Lord declares that it is not good for Adam to remain alone. It is a statement that declares that for the human self to be fully realized there needs to be the presence of 'another', for without this 'other' we cannot know ourselves and are unable to flourish. This 'other' in the case of Adam and Eve was both similar and yet dissimilar. Adam recognizes that this person is of the same raw material as himself – 'bone of my bones and flesh of my flesh' (Gen. 2:23 [NIV]) – yet she is also utterly different: a partner, a companion, a counterpart, a complementary person, but certainly not a competitor. Without having each other Adam and Eve would not have been complete. This depiction is a theological assertion of the structure of the self. The DNA of who we are as persons is intrinsically relational and we are offered the merest of glimpses into this state of innocence. Prior to the temptation by the serpent described in chapter 3, the storyteller informs us in Gen. 2:25 that, '[the man] and his wife were both naked, and they felt no shame' (NIV). What is the theological significance of this piece of information? Is this an incidental morsel of trivia about nudity? Can it be passed over without further attention? It is my view that this highly crafted story of creation includes significant clues that are essential to a correct configuration of the meaning of the narrative, and this reference is pivotal to unlocking the meaning of the tale. Before they chose to disobey the divine injunction Adam and Eve are described as being *without shame*. The Hebrew word that is used here, *bws*, is used in such a way as to articulate that 'the man and his wife were not found in a state of shame as far as their nakedness was concerned'.[1] Indeed the verbal forms used in the Hebrew suggest that Adam and Eve presented themselves (a reflexive verb) as being without shame before each other. In other words they stood before each other, and before the God who created them, without covering, and felt no diminution of themselves and no desire to hide. It is a Hebrew word that is found repeatedly in the Old Testament – 128 times to be precise – which suggests that it plays a significant role in the unfolding story of God's people. Here is a sinless world, a paradise depicted, and the primary characteristic as far as the first couple was concerned was the absence of shame. This ancient account is a depiction of the human condition in a pre-cultural environment. The Adam and Eve story pre-dates any kind of socially constructed understanding of shame. It would suggest that shamelessness is an original, existential description of who we are.

What happens, therefore, when the shameless self endures a rupture, a distortion of some kind? What effect does that have on the self and the sense of being a person? The picture of 'naïve' innocence suffered distortion when the original pair chose an alternative orientation. They heard the voice of the serpent, and their heads turned to listen to what the serpent had to say. The journey towards the breaking of the command began with the turning of their heads away from their creator. The act of disobedience was the consequence of this turning away, the logical outcome of facing away from the community of God. It was this

turning away that was indicative of a desire to sever the relationship of loving dependency upon God. To remain in relationship
meant an acknowledgement of the giftedness of life and the origin
of that gift in the God who had created them. The temptation to
'be as gods' (Gen. 3:5 [KJV]) threatened that dependent connection and struck at the heart of what it was to be human. Dietrich
Bonhoeffer, who so courageously stood against the tyranny of
Hitler's Third Reich, had this to say about Adam, Eve and shame:

> Shame only exists as a result of the knowledge of the division of man
> . . . Shame is the expression of the face that we no longer accept the
> other person as a gift from God . . . When one accepts the other as
> the companion given to him by God, where he is content with un-
> derstanding himself as beginning from and ending in the other and
> in belonging to him, man is not ashamed. In the unity of unbroken
> obedience man is naked in the presence of man, uncovered, revealing
> both body and soul, and yet is not ashamed. Shame only comes into
> existence in the world of division.[2]

The immediate consequence of the turning was the sudden
entrance of shame. It announced its arrival with a new ability to
'know', and this 'knowing' produced an urgent desire to hide.
When God finds the couple crouching behind a tree, they are
too ashamed to come out into the open for their shame is overwhelming. This is the storyteller's way of describing the experience of sin. Ultimately this leads to expulsion from the garden
with no more evening conversations with the God who used to
come looking for them. Yet the guilt that they jointly shared was
merely one aspect of the larger story of their turning away, which
culminated in their shameful expulsion from the place of true
community and harmony with the whole of the created world.
Dietrich Bonhoeffer, commenting on the Genesis account, articulates the narrative in this way:

> Man perceives himself in his disunion with God and men. He per-
> ceives that he is naked . . . laid bare. Hence there arises shame.
> Shame is man's ineffaceable recollection of his estrangement from
> the origin . . . man is ashamed of the loss of his unity with God
> and with other men. Shame and remorse are generally mistaken for

one another: Man feels remorse when he has been at fault, and he feels shame when he lacks something. Shame is more original than remorse.[3]

Bonhoeffer acknowledges that both shame and remorse are present in the Genesis account. Remorse is the human response to the acknowledgement of guilt and as such it is directly connected to a specific misdeed. Shame is far deeper than that, more 'original', to use Bonhoeffer's description, and is often unconnected to specific acts of commission or omission. That original experience resonates with something that lies very deep within the human soul. It is the sense that something is essentially damaged, distorted, infected at the core of our being. It questions our very right to exist before the God who called us into being. The original memory is that we are made for unity and harmony, and shame reminds us of the disunity that now exists. The desire of Adam and Eve to cover their nakedness, by making aprons for themselves, is a sign of their desire to cover that lack of original union. What began for them as the delight of daily open communion with the Creator now manifests itself as terrified concealment.

Why linger on this ancient story? We do so for a number of reasons. First, prior to their expulsion from the garden, Adam and Eve knew what it meant to belong and they belonged to a 'place'. They belonged 'geographically' in that they were placed, according to the narrative, in a location, a habitat, a space created for them in which they could flourish. I use the word 'geographically' with some degree of caution as the mythical elements of the story need to be kept in mind. Yet the storyteller takes care to give us geographical details of the location of the garden, and the resultant expulsion from this home constituted a severe loss. The shame which followed from their tragic choice led to their dislocation from place; in fact it led directly to exile. The theme of shame as exclusion and exile becomes a repeated refrain as the biblical narratives unfold. The exile of Adam and Eve foreshadowed the sense of exile experienced by the Israelites in Egypt before their deliverance. Responding to the catastrophe of shameful exile in Babylon becomes a challenge of acute proportions for the later generation of prophets and theologians. The connection between shame and belonging is highly significant.

Second, there are psychological dimensions to shame that the creation story alludes to. One of those is the desire to hide or conceal. Adam and Eve exchanged their beautiful, open naïvete for suspicious hiding. No longer was there the freedom to be themselves before each other. We are given a picture of humanity that is at odds with itself, unable simply to be, afraid of being known, wanting to conceal, to run, to cover up. Depicted in these terms the creation story has a sadly familiar and contemporary ring to it. Yet hiding was not the only psychological distortion that the story portrays. Once their misdemeanour is exposed, the instinctive response of Adam is to blame, to point the finger, to refuse to accept responsibility for his own actions. Blame had never been part of the original creation; it was not necessary, it was too aggressive, too violent a feature to have any place in the garden. Yet after their joint turning away from God, blame appears, ugly and destructive as always.

Third, the story of the pair hiding from each other also includes their hiding from God. God comes looking for them, in much the same way as Christ himself would later declare that he came to seek and to save the lost. God's searching eye finds them crouching, cringing, wanting not to be found. Theirs is a spiritual crisis as well as a psychological one. What began as a spiritual relationship of beauty now becomes tarnished, characterized by avoidance and the averted gaze. They dare not look God in the eye any longer.

Last, the creation story illustrates how the shame that the original couple experienced is connected to the body. The mention of nakedness and the subsequent desire to cover that nakedness suggests that the distorting effect of sin has a deep connection with the very physicality of our being. Does the Bible have anything to say about the role and significance of our flesh and blood, both in the experience of shame and its redemption and healing? Is there a connection therefore between the original nakedness in the garden and the utter redemptive nakedness of Christ's exposed body on the cross?

It is now necessary to turn to some New Testament texts to explore how the coming of Christ in our world redeems, restores and heals the shamed. Staking a claim for shame as a theological category is not to insist that it is the only necessary paradigm through which to interpret Scripture, but merely to insist that the question of shame needs to be heard. This is necessary not only because it is tragically so evident in our world today but because it is also a pervasive theme throughout the pages of Scripture, if we but know how to look for it. When approaching the question of the place of the crucifixion in the wider narrative of the gospels, it is my contention that there must be a 'red thread' that joins together the disparate stories of Jesus' encounters with the people of his day and the climatic events at the end of his life. In what way do the gospel stories cohere together to form one narrative? Could it possibly be true that shame is the underlying current that ties together the loose ends and incidental occasions and makes the crucifixion take on a different hue? All four gospels tell their stories of Jesus in such a way that the crucifixion and resurrection of Christ is the culmination of their narrative. These differing narratives weave a tale which depicts the unfolding of the plot of the Christian faith, namely the story of how the redemption or salvation of humankind is effected. Yet the history of Christian theology reveals a bewildering and at times highly divergent palette of interpretations as to what has actually been achieved by Christ. What precisely is the nature of the threat that distorts human existence, and by what mechanism or process has that threat been dealt with?

Let us examine one incident from Mark's gospel which functions critically in the unfolding narrative of Jesus. It is the story of when Jesus encounters blind Bartimaeus in Mark 10:46–50. If an atonement theology is framed in such a way that it simply and only deals with the question of individual guilt and its aftermath, then we immediately encounter problems in interpreting the story of Bartimaeus in a coherent way. Do we simply say that he was a 'sinner' included in the blanket judgement of Paul in Romans 3:23: 'for all have sinned and fall short of the glory of God' (NIV)? In one sense this is of course true, yet if we remain with the gospel narrative as it is given to us, then guilt is not the primary emphasis of the story. Bartimaeus is described as sitting outside the city of Jericho, stumbled upon as Jesus and his disciples were leaving. This position – outside the city gates – is significant. He remains an outsider, excluded, not welcome inside the walls of the city where there is safety, commerce and community, but outside, compelled to feed off the scraps that society left behind or people donated to him. He sits therefore in a place of exclusion, a place of shame. This shameful place is emphasized by the attitude of the disciples who rebuke him and do not allow him voice. Those who are shamed are not only excluded but are silenced, for they have no right to speak or to be heard. His shameful status is further underlined by the name by which he is known, Bartimaeus. It is a name of Hebrew origin formed from two separate words, *bar*, meaning 'son of' and *tame* meaning 'foul' or 'unclean'. His name, 'son of filth',[4] was a taunt used by locals to further heap disgrace upon him. So the pausing of Jesus to pay attention to this poor beggar was a revolutionary pause. In that one gesture he signals that this outsider is noticed, his voice has been heard, his request taken seriously. Jesus refuses to be constrained or influenced by the cultural expectations of his day; he rejects the commonly accepted definitions of who is an insider and who is not. Jesus effectively looks at the shame of this man and counts it as nothing. He scorns it (Heb. 12:2) and in so doing prefigures all that he will ultimately accomplish on the cross. His action was both intensely personal – in that poor Bartimaeus received his sight – and simultaneously profoundly political. If this man, this blind beggar, this complete nobody, is to be included now into the very fabric of normal society, then this demands a complete overhaul of the way in which society is structured.

If shame is the underlying motif in the story of Bartimaeus, then this narrative undercurrent should impel us towards the denouement of the story of Jesus, the crucifixion. This event has become a stumbling block. What does it represent? What was achieved through it? Paul's magisterial letter to the Romans offers us an insight into the way in which the apostle extrapolated meaning from the event. Many commentators regard Paul's letter to the Romans as the fruit of many years of reflection on the nature and extent of the gospel. It was probably written in Corinth during a time of relative peace in the midst of an arduous schedule of travelling around the Mediterranean churches. It is therefore considered to be his summary of the whole gospel, covering as it does the issue of both the continuity with the Jewish messianic expectations and simultaneously the radical discontinuity with much of the Jewish tradition. One might expect therefore that the paradigm of 'guilt and forgiveness', which has so dominated theological thinking for centuries, particularly in the West, would be clearly laid out for all to see. It is surprising, to say the least, that such language is almost completely absent from the letter. At no point does Paul speak in terms of forgiveness and in only one sentence is there any allusion to 'guilt'.[5] In the light of this evidence one is compelled to come to the conclusion that Paul was operating under a different paradigm altogether.

A clue to this alternative paradigm is offered in the opening few sentences of his letter, although it is easy for us, living as we do at such a distance from the original circumstances of the letter, to miss the impact of Paul's shocking use of the Greek language. Paul begins his letter by explaining that his vocation is to bring the liberating message of the gospel of Jesus Christ to everyone, whatever their ethnic background. He writes to the fledgling church in Rome, a collection of Christian communities, scattered throughout the city, composed of Jewish converts, slaves, Gentiles and the sophisticated elite of Roman society. Within the Graeco-Roman culture clear boundary lines were drawn between those who were honoured and those who did not or could not receive honour. This newly founded Christian community in Rome to which Paul was writing was steeped in this surrounding culture, a culture characterized by a fierce competitiveness, stemming from a fear of being found to be without honour. The only way to ensure that one's honour was maintained and protected was to boast of one's achievements, and to put others down who might threaten one's status. It was a brutal world, where only those with the right connections, the right education and sufficient financial means could survive. Scholars have shown that the entire machinery of the Roman Empire, founded upon the complex interplay of sheer force, patronage and propaganda, was held together by an underlying dynamic of honour and shame.[6] There was an expectation that honour should be given to those who positioned themselves higher up the social pyramid. In fact the 'duty of honour' was more important than the 'duty to obey'.[7]

Into this world the gospel was introduced and it immediately began to subvert the foundations upon which society was built. One of those groups who belonged to the category of 'the shamed' were the Barbarians. This was a term applied to the non-Greek-speaking peoples and was used pejoratively. The New International Version has sanitized its translation of Romans 1:14 when it renders the verse, 'I am a debtor both to Greeks and non-Greeks, both to the wise and the foolish.' Yet the original language for non-Greeks is the word *barbaros*, an abusive term. It was a term coined to describe those unruly tribes not yet under the orbit of Roman rule. Their language sounded foreign and absurd to the sophisticated Romans – a mere babbling of infantile sounds: *babbababba* – hence the pejorative *Barbarians*. If the verse was translated more colloquially as 'I am a debtor both to the sophisticated and the rabble, the educated and the stupid', then we would catch something of the flavour of Paul's language. As Jewett has stated, 'barbarians were considered sub-human and incapable of being civilized'.[8] One of the lands that was considered to be the home of the most barbaric of peoples was Spain, yet it is to this very region that Paul wished to travel in order to take the liberating gospel. Would the church in Rome be willing to support him in this venture? That is the key question that unlocks the purpose behind this most theological of Paul's letters. If the Roman church were to be able to unequivocally join him in this missionary venture then they would need to be deeply and profoundly conscious of the way in which the gospel of Jesus Christ both subverts and inverts the prevailing culture of honour and shame. Paul goes on to describe the priorities of his mission: 'first for the Jew, then for the Gentile' (Rom 1:16 NIV1984). In so doing he cuts across the prejudices of the educated elite of Roman society who considered themselves vastly superior to the Jewish race. This good news will go to the Jews *first*! And only afterwards to the Gentiles! We are forced then by the sheer brutal power of Paul's rhetoric to ask why he opens his letter in this way. Why does he set out to antagonize and provoke by deploying offensive language?

The answer may lie towards the end of his letter to the Romans. He explains in chapter 15 that the gospel is good news for everyone – even those outside the Jewish faith. This notion is not in reality a new idea, for he is able to cite both the Psalms and Isaiah showing that the 'nations' or the Gentiles will one day sing the praises of Yahweh. To this end Paul feels the overwhelming vocation to take this good news to the Gentiles and writes that he wishes to travel to Spain to achieve his goal. 'I plan to do so when I go to Spain. I hope to visit you while passing through and to have you assist me on my journey there, after I have enjoyed your company for a while'

(Rom. 15:24 [NIV1984]). He has made his plans for this journey, yet wishes to include the church in Rome in this missionary venture. How could he summon their support if it meant giving away the grace of God to those who were considered to be heathens, barbarians, Gentiles? He begins his letter by declaring that those who have received grace are now called to pass it on to those outside the Jewish faith (Rom. 1:5). Paul was acutely aware of the divisive, hierarchical nature of Roman society and yet he boldly strides across these accepted boundary lines, claiming that the gospel of Jesus Christ subverts the entire social system. This inclusive gospel is however, for Paul, not a source of shame as he so confidently asserts, 'I am not ashamed of the gospel, because it is the power of God for the salvation of everyone who believes' (Rom. 1:16 [NIV1984]). The Greek word that he uses here for 'ashamed' is *epaischunomai* and it is a compound word, meaning 'to place a sense of disfigurement or disgrace upon someone'. It is to load someone with a burden of disrepute and revulsion. Paul says that when he associates himself with the gospel of Jesus Christ, which to some is nonsense and to others is abhorrent, he feels absolutely no disfigurement at all. Robert Jewett in his commentary on the book of Romans states that this declaration 'sets the tone for the entire letter' and is the key text which unlocks the setting in which the letter was composed.[9] By making this declaration Paul invites his readers in the church in Rome to view both themselves and the gospel in the same light. Paradoxically, true honour and the removal of shame is found in the life, death and resurrection of one man who had died an ignominious death in a small province of the Roman Empire. To quote Jewett again, 'There were deeply engrained social reasons why Paul should have been ashamed to proclaim such a gospel; his claim not to be ashamed signals that a social and ideological revolution has been inaugurated by the gospel.'[10]

Paul continues in his letter to articulate the radical implications of the coming of Christ into the world. In chapter 12 he writes that the members of the community are to take the lead in honouring one another in brotherly love (Rom. 12:10) as a key distinctive and defining mark of their Christian discipleship. Again it is hard for us to appreciate the force of his words. The Greek word that he uses here – *proecegeomai* – carries the sense that each person is to compete, not in putting others down, but rather to compete to show honour. And to whom is this honour to be shown? He tells us in verse 16: 'Do not be proud, but be willing to associate with people of low position' (NIV). For Paul, the meaning of the gospel was not to be understood primarily as a private, individual and inner experience of the grace of God in Christ. This is how the gospel has been interpreted for centuries in the western world. Instead, the gospel was to have a far more subversive impact than that. The entire way in which Roman culture was organized and managed was now under threat from this tiny, irrelevant, Christian community who based their hope on the death and resurrection of an unknown peasant from Israel. Instead of competing against one another for honour, the Christian community was to practise the exact opposite. They were to compete in giving honour to the lowest of the society, to search for those who had been shamed, ignored, bypassed and forgotten. It is those people that the church had to seek out and in so doing invert their hopeless world, showering them with the grace that provides honour without charge. For the apostle Paul, Christ's mission was profoundly pertinent in addressing a brutal society that felt no qualms in leaving the shamed to suffer on their own. The gospel was such good news because these lost people could be found, healed and restored, and their honour was derived not from anything that they possessed or achieved but simply and only because they could stand before the face of Jesus Christ with their heads held high. In the light of all this, the question is then posed to the Roman community: 'I am going to take the gospel to Spain; will you support me in this?' Their answer to this one key question would reveal much about the extent of their understanding of the revolutionary way in which the story of Jesus addresses the question of shame and honour.

The writer of the book of Hebrews likewise addresses the question of how the crucifixion of Christ removes the burden of shame from despised people and replaces it with honour. The letter begins with a depiction of the glory that inherently belongs to the Son of God. The term 'glory' (*doxa*) is often paired with 'honour' (*time*) in the New Testament. They appear together as bedfellows and represent the exact antithesis of shame. When the writer uses such terms in his letter, therefore, we need to be alert to the particular sensitivity of such phrases. In a culture which was as highly stratified and competitive as the Mediterranean in the first century, any references to honour and glory would immediately provoke interest. So the letter does not hesitate in insisting at the very outset that the Son is the radiance of God's glory (1:3) and that he now sits at the right hand of the majesty in heaven (1:3). The usage of the term 'the right hand' is deliberate. The right hand was the honoured hand in comparison to the left hand, and those who attended feasts and sat at the right hand of the host occupied the most honoured position.[11] Having outlined to his readers the honoured and glorious place that the crucified and shamed Christ now occupies, the writer goes on to state that it is the intention of the Father to bring many into this place of glory too (Heb. 2:10). Although we are merely eavesdropping on a distant conversation and can only fully hear one voice, it is clear that questions of honour and shame are very live topics in the Christian community to which the letter was written. It is as if the pressing issue being addressed concerns how one can hold one's head up high with dignity as a follower of Christ in a society which militated against every value that Jesus Christ espoused.

One of the ways in which this beleaguered Christian community could maintain a sense of honour was through an appeal to an alternative set of values. These values, embodied in the church community, could sustain its members and it was because of this key support mechanism that the writer urges his readers not to give up meeting together (Heb. 10:25). Through this avenue of mutual support their sense of honour could be maintained in the midst of a hostile society. Yet the writer knows that this human support alone is not sufficient and he needs therefore to demonstrate how the awful question of shame was dealt a final blow in the crucifixion of Christ. The key phrase in the whole argument is found in chapter 12:2 where we read, 'keeping our eyes fixed on Jesus, the pioneer and perfecter of our faith. For the joy set out for him he endured the cross, disregarding its shame, and has taken his seat at the right hand of the throne of God' (NET). This sentence comes at the conclusion of a lengthy passage in the letter in which the writer was acutely aware of the way in which this Christian community had suffered at the hands of the surrounding dominant culture. He enumerates the way in which this has happened in chapter 10:32–34 (NIV):

Remember those earlier days after you had received the light, when you
endured in a great conflict full of suffering. Sometimes you were publicly exposed to insult and persecution; at other times you stood side by
side with those who were so treated. You suffered along with those in
prison and joyfully accepted the confiscation of your property, because
you knew that you yourselves had better and lasting possessions.

What the writer highlights here is the way in which Christians
had been made into a public spectacle (*theatrizo*). They had been
paraded in full view of the local community, laughed at, scorned,
ridiculed, exposed to insult and publicly shamed. This is what
happens in any society where there is a competitive hierarchy of
honour and shame. There have to be winners and losers and this
must be demonstrated in the public arena. These poor early Christians had suffered in this shameful way and their plight is taken up
by the writer of this letter. The response is to list all those heroes
of the faith (ch. 11) who had also suffered such public persecution
and shaming. At the end of the list the writer explains how each of
them had been hated and excluded by society for their faith; they
were 'destitute, persecuted and mistreated – the world was not
worthy of them. They wandered in deserts and mountains, and in
caves and holes in the ground' (NIV1984). Here is a depiction of the
most profound forms of shaming, for these heroes no longer had
homes to dwell in, no place to call their own, no recognition of their
full humanity. They had been stripped of anything that gave them
dignity and honour, yet their faith had enabled them to persevere.

The argument of the writer then moves on to the case of Jesus
himself. Jesus belongs to this line of shamed 'heroes'. He too was
excluded, mocked and ridiculed. He too had no place to lay his
head at night; he too was finally stripped of any semblance of
dignity and raised up on a cross outside the city walls. And there,
precisely at that place of ultimate shaming, Christ looks upon
the shame that he is enduring. The writer uses a word which is
usually translated as 'scorn' (*kataphroneo*) and one which literally
means 'to think against' or 'to despise', to consider as nothing
at all. It is a powerful rhetorical device to assert that Christ on
the cross effectively shamed shame. The moment of crucifixion
is thus depicted as the entering into the place of shame in order
to rob shame of its power to humiliate. There is a constellation of

shameful aspects surrounding Christ's crucifixion. The location of Golgotha, outside the walls of the city, is significant. It is a deeply symbolic place, a place for those who do not belong to society, the unwanted, the scum of the earth. Furthermore, his crucifixion exposed Christ in his nakedness. His clothing had been removed and became the object of desire, a trophy for those who had been complicit in his death. To be naked had become over the centuries a deeply shameful thing. The innocent nakedness of Adam and Eve had been replaced with shameful nakedness, as we see so vividly recorded in the story of Noah and his sons in Genesis 9. Furthermore, crucifixion was a form of death reserved by the Romans only for those who were considered beneath contempt. If the intent of execution was to inflict torture, then it would have lasted over a period of days, elongated to its maximum extent. Death through crucifixion was, by comparison, relatively swift, for the weight of the body upon the diaphragm would have caused asphyxiation. The intent of crucifixion was rather to heap shame on the victim to an ultimate extent and as such was reserved only for slaves and those who were not Roman citizens. In the culture of the time there could have been no more perfect way to shame someone. Finally the experience of the crucifixion was intentionally a public spectacle, intended to inflict maximum humiliation and ridicule, such that Paul was able to later refer to this by quoting the Deuteronomic text, 'Cursed is everyone who hangs on a tree' (Gal. 3:13).

This combination of shaming events is presented by the gospel writers to illustrate for us the depths to which Christ was shamed. This entrance is more than simply exemplary. It is done 'for us' and 'with us'. This is the force of the argument in Hebrews 2:10 where the writer speaks about the way in which Christ would taste death for everyone for, 'in bringing many sons [and daughters] to glory, it was fitting that God, for whom and through whom everything exists, should make the author of their salvation perfect through suffering' (NIV1984). The acuteness of the suffering of Christ was, in human terms, the endurance of the most intense shaming. Yet this shaming has now been rendered impotent and, mysteriously, those who have been caught up in his work on the cross have now been brought to 'glory', the exact counterpart to shame. In so doing Christ's actions draw a deep resonance from within all those who have ever entered into their own shamed condition.

EXERCISE: BIBLIODRAMA

Bibliodrama is a mode of engaging with a biblical text which invites us to do some imaginative 'gap filling'. In bibliodrama we allow the biblical text to inspire our thinking, and we engage our own sense of how a character might think or feel. We attend to the gaps of the text, the things we are not told, and fill them with our own ideas. Bibliodrama aims not at interpretation but at engagement. We might expect to learn as much about ourselves and the other members of our group as we do about the meaning of the text. There is no 'wrong' bibliodrama. There are only a variety of creative suggestions about what the text might have said, but does not. Bibliodrama invites imaginative engagement with thoughts and feelings evoked by biblical narratives and gives participants the opportunity to place themselves within the drama of Scripture as acting figures.[1]

Instructions for Using Bibliodrama in a Group Setting

Groups should create safe space for this activity by stressing that each person should participate as they feel willing. Members should also commit to confidentiality of any sharing that takes place as a result of the bibliodrama exercise.

In the group setting:

1. **Warm-up exercise:** Give each participant a copy of the text in a standard translation (NRSV, NIV, etc.). Ask them to read the text aloud individually while walking around the room. Participants

should watch for phrases or sentences that seem important and should read those with various tones and inflections, repeating a phrase until they find the expression that seems to fit. They should allow themselves to voice the text in whatever way seems right to them. The group returns to the main circle and shares any phrases from the text that particularly inspired them.[2]

2. **Second warm-up exercise:** Assign roles and have the group act out the movements of the text while one participant reads the text aloud. Repeat the motions a second time without having the text read.[3]

3. **Reflective discussion:** What themes and motifs are emerging? What did you find most compelling in the text in either of these two exercises? Invite participants to repeat either the word or phrase, or motion that most signified the way the text was engaging them.[4]

4. **Imaginative discussion:** What are the emotions and gaps of the text? Who are the characters in the text? How might they feel? What are their relationships? Who else should we include in our scene? How might we imagine them?[5]

5. **Setting the scene:** Allow participants to select the character they want to play. Ask each character to identify the way they are imaginatively engaging with that character. What is the character thinking, feeling, etc.? Where are they in the scene?[6]

6. **Action:** Act out the scene. Put the Bible away and do not attempt to use the words of the text or its sequence necessarily.

7. **Reflection:** What was most meaningful for you in this exercise? What did you learn about your character? What did you learn from another character? What did you learn about yourself?

Suggested Texts

For engaging with the theme of shame, groups might explore Luke 7:36–50; Luke 8:40–56; Luke 19:1–9; and John 18:15–27.[7] For engaging the broader themes of atonement, groups might consider bibliodrama exercises based on any of the passion narratives.

9

THE CROSS AND THE POETIC IMAGINATION

Katie M. Heffelfinger

The Suffering Servant and Christian Worship

Worship is central to the integrative approach that informs this book. Morning worship and daily Eucharist framed the days of the seminar in which these chapters were originally presented. These services expressed our community's commitment to rooting theological study in the life of faith. During one of the Eucharist services, we affirmed our faith together in the following words:

> We believe in God, who gave his Son into the world not to condemn the world, but that through him the world might have life. He was despised and rejected by others; a man of suffering and acquainted with infirmity; and as one from whom others hide their faces he was despised and we held him of no account. Surely he has borne our infirmities and carried our diseases; yet we accounted him stricken, struck down by God, and afflicted. But he was wounded for our transgressions, crushed for our iniquities; upon him was the punishment that made us whole, and by his bruises we are healed (adapted from John 3:17; 10:10; Isa. 53:3–5).

Similar examples in Christian liturgy, and especially in Christian hymnary, abound. This chapter asks: when Christians read and sing the fourth servant song (Isaiah 52:13 – 53:12) in worship, what does it mean for us to take these poetic words seriously as our own words? That is, what does the poem's 'we' language impel us to do and to be?

Christians have been using Isaiah 52:13 – 53:12 to voice their claims about Jesus since the New Testament period (e.g. Acts 8:27–36). In this chapter, I will not examine or seek to justify such Christian use of the text, nor will I argue that Christian reading of Isaiah 52:13 – 53:12 must necessarily make christological claims. Instead, I will contend that when Christians do use the words of the fourth servant song to speak about their faith in Jesus in worship, this text must be more than an arrow pointing towards New Testament texts. When we recognize connections between what the New Testament authors claim about Jesus' servanthood and Isaiah's depiction of the suffering servant, we are not finished with this text. Instead, if Isaiah 52:13 – 53:12 can be read as saying words that we also affirm as true about Christ, that ought to intensify our interest in the details of the passage.[1] It does the very opposite of giving us permission to claim that the text refers to Jesus and then to move on from reading it closely. This text is much more than a list of details to map onto New Testament stories. Instead, Isaiah 52:13 – 53:12 offers the worshipper a potentially transformative encounter through its poetic shape. For the reader committed to living with it as Christian Scripture, it is a formational text. The song invites us to re-utter it. If we take up the song's invitation, it can produce a (re)ordering of our imagination, and the (re)formation of our emotions. In Christian worship, the poem invites speech that shapes us not so much through a doctrinal (i.e. christological) claim, as by putting words about the significance of that claim on our lips, and by voicing emotions appropriate to that claim.[2]

The Problem of Poetry

We tend to neglect poetry in our churches. We are uneasy about poetry. We often think it is just a bit beyond us, or that it says in complicated language what could be said simply.[3] The 'plain truth for plain people' battle-cry of my own Wesleyan background might be echoed by many if they heard that they might be asked to discuss a poetic text at this week's Bible study.[4] Thus, poetry tends to suffer neglect in modern western Christian worship and discipleship. And contemporary culture's embrace of story reinforces the sense that poetry is difficult, mysterious and obscure.

One of the reasons we find the poetry within Scripture difficult may be that our expectations do not fit well with poetry. Our ideas about what we ought to do with biblical texts are based on narrative and logic. We think that we are supposed to come away from Bible study with a kernel of truth to work into our view of the world. We expect the preacher to make clear points about what this text says for our lives today. We have cognitive expectations. We want to learn truths. We expect to be informed. But poetry resists our assumptions that its primary reason for existence is to inform us.[5] It may be that our 'problem with poetry' is not that poetry is obscure, but that we are asking it to be what it is not. We are asking questions it was never designed to answer.

This scenario is perhaps particularly true of Isaiah 52:13 – 53:12. Treatments of the fourth servant song have commonly embraced a 'storyline' of one sort or another to make sense of this strange poem. From those who see the text as foretelling Christ's passion to those who see it as recounting the life of the prophetic poet responsible for the surrounding chapters, interpreters of all theological stripes have sketched a narrative that they see lying behind the poem's details.[6] But Isaiah 52:13 – 53:12 is not a story and it does not make particularly good sense as a story. Promises of glory sit at the beginning and end of the passage, burial imagery appears in the middle, and a conditional claim about length of days comes after references to death as having happened. This poem makes a very poorly organized story. David J.A. Clines has asked about Isaiah 52:13 – 53:12, 'what if the force of the poem – to say nothing of the poetry of the poem – lies in its very unforthcomingness, its refusal to be precise and to give *information*?'[7] Clines' question is an important reminder that the task of reading poetry is rarely about mining it for cognitive truths. Rather, the fact that this passage is poetry suggests that when we read it, we should begin with poetic expectations.

What does reading with poetic expectations look like? It will mean reading more for the encounter and experience offered by the text than for cognitive claims. It will mean reading emotionally. It will mean reading with an eye to the way things are said as being equally important to what is said.

Reading with poetic expectations begins with recognizing how the particular form of poetry we read in the Bible communicates its message. The majority of biblical poetry is lyric poetry, and Isaiah 52:13 – 53:12 is no exception.[8] Lyric poetry is a type of poetry that does not tell a story and, without story to hold it together, tends to gain its unity from the address of a voice, by the force of its imagery and the power of its language. It often juxtaposes ideas rather than linking them explicitly, and works by a sort of resonance between images rather than by logical chains or the progression of time.[9] The development of a character, which is so important in narratives, is absent. Instead, the voice of the text confronts us directly. Dialogue between characters disappears, and we find ourselves immediately involved in the text's expression either as its audience or by having its words made our own.

So, poetic texts like this one invite us into a much closer encounter than the observer stance offered by narrative. Lyric poetry confronts us with the 'utterance of a voice'.[10] It places us in the presence of its speaker. What we experience in that speaker's presence is an empathy-building encounter. Lyric poetry is a heavily emotionally charged form.

Whenever a speaker addresses another, that speaker uses a particular tone. This is true in general human interactions, and it is true in literature, even if we have to work harder to discern it in the latter case. However, with lyric poetry, we are so often addressed directly by the poem that whatever tone the voice of the text takes has emotional import for us as the audience. Whether the voice of the text is angry, affectionate or indifferent, that tone is often directed at us, drawing us naturally into the emotional world of the poem. Thus, through its form the poem produces a certain level of emotional response, and the fact that it so often addresses us intensifies its emotional charge.

The 'problem of poetry' has an impact on our emotions as well. Poetry does not make things easy for us, even after we have abandoned our narrative expectations. Poetry plays with words and revels in tensions. It is 'difficult fun'.[11] And, because poetry demands our full attention, it shapes our imaginations more intensely than that which we grasp quickly and easily.

If 'figur[ative language] . . . figure[s] the mind' so intensely
precisely because of the emotional and imaginative effort it
demands of us if we are to unpack it, then poetry figures us when
we give ourselves attentively to it.[12] The development of such
habits of attention is what Simone Weil points to as the attitude
appropriate to prayer and genuine empathy.[13] We are formed as
ethical people who can look upon the face of another and feel
compassion by practising such encounters with the emotional,
speaking voices who confront us through poetic texts.[14] And
we are formed as people ready to attend to the presence of God
by developing our ability to attend to what is other than us.[15]
So we might affirm with Mary Kinzie, 'the aesthetic mission is
also a moral one'.[16] And, inspired by Weil, we might come to see
reading biblical poetry as a spiritual discipline that forms us in
habits of prayer.

The Servant Song as Our Utterance

As the utterance of a voice, lyric poetry is 'uniquely disposed to
be re-uttered'.[17] When we speak Isaiah 52:13 – 53:12 in worship,
we engage in re-utterance. We are reading poetically, and we are
reading in a way this passage particularly invites us to, through
its poetic form.

However, re-utterance is necessarily an act of taking on speech
that has been spoken before, and the context for which the words
had their first meaning is fruitful background for our re-speaking.
The fourth servant song is part of a larger section of the book
of Isaiah commonly referred to as Second Isaiah. This unit is a
series of prophetic poems with some overarching features that
should be seen as 'context' for Isaiah 52:13 – 53:12. One of the
most marked features of this section is the overwhelming dominance of the divine voice. While many prophetic books include
stories about the life of the poet (e.g. Amos, Isaiah of Jerusalem)
or recount words of the prophet which appear as very much his
own words (e.g. Jeremiah's laments, Ezekiel's vision reports),
the prophetic poet of Isaiah 40 – 55 is 'anonymous' and seems to
disappear behind the divine voice whose words he proclaims. The
loquaciousness of the LORD's voice in these chapters is one of the

ways that poetic style conveys the book's message. These chapters answer the book of Lamentations, where the people plead with God to be Zion's comforter. In Lamentations, God is entirely silent.[18] Second Isaiah is a sharp contrast to Lamentations. The LORD speaks from the very beginning, explicitly ending the divine silence and claiming to be Zion's comforter (Isa. 40:1; 51:12). In this way, Second Isaiah reinforces the promise of comfort through the frequency of divine speech.

Since the divine voice speaks so much in Second Isaiah, when other voices speak they draw attention to themselves and are particularly important to interpreting passages in which they occur. The 'we' speaks extremely rarely in Second Isaiah. In one other instance they speak a short line (Isa. 42:24). The fourth servant song is the only extended example of 'we' speech in the whole fifteen chapters. The use of 'we' language in the fourth servant song, then, is no accident. It is the means by which the prophetic poet puts words onto the audience's lips. The 'we' creates a space for the audience to imagine themselves as speakers alongside the prophetic poet. While 'I' language could confront the audience and offer the potential for individuals to speak the words as their own, 'we' language almost seems to compel the audience to include themselves among the speakers. The prophetic poet cannot be speaking this 'we' language alone – others are necessarily involved – and in the context of the original proclamation the 'we' must certainly include the Judean exiles to whom the prophet spoke.

If the fourth servant song's 'we' language invites readers to make its words their own, the poem certainly does not invite them to do so alone. The 'we' language is explicitly and repeatedly plural. If we are tempted to speak about the cross in ways that singularly focus on our individual standing before God, this text puts more corporately oriented words on our lips. To the extent that we make these words into words about Christ by speaking them as our own confession, then we cannot be thinking primarily about what we as individual members of the congregation have or have not done, the ways we have or have not recognized Christ, or the suffering endured as solely for us as individuals. These words are the words of the assembly who speaks them, and for that matter, they are the words of the 'cloud of witnesses' (Heb. 12:1) who have spoken them throughout the centuries. They are a corporate confession of our failure to recognize Christ in our midst. They are a corporate confession of transgression, and they are a corporate affirmation of our healing. In these ways, the words of the song point us to an atonement theology with communal implications. The healing that comes through the servant's suffering impacts not merely individuals, but communities and the relationships between and among them.

The 'we' language clusters in 53:1–6 where there are no fewer than sixteen first-person plural forms. These six verses move through three distinct forms of 'we' speech. First, the 'we' speak as subjects of their own action (vv. 1–3). They describe their hearing (v. 1) and seeing (v. 2), and they tell us how they evaluated what they heard and saw (v. 3). A cluster of possessives comes next (vv. 4–5). The 'we' claim the 'infirmities' (v. 4), 'diseases' (v. 4), 'transgressions' (v. 5) and 'iniquities' (v. 5) as their own. Finally, 'us' language begins to emerge in the final verses of this section (vv. 5–6). The servant's punishment has 'made us whole' (v. 5) and 'the LORD has laid on him the iniquity of us all' (v. 6). In each of these instances the 'us' indicates that the speakers are the object of another's action, and the same could be said for the claim that 'by his bruises we are healed' (v. 5). There is a gradual shift in these forms of first-person speech. The action in the poem moves out of the speakers' hands. They gradually give over their agency to another. The activity of the 'we' diminishes and their expression of the consequences of their activity increases. Finally, what the servant accomplishes stands in stark contrast to what the 'we' did not. The actions of the 'we' do not result in their deliverance. Even the servant who suffers is not the primary actor in these six verses. There is a heavy concentration of passive verbs in this passage.[19] God is the actor who accomplishes wholeness and healing (v. 5) through the servant.

When we speak these words as our own in worship, the poem forms us in two important ways. First, our own voices remind us that God is working and has worked in the lives of many others, and God's work in us is intimately bound up with God's work in them. The poem's 'we' language unites us in our expression and reminds us of the necessary relationship between our deliverance and our relationships. Second, the words the poem gives us to speak recognize the ineffectiveness of our own activity. By moving the 'we' away from what they hear, see and judge, to what is done on their behalf, the poem invites us to let go of our pretences about control over our lives. We first confess our corporate failings. We say what we did not see. We express what we did not recognize. But, paradoxically, by reminding us of what we did not see, the poem puts our transformed perception on our lips and reminds us, not only that we did not see it at first, but also what it is that we did eventually come to affirm. In this way, the poem keeps our faithful commitment central to what we say, but will not allow us to be too proud of ourselves for that recognition. There is a potential antidote to triumphant attitudes in speaking this poem together in worship. If we regularly remind ourselves of what we did not see at first, but came belatedly to realize, then we practise humility in our confession itself. Of course, many streams of Christian teaching on salvation emphasize the ineffectiveness of our personal activity in the equation. One does not need to take a Calvinist perspective on predestination to affirm that reconciliation between God and people begins with God, and that no one comes to faith through their own effort (see for example John 6:44, 65). When we speak this poem, it gives us words to speak that affirm that the activity that brings about results for us is entirely God's activity. Our recognition of that activity is important, certainly, or we would not be confessing that we did not see and perceive from the beginning, but it is the activity of God that we find ourselves recognizing and affirming, rather than our own.

The Servant Song and Christian Imagination

When we speak these words in worship, we are formed not only by the words we say about ourselves, but also by the imagery we find ourselves using for our human condition and the salvation accomplished for us. The poem 'figure[s our] mind[s]' through arresting images that we must unpack.[20] This is not a doctrinal or creedal statement in the strictest sense. It is more akin to sung theology, offering us a set of images as lenses through which to glimpse larger truths of God.[21]

Because its central metaphors for the suffering of the servant are so familiar, we sometimes overlook the poem's frame. The divine voice speaks the opening and closing lines of the poem, and these focus on the glorification of the servant. The servant will be 'exalted', 'lifted up' and 'very high' (Isa. 52:13). This is the first perspective that we hear in the poem, and more importantly, it is God's perspective.[22] The 'we' are human voices, and they may well get things wrong. In fact, we know they get things wrong because they tell us about their misperception of the servant (Isa. 53:3–4). But the divine voice which speaks about the glory of the servant sets his suffering in its proper context. Exaltation is always in view. The poem tells us from the very beginning that we are to read the suffering servant as a glorified figure. In this way, the poem highlights the 'we's' misunderstanding. The readers already know that, however shocking it may seem, this 'despised and rejected' (Isa. 53:3) one is honoured by God.

When we speak these words in worship, the frame gives us an important context for our speech about the cross. As one author in this volume says of Jesus and the cross, 'it is not the first or last thing we should say about him'.[23] The divine voice makes the first and last thing this poem says about glorification. When we voice these words in Christian worship we are directed to see resurrection as the indispensable context for Christ's crucifixion. The gospels' story does not end with suffering, and for this poem it neither begins nor ends in suffering. The poem offers us a way of imagining redemption that is exaltation from the beginning, whether 'we' can see the glory through the suffering or not.

The question of who sees what is an important one for reading this text as forming our theological imaginations. The poem invites us to have our perception (re)ordered by its vision and by the way different voices tell us what they see. Appearance is a central factor in the initial judgement the 'we' make of the servant. They tell us about the servant's appearance, that there was 'nothing in his appearance that we should desire him' (Isa. 53:2). While the 'we' are the ones who misapprehend the servant, the familiar imagery of a 'marred' and 'startl[ing]' appearance (Isa. 52:14–15) is actually in the divine voice's description of how others respond to the exalted servant. So, his disturbing appearance is embedded in claims about his exaltation. We are forced to deal with the tension between glory and this 'astonish[ing]' vision.

No wonder 'kings . . . shut their mouths' (Isa 52:15). Our vision is (re)formed by being forced to imagine a way in which being 'marred . . . beyond human semblance' can be a vision of glory. By juxtaposing these ideas which typically live in different contexts in our minds, the poetry drops us into the middle of a metaphor. We are forced to reconsider both what disfigurement is and what glory is. Whatever sort of glory the servant has, it is not the kind we are accustomed to recognizing, as the testimony of the 'we' will bear out. It is a glory that is seen precisely in the 'marr[ing]', if only we have eyes to see. The suffering, too, is transformed by being accounted as glory. This act of (re)imagining both terms (re)forms our imaginations as we begin to unpack its transformed view of both suffering and glory.

In much the same way as the Christ hymn in Philippians 2 re-orders our perceptions of what 'glory' is, when we speak these words as our words about Christ they force us to re-examine our commitments to honour and glory. The glory of God in Christ appears shining through physical brutality and intended humiliation. We who would honour him cannot do so through the world's ideas about honour, or by lifting ourselves and our service up to be revered. When we speak these words as our own in worship, and especially when we speak them as words about our Saviour, we hear the divine voice challenge our notions of what it means to be exalted. These words urge us to look for our Saviour's presence precisely in those places that we think have the least honour, where our humanity does not naturally see beauty. These words can become words for us about the Saviour who invited us to see him in the face of the stranger, the sick and the imprisoned (Matt. 25:31–46). When we speak such words in worship, we are formed through our worship into people who view the world, and especially the people and places deemed least 'honourable' by the world, as meeting points with our Saviour. These words shape us into people who are readied to give due reverence to others in our midst. Such glorifying does not exalt the powerful and revere the beautiful, but honours each person we encounter as bearers of the image of God. In this way, we are formed to participate in God's project of 'lift[ing] up the lowly' and 'fill[ing] the hungry with good things' (Luke 1:52–53), not as acts of charity but as rightfully honouring those in whom we have learned to glimpse Christ's glory.

The poem's despised and wounded servant (re)orders our perceptions in a second way. When we speak these words as words about our Saviour, we also discover that our speaking offers us a distinctive vision of deliverance. 'We' confess that the servant was led like a lamb to the slaughter and twice proclaim that 'he did not open his mouth' (Isa. 53:7). 'We' know that 'he had done no violence' (Isa. 53:9). This poem by no means depicts a non-violent deliverance. In fact, it lays particular emphasis on the pain, bruising and crushing the servant must endure (Isa. 53:5, 10). However, the words repeatedly emphasize that the servant does not wrest deliverance from the hands of another by violently seizing it. Instead, in an ironic reversal of human expectations, the servant accomplishes deliverance precisely by enduring violence. This endurance goes beyond begrudging acceptance to the point of apparent non-protest. The servant is silent, both in this poem and in the way 'we' describe him. So, this poem's vision embeds within 'we', who speak it, a counter-vision to a fierce view of Christianity.[24] Our salvation was accomplished by one who submitted himself to the violence meted out by others, and who not only did not resist by returning violence, but also did not raise his voice in protest.

The poem offers us some particularly troubling words in this connection. We say that 'it was the will of the LORD to crush him with pain' (Isa 53:10).[25] These words, when spoken as our testimony about Christ, can certainly begin to sound like the problematic sort of theological statement that pits the Father against the Son, an approach that the authors of this volume have repeatedly rejected. When we make the theological move of voicing these words as our own in Christian worship, we must make that move carefully, considering that this speech was not written originally for that context, and not all of its language will be entirely appropriate without reference to broader theological tradition. There is good reason, within the poem itself, to embrace a view that suggests that 'crush[ing the servant] with pain', when spoken about Jesus, was the willing activity of the whole of the Trinity. The poem's emphasis on the servant's silent and un-protesting participation can allow us as Christian worshippers to give thanks for Jesus' prayer in the Garden of Gethsemane: 'not my will but yours be done' (Luke 22:42). In addition, when we speak these words as Christians with a sense of the ultimate inseparability of the Trinity in mind, we must conclude that our confession includes the Son's willing submission to vulnerability within what it means to speak about the 'will of the LORD' (Isa. 53:10).

Finally, when we speak these words as our own, the imagery of the poem re-figures our sense of the relationship between Christ and ourselves. The poem gives us a compelling image with which to speak about ourselves: errant sheep. The 'we' are an unruly flock each turning to their own way (Isa. 53:6). The wandering is a way the poem depicts sin. It juxtaposes its language of wandering with 'iniquity'. And although the language of 'iniquity' is quite strong, that harshness contrasts with the implications of the wandering sheep image. By moving the sin language out of the human sphere, the blame element is softened somewhat. Or, at the very least, we are reminded of the naturalness of our sin. It is in the nature of sheep to stray; it is part of their being as sheep. Sheep must be kept within folds, or minded by shepherds if they are not to be lost (cf. Matt. 18:12–13; John 10:1–16). We might likewise affirm that the inherent tendency to sin is a basic human trait. It is not that it is not a problem, indeed it is a problem that merits the strength of a term like 'iniquity', but it is also a core part of what it is to be who we are, just as wandering is for sheep. So, when we speak these words about Christ, we are given an image through which to reconsider what the atonement accomplishes. The 'iniquity' that is laid upon Christ the servant is the iniquity that is common to us all. It is the brokenness that is embedded in our human condition, a horrific brokenness.

In the context of speech about ourselves as iniquitous wandering sheep, we find ourselves speaking shocking words about our Saviour, comparing him to 'a lamb that is led to the slaughter, and . . . a sheep that before its shearers is silent' (Isa. 53:7). By matching its language about the servant to its language about the 'we', the poem creates a radical identification between the servant who accomplishes redemption, and the 'we' who acknowledge that it was for them. Here we are given words for Christ who entered our human condition, who became as we are, and who embraced the results of who we are alongside us and for us. This truly is a vision of 'God with us', and a Saviour who was 'found in human form' (Phil. 2:7). The lamb imagery carries within it both an intensified sense of vulnerability and wider biblical connotations. The slaughtered lamb points in at least two biblical directions, and probably carries resonances of both. Lambs were part of the list of approved animals for sacrificial offerings, including the sin offering (Lev. 14). The lamb was also the animal at the centre of the Passover ritual, a ritual of identification and protection (Exod. 12).[26] Christian tradition has associated Jesus with each of these sets of lamb images. In the Eucharist we say, 'Christ our Passover has been sacrificed for us, therefore let us celebrate the feast', reminding us that each of the gospel narratives testifies to Jesus' death and resurrection occurring within the context of the Passover.[27] By giving us words to speak about Jesus as the lamb, precisely in the context of our being sheep, this poem, when spoken as Christian testimony, reminds us of the radical identification with us that Jesus' incarnation, death and resurrection entail, both as the Passover lamb who marks us as God's own through his blood, and as the lamb of God who is the bearer of our sins.[28]

The Servant Song and Emotional Formation

Finally, when we speak this text in Christian worship it has the potential to form our emotions. The sort of poetic reading that I am proposing in this chapter is an inherently emotional mode of reading. When we re-utter a poetic voice's emotional words, we cannot do so dispassionately. In adopting their speech, we also adopt their tone. This emotionality is entirely appropriate, since it is hard to imagine how we could speak about the atonement unemotionally. Indeed, we are probably in danger within the contemporary church of making our speech about the cross too cognitive and not emotional enough. Our doctrinal discussions have a tendency to focus on the objective realities of what the cross accomplishes, but 'love's redeeming work' can hardly be appropriated by minds without impacting the heart.[29] Speaking the words of Isaiah 52:13 – 53:12 in worship valorizes our emotional response to atonement by placing intensely emotional and biblical words on our lips. It also shapes our emotion by involving us in the emotional responses that Scripture offers.

Jeremy Begbie has suggested that Christian worship might be seen as 'a school of the emotions' and that our emotions are part of what God is in the process of redeeming.[30] In Christian worship we are formed as people whose emotions are shaped by Christian virtues. When we speak Isaiah's profoundly emotional words as our words about Christ, worship 'schools' our emotions by offering us redeemed emotions to live into, even as we speak about our redemption.

One of the most obvious ways that this poetry shapes our emotions is through its confessional attitude. The poem puts humble words onto our lips and invites us to live into the attitude which recognizes its own error. But the 'we' of this text do more than simply acknowledge their mistake. There is real pain in the irony that the 'we' have misjudged the very person who was 'crushed for [their] iniquities' (Isa. 53:5). The passage moves back and forth in a tight alternation between what the 'we' reckoned, and what the servant has done for them. The 'we' say what they perceived about the servant in verses 2 and 3, and move on to what they say the servant has done for them in verses 4 and 5. However, right in the middle of that shift, they proclaim, 'we accounted him stricken, struck down by God, and afflicted' (Isa. 53:4b). On either side of this further confession is testimony about the servant's work: 'carry[ing] our diseases' and being 'wounded for our transgressions' (Isa. 53:4, 5). By placing misperception and the benefit gained by those who misunderstand into such tight relationship, the poem gives us ironically self-convicting words to proclaim. The irony raises the emotional impact of the poem and has the potential to (re)form our emotions if we enter into its confessional mode.

A second way that this poem (re)forms our emotions is through its vivid imagery of real pain. The poem does not hold back in its description of the suffering the servant endures. It uses phrases like 'crush him with pain' (Isa. 53:10), 'stricken, struck down by God' (Isa. 53:4), 'despised' (Isa. 53:3) and 'wounded' (Isa. 53:5). Pain permeates the chapter. This poetic, emotionally freighted language has the potential to build compassion in those who speak it. It forces 'we' who speak it into an encounter with the sufferer imagined by the poem. Its vision of the 'marred' and 'wounded' suffering servant confronts any self-protective walls we may have constructed between ourselves and the cruelty of the world in which we live. We are faced with brutality in this poem, and it is brutality that we confess was visited upon our Saviour for our sake. In making this confession we come face to face with the Saviour who meets the world in its suffering and brokenness, and we are forced to recognize the brokenness of our world for what it is. By speaking the words of the text in their honesty about human pain, we open ourselves to be formed into more compassionate people.

Conclusion

Isaiah 52:13 – 53:12 is a powerful and living text. It is a text that has the potential to shape those who speak it in the context of worship by (re)forming their imaginations, and by (re)shaping their emotions. Its lyric mode invites us to make its words our own, and as we speak them about our Saviour we find its words a rich confession of our own condition. It shapes us into people whose vision of our Saviour reveals his glory shining through suffering and apparent disgrace. It gives us words that highlight our own misperception even as they remind us of what we have come to believe. It forms humility and compassion in us and reminds us of the intimacy of the incarnation by giving us parallel images for ourselves and our Saviour. Reading this poem as our own words has the potential to enable us to become 'communities of obedience and praise which, with marvellous indifference to categories of explanation, act with power, courage, freedom, and energy toward a new world envisioned, imagined, and promised by this text.'[31] Such reading is appropriately poetic reading, and it is formational Christian reading. Through such reading we are invited to participate in the continued unfolding of the living word.

10

THE CROSS AND THE HEALING OF THE SELF

Heather Morris

My great-grandfather was converted to Christ when he was about eleven years old. His name was Abram Kingston. He grew up on the family farm near a village called Drimoleague in West Cork. It was a busy day on the farm and his parents asked him to stay home from school to help out. Towards the end of the day his mother asked him to walk into the village to buy something from the shop. It was a lovely afternoon and Abram was enjoying the walk until up ahead and coming towards him he saw the schoolmaster on his way home. What was a boy skipping school going to do? Rather than face the schoolmaster's wrath, Abram jumped over the wall which ran beside the road and found himself in a quarry.

There was a man there. His name was Samuel Jagoe and he was praying. The quarry was usually a quiet spot where he was undisturbed. However, when Abram arrived, Samuel stopped praying and the two of them chatted. The conversation lasted longer and became more significant than either of them had suspected. After a time, on rough ground in a quarry in West Cork, Abram and Samuel knelt together and Abram made a commitment to follow Jesus.

I love that story. I want my children to know it as they grow. I want them to know how God worked in the life of their great-great-granddad. It brings shivers to my spine to think of days like that on which so much seems to turn; days like that which influence succeeding generations. The implications of that day so many years ago have trickled down through the generations of my family, touching the lives of my grandparents, who spent most of their adult years as missionaries in Nigeria, my parents' lives, my own life and the lives of my children.

God was powerfully at work that day. It was a life-changing event. While there are a couple of different versions of the story, the fact is that it did happen and it has touched my life. All of the above statements are true of both my great-granddad's conversion, and of the cross. But what happened at Calvary is different because this is an event that we do not just know, tell or even own. It is an event which human beings are called to appropriate, to step into. As we do that, God, through his Spirit, begins to change lives.

The atonement stands as an historic event, its influence not trickling narrowly through one family's generations, but flooding through the world and all time. But there is even more to it than that. When we speak and reflect on the atonement, we speak and reflect about an event in and through which God was perfectly and completely at work, and in which God continues to be at work. One might say that the kingdom of God *is* and is coming.

Whether or not you agree with Tom Torrance's particular theological emphasis, listen to the way in which he describes the past, present and future influence of the atonement:

> During my first week of office as Moderator of the General Assembly of the Church of Scotland when I presided at the Assembly's Gaelic Service, a highlander asked me whether I was born again, and when I replied in the affirmative he asked when I had been born again. I still recall his face when I told him that I had been born again when Jesus Christ was born of the Virgin Mary and rose again from the virgin tomb, the first-born from the dead. When he asked me to explain I said: 'This Tom Torrance you see is full of corruption, but the real Tom Torrance is hid with Christ in God and will be revealed only when Jesus Christ comes again. He took my corrupt humanity in His Incarnation, sanctified, cleansed and redeemed it, giving it new birth, in his death and resurrection.'[1]

Whatever view of the atonement one holds, I would want to maintain that it cannot be relegated to an isolated, even interesting, or even significant, historical event. The atonement must be understood as also having present-day and future consequences. It is a story of the past, a story of the present, and a story of the future.

In what follows I want to stand unapologetically at the foot of the cross which shines forth through all of time. I want each of us to step into the story of the cross, to re-claim that meta-narrative as the context for individual healing, and more broadly, for pastoral care. I want to re-claim that story and reality, not in a simplistic way which seeks to crudely see parallels between individual lives, or indeed the life of a community and the gospel story. Re-claiming the meta-narrative is more akin to stepping into the story in the way in which Lucy, Edmund, Susan and Peter step through the wardrobe into the story of Narnia so that their lives unfold within that bigger unfolding story. Gerard Loughlin describes it as being mastered by God's story, being 'written into a narrative that is larger, longer and stronger than our own'.[2]

Learning to place ourselves within the meta-narrative is an appropriate way to think about the connection between the story of the cross and pastoral care. Caring for people requires paying close attention to their stories. And, as Martha Nussbaum says, 'certain truths about human life can only be fittingly and accurately stated in the language and forms characteristic of the narrative artist'.[3] In what follows I will draw heavily upon stories. I do this for two reasons: to illustrate my claim that the story of the cross is central to human healing and to invite us into that story.

At the Cross We Meet God

When we step into the story of the cross we are immediately confronted with the realization that at the cross we meet God. God is powerfully engaged and actively involved in reconciliation through the cross. In 2 Corinthians we read that 'God was in Christ, reconciling the world to himself, no longer counting people's sins against them' (2 Cor. 5:19 [NLT]). Sin is disruptive and destructive, it alienates human beings from each other and from God, and such is the depth and breadth of God's love and faithfulness that God's response to sin and human need is not distance but engagement.

Genesis 3 recounts the story of the fall. We are told that Adam and Eve eat of the fruit of the tree, and then, realizing that they are naked, sew fig leaves together and make coverings for themselves. When they hear God walking in the garden in the cool of the day, instead of meeting God Adam and Eve hide. When God calls them, they admit that they are naked. It is at this point that everything changes. God says to Eve, 'I will greatly increase your pangs in childbearing; in pain you shall bring forth children' (Gen. 3:16) and to Adam 'cursed is the ground because of you; in toil you shall eat of it all the days of your life' (Gen. 3:17). These are heart-wrenching words to speak and to hear.

What does God do next? Does God withdraw from or create distance from them? No, 'the LORD God made garments of skins for the man and for his wife, and clothed them' (Gen. 3:21). Sin is a rupture. There is tragedy in having to live with its painful consequences. Yet God still makes clothes for them. God's love is radical, determined and stubborn. It is there in the loving Father who runs to meet the son who has shamed him (Luke 15:20); in the God who provides for the people of Israel who in the face of that provision moan and wish that they were back in Egypt (Exod. 16). John Swinton puts it like this: 'God's response to evil is practical, embodied, costly and painful . . . As God seeks to redeem creation and put an end to evil and suffering, God moves towards creation through radical gestures of redemption.'[4]

William Willimon recounts a story which a mother told him:

'Our son has been putting us through hell,' she said. 'Didn't even know where he was for months until last night. My husband and I were eating dinner, and suddenly, without warning, he burst through the front door and begins cursing us, demanding money, refusing to join us at the table. After an ugly scene, he stormed down the hall and slammed the door to his room . . . Well, my husband gets up, goes over to the kitchen, pours himself a drink, turns on the TV, and slumps down in his chair. That's how he handles these moments. I walked down the hall and said "Son, can we talk? I just want to talk." I could hear him curse me from inside his bedroom. I tried to open the door. It was locked. So I went to the garage, got a big hammer, walked back in, stood before my son's bedroom door. Took about a third of the door with it. Then I lunged at my surprised-looking son, grabbed him around the throat, and said, "I'm not going to put up with this . . . anymore. You are better than this! I gave birth to you, went into labor for you, and I'm not giving you away!"' . . . I believe God is something like that.[5]

At the cross we meet a passionate God. We meet God, who knows, feels and bears the world's brokenness, and loves the world with a scandalous, shocking love. We meet God who will do all that is possible to break down barriers and make healing possible. Healing of the self, no matter what the issue, is possible because of God's character.

At the cross we meet the triune God. The atonement is an act of the Trinity. This has become a recurrent theme of this volume. Rowan Williams puts it straight and clear: Jesus crucified is God crucified.[6] The cross is not the action of God the Father over and against an unwilling Jesus. God acts together on the cross. In her assessment of the theology of Anselm of Canterbury, Ellen Charry writes that for Anselm 'Christ's Incarnation and death are a humble offering of God to God'.[7] This claim is incredibly significant. Understand its meaning, and accusations of 'cosmic child abuse' are immediately undermined.[8] God's sacrifice has profoundly personal implications. But the cross is not all about us. It is all about God.

This is God, who 'was crucified, died and was buried'.[9] Nothing, neither violence nor suffering, nor the worst that human beings can do to each other, has been able to quench God's saving power. As Hauerwas writes, 'the sacrifice of the Cross is complete, lacking nothing, sufficient for our salvation and the salvation of the world'.[10]

We may wrestle with how it happens, there are certainly many biblical pictures to help us, but the atonement is effective. Salvation has been offered in Jesus and made effective through his death on the cross. As the apostle Paul writes, 'since all have sinned and fall short of the glory of God; they are now justified by his grace as a gift, through the redemption that is in Christ Jesus' (Rom. 3:23–24). Healing of the self demands that human beings do not merely know that truth, but that they trust that it is so.

John Wesley battled with assurance. The question of when he was converted is hotly debated and is not an issue for this chapter.

There is however no doubt that, despite, and in the midst of, many good works and a faithful Christian life, he struggled to believe and really know that he was loved by God. He struggled to believe and to feel that what happened on the cross applied to his life. On 24 May 1738 he went to a service in Aldersgate Street in London. This is how he describes what happened that evening in his journal:

> In the evening I went very unwillingly to a society in Aldersgate Street, where one was reading Luther's preface to the Epistle to the Romans. About a quarter before nine, while the leader was describing the change which God works in the heart through faith in Christ, I felt my heart strangely warmed. I felt I did trust in Christ alone for salvation; and an assurance was given me that He had taken away my sins, even mine, and saved me from the law of sin and death.[11]

At the cross we meet God, and God is trustworthy, faithful and unfailing. God calls us to trust that the work of Jesus on the cross is for all, and for us.

The experience in Aldersgate Street was a turning point for Wesley. He was propelled from that point onwards by the Holy Spirit, preaching on the streets (which he really did not want to do) and setting up bands and classes. The accusation was made about him that he was an enthusiast, feigning the gifts of the Spirit and losing a sense of rationality.[12] As an illustration of the derogatory implications of the term 'enthusiast' at that time, there is an historical plaque in the church at the crematorium in Harold's Cross which praises a clergyman about whom there was 'no trace of enthusiasm'.[13] Wesley's foundation of confidence in God was the springboard into service. Again, we are reminded that the cross is an historical and present event which needs to be appropriated, by those we serve in ministry and by ourselves.

At the Cross We Meet God Who Is Wounded

At the beginning of June last year I fell off my bike when I was cycling from our home in East Belfast into Edgehill College, which is close to the centre of Belfast. I do not remember what happened.

I was knocked out when I hit the ground, but whatever happened I managed to land on my face. There were virtually no injuries except to my face! Our CSI skills are not great but we reckon I must have gone straight over the handlebars. I will spare you the details but part of my recuperation demanded being without a front tooth for considerable periods of time. I even had to preach one week without my tooth. Now I had not worried about vanity as being one of my besetting sins, although I do have many others. I am quite at ease about my appearance but I really did not like being so obviously, and publicly, wounded. Initially, I blamed my feelings on other people. People do treat you differently and give you much less eye contact when you have such obvious wounds. But on reflection, the problem lay with me. I did not like other people seeing me like this. I did not like looking in the mirror and seeing myself wounded.

We are wounded and we do not like it. It seems to me that human beings would often rather pretend that it is not so, and perhaps that is a part of our and the whole of creation's fallenness. But at the foot of the cross we see that Jesus is wounded too.

We are met in our woundedness by a wounded God. Salvation has not bypassed suffering. We are met in our woundedness by a wounded God who does not look away in horror, who does not avoid eye contact, but who whispers, 'I love you'. Alastair Campbell explicitly links the recognition of wounds with the atonement. He writes:

> Christ, the Wounded Healer, restores the fractured relationships between God, man, and the whole universe. We do a grave injustice to the incarnate love of God if we try to understand the suffering and death of Jesus merely as some kind of legal transaction paying the 'penalty' for man's sin in a distanced, 'objective' way. Jesus' wounds, in life and in death, are the expressions of his openness to our suffering. He suffered because of His love; his sufferings are the stigmata of his care for us and for the whole world estranged from God.[14]

Such is God's love that God does not shrug off our wounds but bears them. God was incarnate in broken, wounded flesh.

But there is more than identification going on in Jesus' wounds. It is a wounded God who heals. 'He himself bore our sins in his body on the cross, so that, free from sins, we might live for right-eousness; by his wounds you have been healed' (1 Pet. 2:24; cf. John 20:24–28). He still shows us his hands and his side. These claims draw us back to Bonhoeffer and his recognition that 'only a suffering God can help'.[15] However, the other part of that truth is that those wounds are visible in Jesus' resurrected body (John 20). Jesus who was dead is now alive. Moltmann rightly reminds us that the context is the resurrection, the victory which Christ has won in his death and resurrection.[16] God is wounded too. But here woundedness is not a sign of weakness but a sign in flesh and blood of God's love. It is a sign of the lengths to which God will go to offer forgiveness. It is a sign of God's identification with human beings and of God's unfailing presence.

In our trauma we are met by the presence of Christ. In her book *Trauma and Grace*, Serene Jones has a chapter entitled 'The Unending Cross' in which she reflects on the end of Mark's gospel: 'So they went out and fled from the tomb, for terror and amaze-ment had seized them; and they said nothing to anyone, for they were afraid' (Mark 16:8). She reminds us that in the midst of the women's trauma Jesus was there: 'in a world filled with vast and unresolved traumas Jesus comes to us anyway, in the midst of our faltering speech, our shattered memories, and our frayed sense of agency. This is truly what grace is, in its most radical form: not the reassuring ending of an orderly story, but the incredible insistence on love amid fragmented, unravelled human lives.'[17]

We must not let familiarity fool us into feeling comfortable with the cross. The foot of the cross is not an easy place to be. The cross is horrendous. When we are there, we are in the midst of blood, unanswered questions, apparent abandonment, darkness and evil – both individual and corporate. Wounded and offering healing, wounded and victorious, wounded and liberating, God is there.

Finding Healing at the Foot of the Cross

The encounter with Christ, possible because of God's character and God's action, opens up a new world. It makes it possible for human beings to recognize that they are at the same time both loved and wounded.

First, we are greatly loved. Ellen Charry judges that for Julian of Norwich, God:

> is nothing but love, compassion and mercy. It is God's love for us that enables us to love ourselves, God's compassion that commits him to holding on to those whom he loves no matter what they do, and God's endless well of mercy that models who we are to become . . . In the passion, Christ . . . has shown us that we must trust God's judgements more than our own, for he sees the good in us even when it is visible only to himself.[18]

Second, at the cross we recognize that we are loved and wounded. Henri Nouwen asserts that human beings need to recognize that they are wounded as a step towards receiving healing. He writes, 'Therefore ministry is a very confronting service. It does not allow people to live with illusions of immortality and wholeness. It keeps reminding others that they are mortal and broken, but also that with the recognition of this condition, liberation starts.'[19]

Healing thus does not come through the perpetuation of the pretence that we are not wounded. Personal pain and the woundedness of a broken world are real. The Christian's task is not, and never has been, to pretend this is not so. Affirming and living in the reality of hope, affirming and living within the reality of the benefits of the cross, does not mean pretending that human beings are not wounded. Actually the reverse is true. Living in the reality of hope, appropriating the truth and benefits of the cross, demands the acknowledgement that we are wounded. And this is only truly possible in the light of God's love, understanding, identification and victory.

At the foot of the cross we are drawn to recognize that sin is a reality, and a grave reality at that. At the foot of the cross we are drawn to repentance and confession: 'My sacrifice, O God, is a broken spirit; a broken and contrite heart, O God, you will not despise' (Ps. 51:17).[20]

In their discussion of self-esteem, Joanna and Alister McGrath paint a scene that may be familiar. They write:

> the concern to promote positive self-esteem often seems to rest upon highly questionable theological foundations. Central Christian ideas

– such as the reality of sin and the demand for humility . . . seem to have been abandoned or compromised. The price paid for positive self-esteem is often a dilution or distortion of the gospel . . . so, many Christians find themselves facing a dilemma. They are confronted with one group of Christian writers urging them to have a strongly positive view of themselves and another group urging them to have an equally strong negative view of themselves. But which is right?[21]

The two truths need to be held together. We are wounded, broken, sinful; and we are loved at a depth that we will never fully understand. Where do we see the truths of human brokenness and divine love most clearly? We see them in the cross of Jesus. We see the reality of the cost of sin in Jesus' wounded hands and side. We hear it in Jesus' cry of dereliction. We see the immensity of God's love in the fact that Jesus is there.

The two truths of human brokenness and divine love offer healing to our woundedness. Frank Lake writes:

> The master image of the Cross of Christ is capable, as the Holy Spirit applies its truth, of transforming the ruined archaeology of the self, with patience removing the ivy of our defences against the pain of exposure of old and jagged wounds, and with the salve of God's own loving and willing woundedness, of so richly using those primal occasions of anguish that they become the deepened foundations of our power to praise Him.[22]

What we encounter in the cross of Christ is an invitation to offer our own woundedness to the healing balm of God's love.

When we enter into the reality of the cross we meet God: powerful, passionate, loving, humble and wounded. There we meet Jesus, who came and stood among disciples who were frightened, grieving, doubting, wounded, and showed them his own wounds and said, 'Peace' (John 20:19, 21).

Conclusion

I have been arguing that we ought to appropriate the meta-narrative of the cross as the context for individual healing and pastoral care. Healing of the self is made possible by the character of God who is passionately engaged with us and whose immense love is revealed in the cross. By stepping into this meta-narrative and by living our lives in and through it, we are invited not just to know the truth of God's love, but to trust it. In such a context we are able to face up to our own woundedness. The ability to see ourselves as both wounded and loved is the necessary condition of the healing of the self. Thus, the cross is the essential place for a Christian approach to personal healing, both in our individual lives and in the care we offer to others pastorally.

EXERCISE: PRAYER CLINIC

The seminar concluded with a prayer clinic followed by the Eucharist. Students had opportunities for private reflection, prayer ministry and later to be anointed with oil as part of the Eucharist service.

If you have been reading this book with a group, you might consider using some of these ideas as part of a concluding day retreat, along with the bibliodrama workshop and a closing service of worship. Alternatively, you might consider some of these ideas as prompts for creative expression in your own prayer life as you continue to work through issues related to the meaning of the atonement in your experience of God.

Meditation on the Cross[1]

Set up a large cross as a visual focus in a quiet worship space. Provide the following instructions and slips of paper and pens:

> Sit before the cross and still your heart before God. Allow the image of the cross to become the focus of your meditation. What does Christ say to you from the cross? How do you respond to the cross? Stay in the meditative silence for as long as you wish. When you are ready, write your response to the cross on one of the slips of paper provided and lay it at the foot of the cross.

Praying with Paint[2]

Set out paints, paper and sticky tape, and post a large cross outline on the wall of the room. Provide the following instructions:

> In an attitude of prayer reflect on the state of your soul. How would you imagine it? Is it rejoicing, broken, healing, wounded, close to God, distant? Paint an image of this sense of your soul. Offer your soul, and your sense of its current state, to God in prayer. As an outward sign of this prayer of offering, you are invited to attach your image to the cross with the sticky tape provided.

Collage of Healing

Set out paper, glue, magazines, pictures, newspapers, and an outline of a cross printed on paper. Invite participants to select various bits that reflect brokenness in themselves or in the world, and to affix these to the cross as a way of praying for God's healing.

Mosaic Prayers[3]

Provide broken pieces of various kinds of objects (we used ceramic tiles), glue, and sturdy paper such as cardboard. Invite participants to collect broken pieces as images of the brokenness in their own lives or in the world and to pray for healing as they assemble them into something new, by gluing them into a mosaic.

Visual Prayer Stimuli

In a room with some reflective music playing, place images that would inspire reflection on the cross. We used some icons, some wooden crosses that could be picked up and held, and posted images related to each of the Stations of the Cross on the wall.

Filling the Cross with Our Brokenness

Provide paper with a large outline of a cross on it along with pens, markers and coloured pencils. Invite participants prayerfully to write or draw within the cross elements of their own brokenness or healing.

Washing Prayer[4]

Provide a bucket with water in it, washable markers, smooth river rocks and a towel. Invite participants to write expressions of their brokenness on the rock and to offer it to God in prayer, then to wash that brokenness away in the water.

Lectio Divina and Journalling[5]

Provide prompts for journalling such as: 'What areas of brokenness do you want to offer to God?' and 'How does the cross of Christ make you whole?' In the same space, leave Bibles and a list of passages that might be relevant for *Lectio Divina*. Some suggestions might be 1 Corinthians 1:17–28; 2 Corinthians 5:15–21; Colossians 1:18–20; Hebrews 12:1–2.

SUGGESTIONS FOR THE USE OF INTEGRATIVE SILENCE

Bibliodrama reflection: Choose one of the characters from the bibliodrama exercise outlined earlier in this section and write a monologue expressing what you imagine that character might say about the cross.

Lament writing: Write your personal lament. What would you like to say to God about your own life? How are Jesus' words from the cross your own? Where is the suffering Christ in the pain you voice to God?

Liturgical composition: Write a prayer of thanksgiving expressing your sense of how the cross has meant healing in your life.

Lectio Divina: Read Hebrews 12:1–2 slowly, meditatively and devotionally, contemplating the import of individual words and phrases for your own life of faith. Express your feelings about this text to God in prayer, and rest in the sense of God's presence.[1]

SECTION 4

CONCLUSIONS

RESPONSES TO THE CHAPTERS

Katie M. Heffelfinger and Patrick G. McGlinchey

In this overview we explore some key themes woven through the chapters. It becomes clear as one progresses through the book that the cross is not an isolated theological construct. For example, one cannot speak of the cross without exploring its relationship to the Trinity and the incarnation. In what follows we ask what the authors are saying about themes that emerge when the chapters are considered together. Additionally, we ask what fruitful avenues of theological engagement are opened up when we consider the implications of what has already been committed to print.

The Cross and the Trinity

Wherever the Trinity appears in *Atonement as Gift*, the authors are clearly driven by the conviction that God's being is, in essence, love (1 John 4:16). This perspective emerges most strikingly where Trinitarian thinking merges with the theme of penal substitution. There seems to be substantial agreement among our contributors that caricatured versions of penal substitution which pit the Father against the Son run counter to a scripturally grounded doctrine of the Trinity.[1] Williams, Clutterbuck and Morris each portray God's action on the cross as the fruit of love and are insistent that no dissonance in outlook coloured the activity or the motivation of the divine actors. This view reflects not only the logic of the Trinity but the abundant scriptural evidence highlighting the Father's loving initiative in redemption and the Son's voluntary embrace of suffering and death (John 3:16).

Heather Morris's Trinitarian-inspired unease with viewing the cross as 'merely a legal transaction' strikes this author as an echo of Joseph Ratzinger's 1960s discussion of the atonement. In *Introduction to Christianity*, his best-selling book, the future Pope looked somewhat askance at a theory of atonement which saw the cross as quintessentially a 'mechanism of injured right'.[2] His intuition was that such a perspective drove an unwarranted wedge between Christ's person and his work. That same insight holds true when we think about the cross in a specifically Trinitarian context. We must be wary of any view of the atonement which loses sight of God's love and sees the cross in categories that relate only to wrath or divine book-keeping. Morris never rejects penal substitution, but her dissatisfaction with the caricature stands as a challenge to any who uphold the theory to thoroughly integrate the love of God into it so that it genuinely reflects Scripture's testimony about God.

Stephen Williams' acknowledgement of a family of penal theories of atonement reminds us that a variety of theologians adhere to some form of penal substitution. Moreover, some of those least identified with the evangelical tradition are arguably the most able defenders of the idea. The scholars he has in mind are James Denney, Karl Barth and Emil Brunner. What stands out about some of these scholars' approaches is that penal substitution is located in a decidedly Trinitarian understanding of the cross. Perhaps most paradigmatic is Karl Barth's discussion of the 'Judge Judged in Our Place' in *Church Dogmatics*.[3] This approach has inspired some subsequent evangelical writers to repudiate crude versions of penal substitution. John Stott's comments in *The Cross of Christ* reveal how a properly Trinitarian view of God must impinge on our understanding of what was happening on the cross. He writes:

We must not, then, speak of God punishing Jesus or of Jesus persuading God, for to do so is to set them against each other as if they acted independently of each other or were even in conflict with each other. We must never make Christ the object of God's punishment or God the object of Christ's persuasion, for both God and Christ were subjects not objects, taking the initiative together to save sinners.[4]

Williams takes up the characterization of Father and Son as subjects rather than objects in the drama of redemption at the close of his chapter. He suggests that if we allow the fact that Christ entered into an experience of humanity's condemnation, this must have implications for how we interpret the impact of that self-identification on the Father (Williams, p. 15). This observation, rooted in a profoundly Trinitarian view of the cross, invites us to replace images of the Father inflicting suffering on the Son with one of the Father willingly embracing suffering for the sake of the world's redemption. Bauckham develops a similar thought when he references Paul reflecting on what it must have cost the Father to give his Son to death on the cross (Rom. 8:32): 'The two forms of suffering are different, but what could "did not spare his own Son" mean at all if it involved no pain? The analogy with what a human father would feel for his beloved son loses any meaning if we are to think of the Father acting dispassionately, unaffected by his loss of the Son' (Bauckham, pp. 58–59).

This challenging slant on what the cross means if the doctrine of the Trinity is taken seriously was brought home to me in a context far away from the lecture room and the theological library. Watching a drama team from Youth With A Mission portray the biblical story in the town square of Randers, Denmark, I was struck when, as the drama neared its denouement with Jesus being nailed to the cross, a silver-haired man stepped out from the crowd, stood with his back to the crucified figure, and spread out his own arms in anguished sorrow. This mission organization had grasped something about the cross which some of our brightest theological minds would invite us to embrace today. It would seem that the more our understanding of the cross is Trinitarian, the more we must conceive the sacrifice of Calvary first and foremost as an act of collaborative love.

Cross and Incarnation

A range of views emerged as our contributors explored the relationship of atonement to incarnation. Richard Clutterbuck challenged the cross-centred theology of Stephen Williams, suggesting that late-medieval and Reformation perspectives on atonement were not the only, nor indeed the best, vantage points from which to view the cross. His plea was for us to see the atonement through the lens of the early Church Fathers and their successors in the Eastern Church. Understood in this light, the cross is not a stand-alone event but one which is set between two of the great pillars of Christian theology, the incarnation and the resurrection. Within such a framework the incarnation emerges for Clutterbuck as being more crucial than the cross since it was only Jesus' identity as God which lent significance to his death. Moreover, his whole life is to be understood as having salvific value should we follow Irenaeus in his doctrine of recapitulation or accept Gregory of Nazianzus' claim that Christ can only heal that which he assumes. Even at the end of Jesus' life, argues Clutterbuck, it cannot be asserted that the cross is the ultimate culmination of the story. It is the world-changing event of the resurrection which lends true credibility to the cross and confirms that Jesus' atoning death is neither 'the first thing or the last thing that we should say about him' (Clutterbuck, p. 23).

The charge that atonement theologies are defective when they seek to isolate the cross from the incarnation is also present in Bauckham, although the chapter does not indicate that Bauckham subscribes to Clutterbuck's larger thesis that the incarnation itself is more fundamental to redemption than the crucifixion. Bauckham's thoughts on incarnation and cross focus more on the impact of Jesus' human experience on the Godhead. His reflections highlight how the eternal Son embraced certain emotions and frailties which would otherwise have been alien to the Godhead as Christ lived a true human life and faced death on the cross. Such a strange reality was deemed to confound traditional assumptions about God's impassibility and open new avenues on the question of suffering and theodicy (see the discussion on pp. 57–60).

Elaine Storkey's insightful reflection on the cross and the reconciliation of gender touched on incarnation again. Here she focused on the problem posed to feminist theology by the traditional incarnational categories in which the atonement was understood. Storkey demonstrated that a core part of the feminist objection to such thinking was a profound discomfort at the idea of a *male* Saviour pleading the sinner's cause to a *male* God and all of the attendant ramifications that would come with that. Storkey's response to this objection is to portray the incarnation and the cross as a standing challenge to a status quo which feminists have rightly labelled unjust, patriarchal and inequitable.

Taken collectively, our contributors are at pains not to disengage the event of the cross from the other aspects of Christ's incarnation. All would concur that we are saved by the life, death and resurrection of the Son of God and that we should not conceive of redemption as occurring in a vacuum. Nevertheless, some contributors would wish to continue to privilege the cross as *the* saving event *par excellence*. Here a decisive action took place which changed the nature of the divine–human relationship even if it did nothing to make God any more gracious than God already was. The incarnation, in these terms, consistently points us to a God who came in search of us and whose vulnerability and self-giving love were never in question.

What Can the Cross Teach Us about the Cosmos?

Among the insights gleaned from examining the cross from multiple angles has been an appreciation of the expansive redemption achieved in the atonement. Our authors suggest there is a cosmological import to the cross. It is entirely appropriate that we set the celebration of our redemption in this broader context. An example of such cosmologically oriented celebration appears in eucharistic liturgies which reference the Creator's role in forming 'interstellar space'.[5] If God, through the cross, is redeeming creation, then it should shape and transform Christian perspectives on many things including 'violence', natural evil, and the suffering associated with both. On this view, these aspects of life in this world are symptoms of the 'not yet' which await the full realization of God's project of 'putting the world to rights' (Bauckham, p. 51).

In Christ's incarnation, God voluntarily enters into the realm of suffering and contingency. All of creation waits with eagerness for the full revelation of God's work of renewal, and this is the outworking of the cross (Rom. 8). In voluntarily subjecting himself to that 'futility' that is now part of being within the created order, the incarnate Son sets not just human beings within a whole new frame, but creation itself. In the incarnation, God makes all of creation part of the redemptive project. As both Elsdon and Russell point out to us, God's radical identification with the created order through the incarnation ought to change our perspective on the cosmos.

First, it allows us to engage the issue of natural evil with some measure of hope. Bauckham suggests that Jesus' radical identification with us removes the suffering in the suffering by reminding us that even when we suffer the incomprehensible, we are not suffering in isolation from the love of God. Elsdon further indicates that the suffering caused by natural evil can be seen as part of the ongoing renewal and life of the created order. In drawing upon Bauckham and Hart's eschatology, Elsdon suggests that the redemption of the whole of creation throughout its aeons means the redemption and recreation of those natural processes that are both life-giving and life-destroying.[6]

Second, Russell reminds us that we are to be part of the renewal of the earth, and Elsdon agrees, setting ecological action within our mandate as redeemed people. However, it is clear for our authors that ecological action is not just one good thing among others in which we should be involved. Rather, they see the redemption of the cosmos as God's activity inaugurated in the cross and this, for them, necessarily changes a Christian perspective on it. Elsdon helpfully places Christian ecology into an appropriately christocentric perspective, suggesting that 'we should approach the question of *what* is being reconciled from the standpoint of *who* it is who effects this reconciliation, and how it is achieved' (Elsdon, p. 41). He points out that Christian ecology is mandated by the claim that Christians live according to their hope in the promise that God is putting the world to rights. One might further add that the idea of modelling our life on Christ means dedicating ourselves to the objectives that we see accomplished proleptically by means of his death on the cross. Thus, we should engage in working out the implications of a ransomed creation in our daily living.

What Can We Learn about Violence and the Cross?

The issue of violence was a recurrent theme of our seminar and appears as a 'red thread' in the essays that make up this book. This fact should come as no surprise. For many people, whether from a church background or not, mention of the cross evokes an immediate mental connection with violence. Indeed, the violence of the cross as an historical reality cannot be denied. However, as our authors remind us, the theological significance and ethical impact of that violence merit our attention. If we can learn to interact with this issue non-defensively, talking about violence and the cross can be an important way for Christians to have a voice about issues of violence in our world as well as about redemption.

As David Tombs reminds us in his essay, discussion of the cross has both intended and unintended consequences. This means that we need to start saying quite clearly what the cross does and does not do with regard to violence. The cross does not condone human violence, quite the opposite. It showcases the horror as something that we should reject precisely by showing the lengths to which God will go to reconcile us. It functions as a reminder of our tendency to dehumanize our enemy and shows us how God, in Christ, embraced our humanity and willingly engaged our desperate situation, becoming a victim of our violence. If, as Storkey suggests some feminists have argued, the cross has been used to romanticize suffering, then as Tombs reminds us, stripping away the artful trappings reminds us that there is no glorification of suffering in the cross. The cross glorifies the humiliated, as Stockitt says, but not violence itself. The victimizers of Jesus are not praised, their activity is never applauded, God makes use of it, but it is evil. As Williams indicates, at the cross God harnesses human evil to redemptive purposes. When we face up to its horror and its capacity to shame and dehumanize, we are charged to recognize the 'awful result' of human violence and to turn resolutely away from it.

Tombs' essay also issues a stark challenge to those of us within the church who wish to preach and call for peace. He says that we can be worse than useless if we preach peace where it does not exist and thereby cover over the realities of the world we live in. Our world is full of violence, and there seems to be no end to it.

In the cross we have words and symbols that impel us to speak an anti-violence message to our world. If the cross has functioned to justify dehumanization and violence in the past, we have misused it and allowed it to be misused. We must clarify this central tenet of our faith. The cross does not proclaim that violence is a good and that the end justifies the means. Rather, if Stephen Williams is right, it calls us to realize that God can redeem and put to good purposes even our very worst actions. In 'holding up the awful result' of our human inhumanity, the cross is a warning about letting violence run amuck in our world. In dehumanizing God's expression of solidarity with our humanity through the incarnation, the cross impels us to look more closely at the humanity of even those we might name our enemy and to work towards reconciliation. In shaming shame, the Christ of the cross glorifies not violence, but those who are oppressed by it. He promotes not passive acquiescence to unjust systems, but offers precisely the dignity necessary to withstand their most corrosive effects.

What Can the Cross Teach Us about Human Relationships?

David Tombs has suggested that reflection on the cross might significantly reshape our moral imagination. Such a role for the cross has wide-ranging implications, not least regarding human relationships. One might say that viewing human relationships through a cross-focused lens reframes our moral imagination in four crucial ways: by demonstrating deep engagement, by shaming shame, by inverting power dynamics and by setting all relationality within the context of the voluntary suffering of love.

First, several of our authors highlighted the level of deep engagement revealed in the cross. Heather Morris movingly points out that 'God's response to sin and human need is not distance but engagement' (Morris, p. 169). Stockitt underlines the notion that the cross is not something done in an exemplary fashion but done both 'for us' and 'with us' (Stockitt, p. 149). For both of these authors, there is a healing and redemptive element in Christ's self-identification with our human brokenness. The level of engagement implied in the incarnation, as well as the cruci-fixion, demonstrates that God's restoration of the divine–human relationship is not accomplished by distance and detachment, but through willing and passionate engagement. Similarly, Bauckham highlights the potent identification of the suffering Christ with those who suffer. For each of these authors, Christ's entrance into our human condition is inherently relational.

Both Tombs and Storkey have pointed to aspects of human relationality which are indisputably broken in our world. And, in each case, truthful perception of both oneself and the other in the broken relational dynamic are important aspects of an approach to healing based on the cross. Tombs advocates a rejection of dehumanization of 'the other'. Storkey highlights our need to admit that both women and men require outside intervention and cannot save themselves. In each case, an approach modelled on Christ's engagement with our otherness can usefully inform our moral re-imagining. The sort of willing self-identification Christ models will not allow us to dehumanize our enemy or to stereo-type those who are not of our gender. As such, following Christ's example is one way we can begin to reform our moral imaginations and relationships in light of the cross.

Second, as Stockitt has highlighted, shame has the power to corrode human relationships. He points out that as it is depicted in Genesis, shame results in fear 'of being known, wanting to conceal, to run, to cover up' (Stockitt, p. 140). Viewed this way, shame inhibits our openness to God and to each other. Thus, the cross's power to shame shame has a direct impact upon the nature of human relational living. Both Tombs and Stockitt point to Christ's crucifixion as inverting the categories of shame. They highlight the centrality of shaming to Roman crucifixions. In the cross, the Romans attempt to exercise power over Christ in this way. However, in his divinity the incarnate Son of God transforms the shameful character of crucifixion. For Tombs this happens through the resurrection, in which Christ's vindication demonstrates that 'God does not abandon the victim, no matter how shamefully he is abused' (Tombs, p. 78). And, while Stockitt's discussion of Christ's transformation of the shame of the cross into glory characterizes it as happening 'myste-riously', it is no less clearly a divinely enacted transformation of shame (Stockitt, p. 149). This transformation creates the possibility of a cross-shaped moral vision of human relationships. Both Tombs and Bauckham see potential in the cross for overcoming dehumanization. Stockitt characterizes shame as undermining our humanity and 'our very right to exist before God', much less our ability to live in harmony with one another. The divine activity of the cross directly addresses this impasse and calls for a transformed perception of ourselves and one another.

Third, the cross inverts our world's power dynamics, shaping moral imagination around the voluntary suffering of love. That idea comes through quite clearly when one considers these chapters together. There is no compulsion in Christ's sacrifice; it is truly a gift freely given. Jesus himself expresses this outlook, saying in John's gospel, 'No one takes [my life] from me, but I lay it down of my own accord' (John 10:18). And the cross is a divine gift of the Godhead. Those authors who emphasize the cross as the activity of the whole Trinity remind us of the inherently voluntary nature of divine self-giving. As Williams points out, the violence and power dynamics of the cross must be considered within a Trinitarian framework. In this light it cannot be said that the Father demands the life of the unwilling Son. The atonement is an act of the Trinity, undertaken within the bounds of Trinitarian interrelationship, not hierarchical coercion. Storkey, likewise, highlights how the doctrine of the atonement transforms our view of power. Her reading of the Christ hymn in Philippians underscores the voluntary negation of power and privilege that were involved in the incarnation. In Christ, God both suffers and renounces power voluntarily. Indeed, both of these activities must be voluntary within the nature of God, as it is impossible that God could be compelled to suffer, or forced to relinquish power. Rather, as Bauckham reminds us, the suffering in the cross is the 'voluntary suffering of love' (Bauckham, p. 59). Further, as Storkey shows, Christ's voluntary relinquishment of power points the way to a 'greater power' (Storkey, p. 91). In each of these inversions, the cross re-forms our moral imagination in ways that call us to Christian living which is authentically vulnerable, freely giving and intentionally anti-coercive.

The Cross and Human Flourishing

How does the cross relate to notions of human flourishing and wholeness? For Bauckham, Christian atonement theology turns on the reality that there is something profoundly wrong with the human condition. Reduced to its core, this sense of things not being right is the outcome of one very defining human experience – the absence of God. Thus, human healing or human flourishing can only come about through individuals finding God and being transformed by his presence in their lives. However, this is only possible, claims Bauckham, if God finds human beings in the midst of their own alienation. The meeting point is the cross where Jesus himself plumbed the very depths of human godforsakenness (Bauckham, p. 55).

Here we see the crucicentric focus of Bauckham's approach to the question of redemption in contrast to the Eastern model presented by Clutterbuck. Humanity's fundamental problem is alienation and only Christ's suffering on the cross can bring an end to that trauma. Of course, it only achieves this effect by virtue of who is on the cross. This willing baptism into suffering and godforsakenness by the Son of God brings about salvation, which Bauckham characterizes as 'forgiveness, healing, new hope, and life out of death' (Bauckham, p. 55).

Robin Stockitt's reflection on the cross and its relationship to shame opens an entirely new window on what might be meant by healing, wholeness and redemption. In a daring theological move he suggests that the existential experience of shame is a more profound problem for human beings than the sense of moral guilt. Stockitt suggests that the redeeming, healing and restoring of the shamed was the prime goal of Christ's ministry on earth and, indeed, of his death on the cross (Stockitt, p. 140). Seen from this perspective, his crucifixion at Calvary was an event of intense shaming that rendered shame impotent by absorbing its full impact. It was this act of loving identification which brought freedom from the sting of shame to all those 'caught up' in his death (Stockitt, p. 149). While this approach undoubtedly raises questions for those who view the traditional paradigm of sin–guilt–forgiveness as the primary prism by which we must view the cross, there is little doubt that Stockitt has succeeded in demonstrating the huge existential impact of shame in human lives. By incorporating Stockitt's insights into our theology, we can rightly view the atonement as necessarily involving freedom from shame as well as guilt.

The final sermonic conclusion to the volume challenges the reader to not only 'own' and 'tell' the event of the cross, but to appropriate its riches. This response entails an act of the imagination by which we enter God's story and allow it to be the template for our own lives. Morris invites us, in the words of Gerard Loughlin, to be 'written into a narrative that is larger, longer and stronger than our own'. Key to her vision of God's healing of the self through the cross is the sheer passionate love of God for his creatures and his desire to see them healed and restored. This truth about God should inspire us to trust that what the cross achieved can become real in our own lives. But healing derived from a wounded God entails recognizing our own woundedness and not running away from it. Only in radical honesty are we enabled to receive the healing power of the cross, God's wonderful pledge of love towards us.

CONTINUING THE CONVERSATION

Katie M. Heffelfinger and Patrick G. McGlinchey

The conversation we have been having about the impact of the cross now enters a new phase. Throughout this book, we have been inviting you, the reader, to join in. Now we hope that you will take up that challenge in your own setting. One way to begin that process within a church context is to read some sections of this book, and do the exercises, with an adult discipleship group. We are convinced that there is great value in giving adults opportunities to integrate theology into their Christian journey and to interact with one another along the way. The exercises and discussion prompts are designed to help you do just that.

There are a number of additional ways that readers could apply the lessons of the book. First, one could incorporate some of the book's themes into creative liturgy and preaching. For example, liturgy that helps worshippers to be more truly honest with God about their struggles may enable them to experience more of God's presence in the midst of suffering. To this end, we would commend resources for applying more of the Bible's lament literature to Christian worship.[1] Creative liturgy might also inspire connected thinking about the way that the cross impacts upon such themes as shame, the environment and reconciliation.[2]

The material in the book would also stimulate more grounded preaching on fundamental life-issues such as shame and emotional healing, which tend to get ignored in the pulpit. Additionally, our interview with Dr Casey and Prof. Williams highlighted the need for preachers to be more attentive to anchoring their proclamation of the cross in classic Trinitarian doctrine. Proclaiming the essential unity of the Father and the Son and their common purpose in redemption highlights the relational foundation to the cross. Beyond guarding against potential caricatures of the cross, such relationally orientated proclamation of the gospel may open people up to the idea that God wants a relationship with them.

Our Irish location has brought home to us the necessity of thinking about the relationship of the cross to reconciliation. However, we are convinced that this essential connection has broad import. It is imperative that we think through reconciliation in ways inspired by the cross. The chapters on gender, enemies and the cosmos have indicated some of the potential fruitfulness of this kind of reflection. We invite you to consider what issues need reconciliation in your setting, and how you might think them through under the influence of the gospel.[3] Throughout this book, we have been intentional about engaging issues requiring reconciliation in a non-polemical manner. One of the ways that we have encouraged this is by listening carefully to people who have different theological starting points, and trying to understand them on their own terms. This is a model not simply for academic discourse but for Christians in all contexts. God has modelled out this risky kind of interaction by entering into our human experience in the incarnation.

We began this project as theological educators committed to the principle of integration. Over the course of this project, we have been increasingly convinced of the importance of this perspective for the future of the church and the formation of its leaders. We would encourage those charged with this role to ground their teaching of all theological themes in the reality of worship and the challenge of discipleship. This kind of approach prevents theology from being an escape to an ivory tower and ensures that neither we nor our students can dodge the real-life issues that confront us.

BIBLIOGRAPHY

Althaus, Paul. *The Theology of Martin Luther* (Philadelphia: Fortress Press, 1966).

Anderson, David E. 'Religion in America.' *Ludington Daily News*, 29 December 1975.

Anselm. *Cur Deus Homo* [*Why God Became Man*]. Pages 260–357 in *Anselm of Canterbury: The Major Works* (ed. B. Davies and G.R. Evans; Oxford: Oxford University Press, 1998).

Anstall, Kharalambos. 'Juridical Justification Theology and a Statement of the Orthodox Teaching.' Pages 482–503 in *Stricken by God? Nonviolent Identification and the Victory of Christ* (ed. Brad Jersak and Michael Hardin; Grand Rapids, MI: Eerdmans, 2007).

Appleby, Scott R. *The Ambivalence of the Sacred: Religion, Violence, and Reconciliation* (Lanham, MD: Rowman & Littlefield, 2000).

Arnold, C.E. *The Colossian Syncretism: The Interface between Christianity and Folk Belief at Colossae* (Grand Rapids, MI: Baker, 1996).

Augustine, *Sermon XXX*.

Aulén, Gustav. *Christus Victor: An Historical Study of the Three Main Types of the Idea of the Atonement* (trans. A.G. Herbert; London: SPCK, 1970).

Bailey, Kenneth E. *Jesus through Middle Eastern Eyes: Cultural Studies in the Gospels* (Downers Grove, IL: InterVarsity Press, 2008).

Balabanski, Vicky S. 'Hellenistic Cosmology and the Letter to the Colossians: Towards an Ecological Hermeneutic.' Pages 94–107 in *Ecological Hermeneutics: Biblical, Historical and Theological Perspectives* (ed. David G. Horrell, Cherryl Hunt, Christopher Southgate and Francesca Stavrakopoulou; London: T&T Clark, 2010).

Balthasar, Hans Urs von. *Unless You Become Like This Child* (San Francisco: Ignatius Press, 1991).

Baltzer, Klaus. *Deutero-Isaiah* (trans. Margaret Kohl; Hermeneia. Minneapolis: Fortress Press, 2001).

Barth, Karl. *Church Dogmatics, Vol. 2: The Doctrine of God Part 2* (ed. G.W. Bromiley and T.F. Torrance; 14 vols; London: T&T Clark, 1957).

— *Church Dogmatics, Vol. 4.1: The Doctrine of Reconciliation* (ed. G.W. Bromiley and T.F. Torrance; 14 vols; London: T&T Clark, 1957).

Bauckham, Richard. *Jesus and the God of Israel: God Crucified and Other Studies on the New Testament's Christology of Divine Identity* (Milton Keynes: Paternoster Press/Grand Rapids, MI: Eerdmans, 2008).

— *Bible and Ecology: Rediscovering the Community of Creation* (London: Darton, Longman & Todd, 2010).

— and Trevor Hart. *Hope Against Hope: Christian Eschatology in Contemporary Context* (London: Darton, Longman & Todd, 1999).

Baxter, Christina A. 'Cursed Beloved.' Pages 54–72 in *Atonement Today* (ed. John Goldingay; London: SPCK, 1995).

Beattie, Tina. *The New Atheists: The Twilight of Reason and the War on Religion* (London: Darton, Longman & Todd, 2007).

Bebbington, David W. *Evangelicalism in Modern Britain: A History from the 1730s to the 1980s* (London: Unwin Hyman, 1989).

Beckwith, R.T. *Christ's Presence and Sacrifice: The Agreed Statement on Eucharistic Doctrine with a Response* (London: The Church Book Room Press, 1973).

Begbie, Jeremy S. 'Faithful Feelings: Music and Emotion in Worship.' Pages 323–54 in *Resonant Witness: Conversations between Music and Theology* (ed. Jeremy S. Begbie and Steven R. Guthrie; Grand Rapids, MI: Eerdmans, 2011).

Berlin, Adele. *Lamentations* (Old Testament Library; Louisville, KY: Westminster John Knox Press, 2002).

Berry, R.J. 'Adam or Adamah?' *Science and Christian Belief* 23 (2012): pp. 23–48.

Bickersteth, Edward H. 'Peace, Perfect Peace, in This Dark World of Sin?'

Bielby, James, and Paul R. Eddy, eds, *The Nature of the Atonement: Four Views* (Downers Grove, IL: InterVarsity Press, 2006).

Blake, Daniel. 'Evangelical Alliance Ease Theology Tensions at Atonement Symposium.' *Christian Today*, 27 July 2005. http://www.christiantoday.com/article/evangelical.alliance. ease.theology.tensions.at.atonement.symposium/3542.htm (accessed 29 December 2013).

Blenkinsopp, Joseph. *Isaiah 40 – 55* (Anchor Bible Commentary Series 19A; New York: Doubleday, 2000).

Boersma, Hans. *Violence, Hospitality and the Cross: Reappropriating the Atonement Tradition* (Grand Rapids, MI: Baker Academic, 2004).

Bonhoeffer, Dietrich. *Ethics* (New York: Macmillan, 1955).

— *Creation and Fall: A Theological Interpretation of Genesis 1 – 3* (New York: Macmillan, 1964).

— *Letters and Papers from Prison* (London: SCM Press, 2002).

Book of Common Prayer (Dublin: Columba Press, 2004).

Booth, Wayne C. *The Company We Keep: An Ethics of Fiction* (London: University of California Press, 1988).

Botterweck, Gerhard Johannes, Helmer Ringgren, Heinz-Josef Fabry et al. *Theological Dictionary of the Old Testament* (15 vols; Grand Rapids, MI: Eerdmans, 1975).

Bradbury, Paul. *Sowing in Tears: How to Lament in a Church of Praise* (Cambridge: Grove, 2007).

Brock, Rita Nakashima. 'The Feminist Redemption of Christ: Visions of a New Humanity.' Pages 55–74 in *Christian Feminism* (ed. Judith Weidman; New York: Harper & Row, 1984).

Brown, R.E. *Death of the Messiah* (2 vols; Anchor Bible Reference Library; New York: Doubleday, 1994).

Bruce, F.F. *1 & II Corinthians* (The New Century Bible Commentary; London: Marshall, Morgan & Scott, 1971).

Brueggemann, Walter. *The Psalms and the Life of Faith* (Minneapolis: Fortress Press, 1995).

— *The Book that Breathes New Life: Scriptural Authority and Biblical Theology* (Minneapolis: Fortress Press, 2005).

Brunner, Emil. *The Mediator* (London: Lutterworth Press, 1934).

Calvin, John. *Institutes of the Christian Religion* (trans. F.L. Battles; Philadelphia: Westminster Press, 1960).

— *Institutes of the Christian Religion* (trans. Henry Beveridge; London: James Clarke & Co., 1962).

Campbell, Alastair V. *Rediscovering Pastoral Care* (Louisville, KY: Westminster John Knox Press, 1981).

Carlson Brown, Joanne, and Carole R. Bohn, eds. *Christianity, Patriarchy, and Abuse: A Feminist Critique* (New York: Pilgrim Press, 1989).

Carr, Wesley. *The Pastor as Theologian: The Integration of Pastoral Ministry, Theology and Discipleship* (London: SPCK, 1989).

Catechism of the Catholic Church (London: Geoffrey Chapman, 1994).

Chalke, Steve and Alan Mann. *The Lost Message of Jesus* (Grand Rapids, MI: Zondervan, 2003).

Charry, Ellen. *By the Renewing of Your Minds: The Pastoral Function of Christian Doctrine* (New York: Oxford University Press, 1997).

Chesterton, G.K. 'The Secret Garden.' Pages 33–48 in *The Complete Father Brown Stories* (London: Wordsworth, 2006).

Childs, B.S. *Memory and Tradition* (Naperville, IL: Alec R. Allenson, 1961).

Christ, Carol, and Judith Plaskow, eds. *Womanspirit Rising* (San Francisco: Harper & Row, 1979).

Coleman, M. 'Fatal Charades'. *Journal of Roman Studies* 80 (1990): pp. 44–73.

Clancy, Robert A.D. 'The Old Testament Roots of Remembrance in the Lord's Supper'. *Concordia Journal* (1993): pp. 35–50.

Clark Kroeger, Richard, and Catherine Clark Kroeger. *I Suffer Not a Woman: Rethinking 1 Timothy 2:11–15 in the Light of Ancient Evidence* (Grand Rapids, MI: Baker, 1992).

Clines, David J.A. *I, He, We, and They: A Literary Approach to Isaiah 53* (Journal for the Study of the Old Testament Supplement Series 1; Sheffield: JSOT Press, 1976).

Clutterbuck, Richard. 'How Great the Debt We Owe: Can Anselm's *Cur Deus Homo* Say Anything to Contemporary Culture?' *Epworth Review* 36.1 (2009): pp. 18–28.

Cocksworth, Christopher. 'Holding Together: Catholic Evangelical Worship in the Spirit'. *Anvil* 22.1 (2004): pp. 5–16.

Congregation for the Doctrine of the Faith. *Declaration on the Question of the Admission of Women to the Ministerial Priesthood* 27. Vatican City, 15 October 1976.

— *Dominus Iesus* (London: Catholic Truth Society, 2000).

Cranfield, C.E.B. 'Some Observations on Romans 8:19–21.' Pages 224–30 in *Reconciliation and Hope: New Testament Essays on*

Atonement and Eschatology Presented to L.L. Morris on His 60th Birthday (ed. Robert Banks. Grand Rapids, MI: Eerdmans, 1974).

Crosby, Fanny J. 'At the Cross There's Room!'

Culler, Jonathan. *Literary Theory* (A Very Short Introduction Series; New York: Oxford University Press, 1997).

da Todi, Jacopone. *Stabat Mater*.

Daly, Mary. *Beyond God the Father* (Boston: Beacon Press, 1973).

Danaher, James P. 'A Contemporary Perspective on Atonement'. *Irish Theological Quarterly* 69.3 (2004): pp. 281–94.

Davis, Ellen F. *Wondrous Depth: Preaching the Old Testament* (Louisville, KY: Westminster John Knox Press, 2005).

Dawes, James. *Evil Men* (Cambridge, MA: Harvard University Press, 2013).

Dawkins, Richard. *The God Delusion* (London: Bantam, 2007).

De Chirico, Leonardo. 'The Cross and the Eucharist: The Doctrine of the Atonement According to the Catholic Church'. *European Journal of Theology* 8.1 (1999): pp. 49–59.

— *Evangelical Theological Perspectives on Post-Vatican II Roman Catholicism* (Oxford: Peter Lang, 2003).

— 'The Blurring of Time Distinctions in Roman Catholicism'. *Themelios* 29.2 (2004): pp. 40–46.

Denney, James. *Studies in Theology* (London: Hodder & Stoughton, 1904).

— *The Death of Christ* (London: Hodder & Stoughton, 1911).

— *The Christian Doctrine of Reconciliation* (London: Hodder & Stoughton, 1917).

— *The Death of Christ* (London: Tyndale, 1951).

Dobbs-Allsopp, F.W. *Lamentations* (Interpretation: A Bible Commentary for Teaching and Preaching; Louisville, KY: Westminster John Knox Press, 2002).

— 'The Psalms and Lyric Verse.' Pages 346–79 in *The Evolution of Rationality: Interdisciplinary Essays in Honor of J. Wetzel van Huyssteen* (ed. F. LeRon Shuts; Grand Rapids, MI: Eerdmans, 2006).

Dombkowski Hopkins, Denise, and Michael S. Koppel. *Grounded in the Living Word: The Old Testament and Pastoral Care Practices* (Cambridge: Eerdmans, 2010).

Doyle OFM, Eric. 'God and the Feminine'. *The Clergy Review* 61 (1971).

Driver, S.R. *An Introduction to the Literature of the Old Testament* (New York: Meridian Library, 1957).

Dunn, James D.G. *Romans 1 – 8* (Word Biblical Commentary 38A; Waco, TX: Word, 1988).

— *The Theology of Paul the Apostle* (Edinburgh: T&T Clark, 1998).

Dyson, Freeman J. *Disturbing the Universe* (New York: Harper & Row, 1979).

Elsdon, Ron. *Greenhouse Theology: Biblical Perspectives on Caring for Creation* (Eastbourne: Monarch, 1992).

Endo, Shusaku. *A Life of Jesus* (trans. Richard A. Schuchert; New York: Paulist Press, 1978).

— *Deep River* (trans. Van C. Gessel; London: Hodder & Stoughton, 1995).

Farley, Edward. 'Four Pedagogical Mistakes: *A Mea Culpa*'. *Teaching Theology and Religion* 8 (2005): pp. 200–3.

Fee, Gordon. *First Epistle to the Corinthians* (New International Commentary on the New Testament; Grand Rapids, MI: Eerdmans, 1991).

Fiddes, Paul. *The Creative Suffering of God* (Oxford: Oxford University Press, 1992).

Francis I. 'Easter Vigil Homily' http://www.catholicherald.co.uk/news/2013/03/30/full-text-of-pope-franciss-homily-at-the-easter-vigil/ (accessed 27 November 2013).

Fraser, Ian. 'Lord, Bring the Day to Pass.'

Galloway, Kathy, ed. *The Pattern of Our Days: Liturgies and Resources for Worship* (Glasgow: Wild Goose, 1996).

Gibson, Mel, dir. *The Passion of the Christ* (2004).

Gillett, David. *Trust and Obey: Explorations in Evangelical Spirituality* (London: Darton Longman & Todd, 1993).

Girard, René. *Violence and the Sacred* (trans. Patrick Gregory; Baltimore: Johns Hopkins Press, 1979).

— *Things Hidden since the Foundation of the World* (Stanford, CA: Stanford University Press, 1987).

— *The Scapegoat* (New York: Athlone Press, 1988).

George, Timothy. 'Symposium on the Declaration *Dominus Iesus*'. *Pro Ecclesia* 10.1 (2001): pp. 5–16.

Godfrey, John M. *The Place of Lament and the 'Catharsis of the Complaint' in Response to the Problem of Evil* (Braemor Series 2; Dublin: Church of Ireland Publishing, 2013).

Grant, Robert. 'O Worship the King, All Glorious Above.' *Church of Ireland Hymnal* (Oxford: Oxford University Press, 5th edn, 2000).

Green, Douglas J. 'When the Gardener Returns: An Ecological Perspective on Adam's Dominion.' Pages 267–75 in *Keeping God's Earth: The Global Environment in Biblical Perspective* (ed. Noah J. Toly and Daniel I. Block; Nottingham: Apollos, 2010).

Greene, Roland. *Post Petrarchism: Origins and Innovations of the Western Lyric Sequence* (Princeton: Princeton University Press, 1991).

Grey, Mary. *Redeeming the Dream: Feminism, Redemption and Christian Tradition* (London: SPCK, 1989).

Gunton, Colin E. *Christ and Creation* (Carlisle: Paternoster Press, 1992).

Gustafson, David M. 'J.G. Princell and the Waldenströmian View of the Atonement'. *Trinity Journal* 20.2 (1999): pp. 191–214.

Haers SJ, Jacques. 'Reconciliation in Times of Worldwide Environmental Crisis'. *Concilium* (2013) 1: pp. 42–52.

Hampson, Daphne. *Theology and Feminism* (Oxford: Basil Blackwell, 1990).

Häring, Hermann. 'Disaster for the World and Human Disaster'. *Concilium* (2004) 1: pp. 57–76.

Harries, Richard. *The Passion in Art* (Ashgate Studies in Theology, Imagination and the Arts; Burlington, VT: Ashgate, 2004).

Hart, David Bentley. *The Beauty of the Infinite: The Aesthetics of Christian Truth* (Grand Rapids, MI: Eerdmans, 2003).

— *The Doors of the Sea: Where Was God in the Tsunami?* (Grand Rapids, MI: Eerdmans, 2005).

Hauerwas, Stanley. *A Cross-Shattered Church: Reclaiming the Theological Heart of Preaching* (Grand Rapids, MI: Brazos Press, 2009).

Hecht, Anneliese. 'Bibliodrama and Exegesis'. *Bulletin Dei Verbum* 66/67 (2003): pp. 6–10
http://www.deiverbum2005.org/Bulletin/BDV%206667_e.pdf (accessed 4 November 2013).

Heffelfinger, Katie M. *I Am Large, I Contain Multitudes: Lyric Cohesion and Conflict in Second Isaiah* (Leiden: Brill, 2011).

Hegel, G.W.F. *Lectures on the Philosophy of World History, Vol. 1: Manuscripts of the Introduction and the Lectures of 1822-3* (ed. and trans. Robert F. Brown and Peter C. Hodgson; Oxford: Clarendon Press, 2011).

Heim, Mark. *Saved from Sacrifice: A Theology of the Cross* (Grand Rapids, MI: Eerdmans, 2006).

Hengel, M. *Crucifixion in the Ancient World and the Folly of the Cross* (trans. J. Bowden; Philadelphia: Fortress Press, 1977).

Heron, Alasdair. *Table and Tradition: Towards an Ecumenical Understanding of the Eucharist* (Edinburgh: Handsel Press, 1983).

Holmes, Stephen R. *The Wondrous Cross: Atonement and Penal Substitution in the Bible and History* (London: Paternoster Press, 2007).

'Hubble's Deepest View Ever of the Universe Unveils Earliest Galaxies' http://hubblesite.org/newscenter/archive/releases/2004/07/text/ (accessed 13 December 2013).

Hughes, John Jay. 'Eucharistic Sacrifice: Transcending the Reformation Deadlock'. *Worship* 43.9 (1969): pp. 532–44.

Hunt, Cherryl, David G. Horrell and Christopher Southgate. 'An Environmental Mantra? Ecological Interest in Romans 8:19–23 and a Modest Proposal for Its Narrative Interpretation'. *Journal of Theological Studies* 59 (2008): pp. 546–79.

Irenaeus. *Adversus Haereses.*

Jeffery, S., M. Ovey and A. Sach. *Pierced for Our Transgressions: Rediscovering the Glory of Penal Substitution* (Nottingham: InterVarsity Press, 2007).

Janowski, Bernd, 'He Bore Our Sins: Isaiah 53 and the Drama of Taking Another's Place.' Pages 48–74 in *The Suffering Servant: Isaiah 53 in Jewish and Christian Sources* (ed. Bernd Janowski and Peter Stuhlmacher; Cambridge: Eerdmans, 2004).

Jensen, Robin. *Face to Face: Portraits of the Divine in Early Christianity* (Grand Rapids, MI: Fortress Press, 2005).

Jersak, Brad, and Michael Hardin, eds. *Stricken by God? Nonviolent Identification and the Victory of Christ* (Grand Rapids, MI: Eerdmans, 2007).

Jewett, Robert. *Romans* (Hermeneia; Minneapolis: Fortress Press, 2008).

Johnson, Elizabeth A. *She Who Is: The Mystery of God in Feminist Theological Discourse* (New York: Crossroad, 1993).

Johnson, Luke Timothy. 'Imagining the World Scripture Imagines'. *Modern Theology* 14.2 (1998): pp. 165–79.

'Joint Declaration on the Doctrine of Justification by the Lutheran World Federation and the Catholic Church' http://www.vatican.va/roman_curia/pontifical_councils/chrstuni/documents/rc_pc_chrstuni_doc_31101999 (accessed 29 December 2013).

Jones, Serene. *Trauma and Grace: Theology in a Ruptured World* (Louisville, KY: Westminster John Knox Press, 2009).

Julian of Norwich, *Revelations of Divine Love* (trans. Grace Warrack; Grand Rapids, MI: Christian Classics Ethereal Library) http://www.ccel.org/ccel/julian/revelations.pdf (accessed 23 December 2013).

Kimbrough Jr, S.T. 'Lyrical Theology: Theology in Hymns'. *Theology Today* 63 (2006): pp. 22–37.

Kinzie, Mary. *The Cure of Poetry in an Age of Prose: Moral Essays on the Poet's Calling* (Chicago: University of Chicago Press, 1993).

Lake, Frank. 'The Theology of Pastoral Counselling.' Pages 127–35 in *Spiritual Dimensions of Pastoral Care: Practical Theology in a Multidisciplinary Context* (ed. David Willows and John Swinton; London: Jessica Kingsley, 2000).

Lederach, John Paul. *The Little Book of Conflict Transformation* (Intercourse, PA: Good Books, 2003).

— *The Moral Imagination: The Art and Soul of Building Peace* (Oxford: Oxford University Press, 2005).

Lendon, J.E. *Empire of Honour: The Art of Government in the Roman World* (Oxford: Oxford University Press, 2001).

Levinas, Emmanuel. *Entre Nous: Thinking-of-the-Other* (trans. Michael B. Smith and Barbara Harshav; New York: Columbia University Press, 1998).

Lewis, Alan. 'The Burial of God: Rupture and Resumption as the Story of Salvation'. *Scottish Journal of Theology* 40.3 (1987): pp. 335–62.

Lewis, C.S. *The Lion, the Witch and the Wardrobe* (London: Lions, 1980).

— *The Last Battle* (London: HarperCollins, 2009).

Liechty, Joseph, and Cecelia Clegg. *Moving Beyond Sectarianism: Religion, Conflict and Reconciliation in Northern Ireland* (Dublin: Columba Press, 2001).

Lincoln, Andrew T. *Ephesians* (Word Biblical Commentary 42; Dallas: Word, 2002).

Loughlin, Gerard. *Telling God's Story: Bible, Church and Narrative Theology* (Cambridge: Cambridge University Press, 1999).

Luoma, Tapio. *Incarnation and Physics: Natural Science in the Theology of Thomas F. Torrance* (Oxford: Oxford University Press, 2002).

Luther, Martin. *Martin Luthers Werke* (Weimar: Weimerer Ausgabe, no year).

Mase-Hasegawa, Emi. *Christ in Japanese Culture: Theological Themes in Shusaku Endo's Literary Works* (Brill's Japanese Studies Library 28; Leiden: Brill, 2008).

Martial, *Liber spectaculorum.*

Martin, Ralph P. 'Reconciliation and Forgiveness in Colossians.' Pages 104–24 in *Reconciliation and Hope: New Testament Essays on Atonement and Eschatology Presented to L.L. Morris on His 60th Birthday* (ed. Robert Banks; Grand Rapids, MI: Eerdmans, 1974).

McCormack, Bruce. 'The Ontological Presuppositions of Barth's Doctrine of the Atonement.' Pages 346–66 in *The Glory of the Atonement* (ed. Charles Hill and Frank James III; Downers Grove, IL: InterVarsity Press, 2003).

McGrath, Alister, and Joanne McGrath. *The Dilemma of Self-Esteem: The Cross and Christian Confidence* (Wheaton, IL: Crossway, 1992).

McGregor, Neil, and Erika Langmuir. *Seeing Salvation* (London: BBC, 2000).

Meyer, Jan, and Ray Land. 'Threshold Concepts and Troublesome Knowledge: Linkages to Ways of Thinking and Practising within the Disciplines.' *ETL Project: Occasional Report* 4 (Edinburgh: Enhancing Teaching-Learning Environments in Undergraduate Courses Project, 2003) http://www.etl.tla.ed.ac.uk//docs/ETLreport4.pdf (accessed 9 October 2013).

Miller, Patrick D. *Interpreting the Psalms* (Philadelphia: Fortress Press, 1986).

Miller, William I. *Humiliation: And Other Essays on Honor, Social Discomfort and Violence* (London: Cornell University Press, 1993).

Mollenkott, Virginia R. *Women, Men and the Bible* (New York: Crossroad, 1989) http://www.ministryforwomen.org/scriptur/mollenk2.asp (accessed 21 December 2013).

Moltmann, Jürgen. *The Crucified God: The Cross of Christ as the Foundation and Criticism of Christian Theology* (trans. R.A. Wilson and John Bowden; London: SCM Press, 1974).

— and Elisabeth Moltmann Wendel. *Passion for God: Theology in Two Voices* (Louisville, KY: Westminster John Knox Press, 2003).

Moo, Douglas J. 'Eschatology and Environmental Ethics: On the Importance of Biblical Theology to Creation Care.' Pages 23–43 in *Keeping God's Earth: The Global Environment in Biblical Perspective* (ed. Noah J. Toly and Daniel I. Block; Nottingham: Apollos, 2010).

Morrison, Alistair James. *The New Masculinity Movement: A Viable Model for Engaging Men with God and the Church?* (Braemor Studies Series 3; Dublin: Church of Ireland Publishing, 2013).

Northcott, Michael S. *The Environment and Christian Ethics* (Cambridge: Cambridge University Press, 1996).

Nouwen, Henri. *The Wounded Healer* (New York: Doubleday, 1972).

Numbers, Ronald W. *The Creationists: From Scientific Creationism to Intelligent Design* (Cambridge, MA: Harvard University Press, 2006).

Nussbaum, Martha C. *Love's Knowledge: Essays on Philosophy and Literature* (Oxford: Oxford University Press, 1990).

O'Brien, Peter T. *Colossians–Philemon* (Word Biblical Commentary 44; Dallas: Word, 2002).

O'Mahony, Kieran. 'To Tear Down and to Build: Replacing Anselm, Reading Paul and John.' Lecture to the Trinity College Dublin Biblical Studies Seminar (15 November 2013).

Oppenheimer, Lady Helen. *The Hope of Happiness: A Sketch for a Christian Humanism* (London: SCM Press, 1983).

Orr, James. *Sidelights on Christian Doctrine* (London: Marshall, 1909).

Owen, Wilfred. 'At a Calvary near the Ancre.'

Parker, Rebecca Ann and Rita Brock. *Saving Paradise: How Christianity Traded Love of This World for Crucifixion and Empire* (Boston: Beacon Press, 2008).

Peacore, Linda. *The Role of Women's Experience in Feminist Theologies of the Atonement* (Eugene, OR: Pickwick, 2010).

Pickering, Sue. *Creative Retreat Ideas: Resources for Short Day and Weekend Retreats* (Norwich: Canterbury Press, 2010).

Plato. *The Republic* (trans. Robin Waterfield; Oxford: Oxford University Press, 1993).

Pöhl, Rudi. 'Bibliodrama is *Lectio Divina* on Stage'. *Bulletin Dei Verbum* 66/67 (2003): pp. 2–22
http://www.deiverbum2005.org/Bulletin/BDV%206667_e.pdf (accessed 4 November 2013).

Polkinghorne, John. 'Scripture and an Evolving Creation'. *Science and Christian Belief* 21 (2009): pp. 163–73.

— *Reason and Reality: The Relationship between Science and Theology* (London: SPCK, 2010).

Quimby, Lee. 'The Unsettling of the Fundamentalist Mindset: Shifts in Apocalyptic Belief in Contemporary Conservative Christianity.' Pages 120–37 in *The Fundamentalist Mindset* (ed. Charles B. Strozier, David M. Terman and James W. Jones; Oxford: Oxford University Press, 2010).

Radford Ruether, Rosemary. *To Change the World: Christology and Cultural Criticism* (London: SCM Press, 1981).

— *Sexism and God-Talk: Towards a Feminist Theology* (Boston: Beacon Press, 1983).

— 'The Liberation of Christology from Patriarchy.' Pages 138–47 in *Feminist Theology: A Reader* (ed. Ann Loades; Louisville, KY: Westminster John Knox Press, 1990).

Ratzinger, Joseph. 'Is the Eucharist a Sacrifice?' *Concilium* 4.3 (1967): pp. 35–40.

— 'Luther and the Unity of the Churches'. *Communio: International Catholic Review* 11 (1984): pp. 210–26.

— *Introduction to Christianity* (San Francisco: Ignatius Press, 1990).

— *God Is Near Us: The Eucharist, The Heart of Life* (San Francisco: Ignatius Press, 2003).

Re-Imagining: A Global Theological Conference by Women: For Men and Women. Minnesota, November 1993.

Richardson, Alan. *Creeds in the Making* (London: SCM Press, 2nd edn, 1941).

—, ed. *A Dictionary of Christian Theology* (London: SCM Press, 1969).

Ricoeur, Paul. *Figuring the Sacred* (Minneapolis; Fortress Press, 1995).

Roberts, M. B. 'An Anglican Priest's Perspective on the Doctrine of Creation in the Church Today.' Pages 339–48 in *Geology and*

Religion: A History of Harmony and Hostility (Special Publication 310; ed. M. Kölbl-Ebert; London: Geological Society, 2009).

Rowland, Tracey. *Benedict XVI: A Guide for the Perplexed* (London: Continuum, 2010).

Russell, Cathriona. 'Environmental Perspectives on the Genesis Flood Narrative.' Pages 461–87 in *Opening Heaven's Floodgates: The Genesis Flood Narrative, Its Context and Reception* (Biblical Intersections 12; ed. Jason M. Silverman; Piscataway, NJ: Georgias Press, 2013).

Russell, Letty M. *The Liberating Word: A Guide to Nonsexist Interpretations of the Bible* (Philadelphia: Westminster Press, 1976).

— 'Authority and Challenge of Feminist Interpretation.' Pages 137–46 in *Feminist Interpretation of the Bible* (ed. Letty Russell; Oxford: Basil Blackwell, 1985).

Saiving, Valerie. 'The Human Situation: A Feminine View'. *Journal of Religion* 40.2 (1960): pp. 100–12.

Sands, Craig. *Moving Beyond Sectarianism: A Resource for Adult Education – Continuing Education* (Dublin and Belfast: Irish School of Ecumenics, 2001).

Santmire, H. Paul. *The Travail of Nature: The Ambiguous Ecological Promise of Christian Theology* (Minneapolis: Fortress Press, 1997).

Schottroff, W. *'Gedenken' im Alten Orient und im Alten Testament* (Neukirchen-Vluyn: Neukirchener Verlag, 1964).

Schüssler Fiorenza, Elisabeth. 'Feminist Theology as a Critical Theology of Liberation'. *Theological Studies* 36 (1975): pp. 605–26.

— *Bread Not Stone: The Challenge of Feminist Biblical Interpretation* (Boston: Beacon Press, 1984).

Sheckler, A.E., and M. J. Winn Leith. 'The Crucifixion Conundrum and the Santa Sabina Doors'. *Harvard Theological Review* 103.1 (2010): pp. 67–88.

Sherman, Robert. *King, Priest and Prophet: A Trinitarian Theology of Atonement* (London: T&T Clark International, 2004).

Sölle, Dorothee. *Suffering* (trans. Everett R. Kalin; Philadelphia: Fortress Press, 1984).

Stalley, R. 'European Art and the Irish High Crosses'. *Proceedings of the Royal Irish Academy Section C: Archaeology, Celtic Studies, History, Linguistics, Literature* 90C (1990): pp. 135–58.

Sterk, Helen. 'Gender Relations and Narrative in a Reformed Church Setting.' Pages 184–221 in *After Eden: Facing the Chal-*

lenge of Gender Reconcilaition (ed. Mary Stewart Van Leeuwen; Carlisle: Paternoster Press, 1993).

Stockitt, Robin. *Restoring the Shamed: Towards a Theology of Shame* (Eugene, OR: Cascade, 2012).

Stott, John. *The Cross of Christ* (Leicester: InterVarsity Press, 1986).

— *Evangelical Truth: A Plea for Unity* (Leicester: InterVarsity Press, 1999).

Swinton, John. *Raging with Compassion: Pastoral Responses to the Problem of Evil* (Grand Rapids, MI: Eerdmans, 2007).

Taliaferro, Charles. 'A Narnian Theory of the Atonement'. *Scottish Journal of Theology* 41.1 (1988): pp. 75–92.

Tavard, George H. 'The Anglican–Roman Catholic Agreed Statements and Their Reception'. *Theological Studies* 41.1 (1980): pp. 74–97.

Taylor, Charles. *A Secular Age* (London: Belknap Press, 2007).

Teresa of Avila, *Interior Castle* (ed. Benedict Zimmerman; Grand Rapids, MI: Christian Classics Ethereal Library) http://www.ccel.org/ccel/teresa/castle2.pdf (accessed 23 December 2013).

Thiselton, Anthony. *First Epistle to the Corinthians* (New International Greek Testament Commentary; Grand Rapids, MI: Eerdmans, 2013).

Thompson, Marjorie J. *Soul Feast: An Invitation to the Christian Spiritual Life* (Louisville, KY: Westminster John Knox Press, 1995).

Townend, Stuart. 'How Deep the Father's Love for Us.'

— 'In Christ Alone.'

Tracy, David. *Blessed Rage for Order: The New Pluralism in Theology* (New York: Seabury Press, 1975).

Trible, Phyllis. 'Depatriarchalizing in Biblical Interpretation'. *Journal of the American Academy of Religion* 41.1 (1973): pp. 30–48.

— *God and the Rhetoric of Sexuality* (Philadelphia: Fortress Press, 1978).

— *Texts of Terror: Literary–Feminist Readings of Biblical Narrative* (Philadelphia: Fortress Press, 1984).

Turl, John. 'Theodicy and Geodesy: Who Is to Blame?' *Science and Christian Belief* 23 (2011): pp. 49–66.

Ullrich, Lothar. 'Reconciliation.' Pages 571–5 in *Handbook of Catholic Theology* (ed. W. Beinert and F. Schüssler Fiorenza; New York: Herder & Herder, 2000).

Weaver, J Denny. *The Nonviolent Atonement* (Grand Rapids, MI: Eerdmans, 2001).

Weil, Simone. 'Reflections on the Right Use of School Studies with a View to the Love of God' http://www.uwo.ca/chaplain/crc/articles/right_use.pdf (accessed 21 December 2013).

Weingart, R.E. *The Logic of Divine Love: A Critical Analysis of the Soteriology of Peter Abelard* (Oxford: Clarendon Press, 1970).

Wesley, Charles. 'Christ the Lord Is Risen Today.'

Wesley, John. *The Works of the Rev. John Wesley* (14 vols; London: John Mason, 1831).

— *The Journal of John Wesley* (Chicago: Moody Press, 1974).

— 'Preface.' *Sermons on Several Occasions* (Grand Rapids, MI: Christian Classics Ethereal Library) http://www.ccel.org/ccel/wesley/sermons.pdf (accessed 21 December 2013).

Wiles, Maurice. 'Christianity without Incarnation?' Pages 1–10 in *The Myth of God Incarnate* (ed. John Hick; London: SCM Press, 1977).

Wilkinson, David. *The Message of Creation* (Leicester: InterVarsity Press, 2002).

Williams, Rowan. *The Wound of Knowledge* (London: Darton, Longman & Todd, 1990).

Williams, Stephen N. *Revelation and Reconciliation: A Window on Modernity* (Cambridge: Cambridge University Press, 1995).

— 'Atonement: The Penal View'. *Books & Culture* 11.1 (2005): pp. 20–22.

— 'What Christians Believe about Forgiveness'. *Studies in Christian Ethics* 24.2 (2011): pp. 147–56.

Willimon, William H. *Who Will Be Saved?* (Nashville: Abingdon Press, 2008).

Wilson Schaef, Anne. *Women's Reality: An Emerging Female System in the White Male Society* (San Francisco: Perennial Library, 1985).

Wink, Walter. *Naming the Powers: The Language of Power in the New Testament* (Philadelphia: Fortress Press, 1984).

— *Unmasking the Powers: The Invisible Forces that Determine Human Existence* (Philadelphia: Fortress Press, 1986).

— *Engaging the Powers: Discernment and Resistance in a World of Dominion* (Minneapolis: Fortress Press, 1992).

— *When the Powers Fall: Reconciliation in the Healing of Nations* (Minneapolis: Fortress Press, 1998).

— *Jesus and Nonviolence: A Third Way* (Minneapolis: Fortress Press, 2003).

Wolterstorff, Nicholas. *Divine Discourse: Philosophical Reflections on the Claim that God Speaks* (New York: Cambridge University Press, 1995).

— 'To Theologians: From One Who Cares about Theology but Is Not One of You'. *Theological Education* 40.2 (2005): pp. 79–92.

World Council of Churches. *Baptism, Eucharist and Ministry* (Geneva: WCC, 1982).

Wright, N.T. *Colossians and Philemon: An Introduction and Commentary* (Tyndale New Testament Commentaries 12; Downers Grove, IL: InterVarsity Press, 1986).

Wright, N.T. *The Resurrection of the Son of God* (London: SPCK, 2006).

Wright, Tom. *Surprised by Hope* (London: SPCK, 2007).

— *Virtue Reborn* (London: SPCK, 2010).

Wyllie, Peter J. *The Way the Earth Works: An Introduction to the New Global Geology and Its Revolutionary Development* (New York: John Wiley and Sons, 1976).

Websites

http://daily.upperroom.org/?page_id=19

http://www.christianityandculture.org.uk/

http://www.creativeprayer.com

http://www.gbod.org/live-the-um-way/responding-to-world-events

http://www.ignatianspirituality.com/ignatian-prayer/the-examen/

http://www.ignatianspirituality.com/ignatian-prayer/the-examen/how-can-i-pray/

http://www.tcd.ie/ise/belfast.

http://justus.anglican.org.

Endnotes

Introduction

[1] The attentive reader of the Table of Contents will correctly infer that Paddy was reading something written by Robin Stockitt, one of the contributors to this volume. While Robin's idea was the initial springboard that set our minds to work, it is by no means the only, or even primary, lens through which this volume examines the cross.

[2] As Clutterbuck's essay will highlight, some scholars have disputed the cross's centrality for the earliest Christians. However, the larger perspective of this volume affirms its centrality to the Christian faith throughout its history.

[3] Edward Farley, 'Four Pedagogical Mistakes: A Mea Culpa', *Teaching Theology and Religion* 8 (2005): p. 201.

[4] See, e.g., Jan Meyer and Ray Land, 'Threshold Concepts and Troublesome Knowledge: Linkages to Ways of Thinking and Practising within the Disciplines', *ETL Project: Occasional Report* 4 (Edinburgh: Enhancing Teaching-Learning Environments in Undergraduate Courses Project, 2003) http://www.etl.tla.ed.ac.uk//docs/ETLreport4.pdf (accessed 9 Oct. 2013). We do not claim exclusivity for the cross as a threshold concept. Instead, we are suggesting that Christianity has several distinctive and essential claims which might be viewed in this way. Among others, one might include incarnation, and Trinity, each of which could inspire similarly integrative discussions.

[5] Meyer and Land, 'Threshold Concepts', p. 1, use the language of 'portal'.

[6] Meyer and Land, 'Threshold Concepts', pp. 4–5.

[7] See, e.g., how Paul works through the reversal of wisdom and foolishness in light of the cross (1 Cor. 1:18–25) and how Mary's song

highlights the reversal of the ways of the world through her Son's coming (Luke 1:46–55).

[8] Meyer and Land, 'Threshold Concepts', p. 2.

[9] Meyer and Land, 'Threshold Concepts', p. 5.

[10] See Luke Timothy Johnson, 'Imagining the World Scripture Imagines', *Modern Theology* 14:2 (1998): pp. 165–79, on the idea of imaginative viewing of the world through the various lenses offered by Scripture's images.

[11] See, e.g., Gustav Aulén, *Christus Victor: An Historical Study of the Three Main Types of the Idea of the Atonement* (trans. A.G. Herbert; New York: MacMillan, 1978); and James Bielby and Paul R. Eddy, eds, *The Nature of the Atonement: Four Views* (Downers Grove, IL: IVP, 2006).

[12] Steve Chalke and Alan Mann, *The Lost Message of Jesus* (Grand Rapids, MI: Zondervan, 2003), p. 182.

[13] E.g. a symposium held by the Evangelical Alliance UK, in London, 6–8 July 2005 (Daniel Blake, 'Evangelical Alliance Ease Theology Tensions at Atonement Symposium', *Christian Today*, 27 July 2005, n.p. http://www.christiantoday.com/article/evangelical.alliance.ease.theology.tensions.at.atonement.symposium/3542.htm (accessed 29 Dec. 2013); and Steve Jeffery, Mike Ovey and Andrew Sach, eds, *Pierced for Our Transgressions: Rediscovering the Glory of Penal Substitution* (Nottingham: IVP, 2007).

[14] In this sense, we are doing 'located theology' in the belief that Ireland and its distinctive voice and history have an important contribution to make, whose relevance extends beyond the boundaries of this island.

[15] The term 'troublesome' here draws on the previous discussion of Meyer and Land, 'Threshold Concepts and Troublesome Knowledge'.

[16] The term 'engaged theology' is that of Nicholas Wolterstorff, 'To Theologians: From One Who Cares about Theology but Is Not One of You', *Theological Education* 40.2 (2005): p. 81.

Section 1 – The Cross and Reality

[1] Hans Urs von Balthasar, *Unless You Become Like This Child* (San Francisco: Ignatius, 1991), p. 57.

1. Where Are We in Relation to Atonement?

[1] The year before I embarked on postgraduate study in theology, David Tracy published his *Blessed Rage for Order: The New Pluralism in Theology* (New York: Seabury, 1975). If it was 'rage' then, what is it now that the boundaries of pluralism have expanded much further?

[2] Gustav Aulén, *Christus Victor: An Historical Study of the Three Main Types of the Idea of the Atonement* (trans. A.G. Herbert; London: SPCK, 1970).

[3] E.g. Hans Boersma's widely publicized study of *Violence, Hospitality and the Cross: Reappropriating the Atonement Tradition* (Grand Rapids, MI: Baker Academic, 2004) and Robert Sherman's eirenic *King, Priest and Prophet: A Trinitarian Theology of Atonement* (New York/London: T&T Clark International, 2004).

[4] I simply reproduce here the argument of Anselm's *Cur Deus Homo*, in B. Davies and G.R. Evans, *Anselm of Canterbury: The Major Works* (Oxford: OUP, 1998).

[5] See R.E. Weingart, *The Logic of Divine Love: A Critical Analysis of the Soteriology of Peter Abelard* (Oxford: Clarendon, 1970). For that matter, Aulén also got Luther wrong! See Paul Althaus, *The Theology of Martin Luther* (Philadelphia: Fortress, 1966), pp. 218–23.

[6] Alan Richardson, *Creeds in the Making* (London: SCM, 2nd edn, 1941); *A Dictionary of Christian Theology* (ed. Alan Richardson; London: SCM, 1969).

[7] Stephen R. Holmes, *The Wondrous Cross: Atonement and Penal Substitution in the Bible and History* (London: Paternoster, 2007), ch. 3.

[8] G.W.F. Hegel, *Lectures on the Philosophy of World History, Vol. 1: Manuscripts of the Introduction and the Lectures of 1822–3* (ed. and trans. Robert F. Brown and Peter C. Hodgson; Oxford: Clarendon, 2011), p. 88.

[9] For a brief account of the influential positions adopted here by Rita Brock, Joanne Brown and Rebecca Parker, see Linda Peacore, *The Role of Women's Experience in Feminist Theologies of the Atonement* (Eugene, OR: Pickwick, 2010), pp. 101–9.

[10] Brad Jersak and Michael Hardin, eds., *Stricken by God? Nonviolent Identification and the Victory of Christ* (Grand Rapids, MI: Eerdmans, 2007).

[11] See the remarks both in the Foreword and the Preface of Jersak and Hardin, *Stricken by God*.

¹² Charles Taylor, *A Secular Age* (London: Belknap, 2007), especially chs 16–17.

¹³ This reference to the form of my obedience to the editors of this volume will be lost on a generation that knows not the hymn: 'Come Down, O Love Divine . . .' Still, I have taken revenge on the editors by referring to myself, the 'I' and the 'me' rather too often in what follows.

¹⁴ John Calvin, *Institutes of the Christian Religion* (trans. F.L. Battles; Philadelphia: Westminster, 1960), p. 35.

¹⁵ S. Jeffery, M. Ovey and A. Sach, *Pierced for Our Transgressions: Rediscovering the Glory of Penal Substitution* (Nottingham: IVP, 2007).

¹⁶ See Jeffery, Ovey and Sach, *Pierced for Our Transgressions*, ch. 5.

¹⁷ James Denney, *The Death of Christ* (London: Hodder & Stoughton, 1911); Denney, *The Christian Doctrine of Reconciliation* (London: Hodder & Stoughton, 1917); Emil Brunner, *The Mediator* (London: Lutterworth, 1934), Book 3, §2. The broad context in which we should read Barth on this point is well set out by Bruce McCormack in 'The Ontological Presuppositions of Barth's Doctrine of the Atonement', in *The Glory of the Atonement* (ed. Charles Hill and Frank James III; Downers Grove, IL: IVP, 2003).

¹⁸ Presumably Barth and Brunner are judged non-evangelical and thus unworthy of inclusion in this volume among defenders of penal substitution in the twentieth century. A comparison of what Denney himself wrote with a widely used edition of his *The Death of Christ* (London: Tyndale, 1951), published by an evangelical publishing house under the editorship of R.V.G. Tasker, shows clearly that this edition unfortunately conceals the fact that it edits out and amends all the bits in Denney judged 'liberal'. Constraints of time prohibit enquiry into substantive differences between conservative evangelical and nonconservative evangelical defenders of penal substitution. (Denney has the merit of being pushed into the other camp by each side.)

¹⁹ James Denney, *Studies in Theology* (London: Hodder & Stoughton, 1904), p. 104. Denney's habit of capitalizing, rather than putting in lower case, the masculine pronoun reference to God, in accordance with the custom of his day, remains welcome, as far as I am concerned. Lady Helen Oppenheimer wrote in the Preface to *The Hope of Happiness: The Search for a Christian Humanism* (London: SCM, 1983), that this habit, which she followed, was a protection against regarding God as 'anthropomorphically masculine'.

20 The way that we read this text (e.g. alternatively, 'God was reconciling the word to himself through Christ') does not affect the point made, which could easily be couched, instead, in the language of such a text as Colossians 1:19, where the fullness of God is said to dwell in Christ.

21 In this connection, Bushnell was taken up positively, though judged inadequate, in connection with the atonement, by the evangelical theologian, James Orr, *Sidelights on Christian Doctrine* (London: Marshall, 1909), p. 135.

22 See Stephen N. Williams, 'What Christians Believe about Forgiveness', *Studies in Christian Ethics* 24.2 (2011): pp. 147–56.

23 The phrase, of course, picks up C.S. Lewis's imaginative analogy of atonement in *The Lion, the Witch and the Wardrobe* (London: Lions, 1980). See the interesting essay by Charles Taliaferro, 'A Narnian Theory of the Atonement', *SJT* 41.1 (1988): pp. 75–92.

24 See Stephen N. Williams, *Revelation and Reconciliation: A Window on Modernity* (Cambridge: CUP, 1995), pp. 155–7.

25 I do, however, stand by a form of it: see Stephen N. Williams, 'Atonement: the Penal View', *Books & Culture* 11.1 (2005): pp. 20–22.

26 A trawl through Jersak and Hardin, *Stricken by God*, illustrates this point. I am not thinking here of more sophisticated investigations which yield the possibility that Anselmian 'satisfaction' is not all that far from the conceptual neighbourhood of punishment or more detailed historical investigations that catch Anselm using 'punishment' language for the atonement in works other than *Cur Deus Homo*. Even where it is acknowledged that Anselm's view is non-penal, it is surprising to find this acknowledgement so casually tucked away in a footnote, as is the case with Boersma, *Violence, Hospitality and the Cross*, p. 158, n.16.

27 Boersma, *Violence, Hospitality and the Cross*, p. 35.

28 Reading Thomas Hardy's fine 'Afterwards', she astonished me by recoiling from what she called this cross-dominated poem of his. The poem has nothing to do with the cross, but it uses the word 'crossing' and that triggered her reaction. 'Cross' and violence seem to be deeply associated in her psyche and not just in the obvious way involved in the fact of crucifixion.

29 However, it is impossible to follow some feminist rhetoric on this point. For example, Lee Quimby castigates fundamentalist American patriotic patriarchalism for accepting 'gender oppositions that divide

women into virgins and Jezebels'. See, Lee Quimby, 'The Unsettling of the Fundamentalist Mindset: Shifts in Apocalyptic Belief in Contemporary Conservative Christianity', in *The Fundamentalist Mindset* (ed. Charles B. Strozier, David M. Terman and James W. Jones; Oxford: OUP, 2010), p. 121. My problem is that, at the same time, she slams fundamentalist mothers who exercise control by home schooling (p. 126). How can fundamentalist mothers be any women's role models if your world is divided into virgins and Jezebels? They are neither.

30 It has sometimes been claimed that Moltmann has no doctrine of the atonement. See, e.g., Alan Lewis, 'The Burial of God: Rupture and Resumption as the Story of Salvation', *SJT* 40.3 (1987): pp. 335–62. That may be so, but insistence on the unity of the Son and Father's experience is a strength in Jürgen Moltmann, *The Crucified God* (London: SCM, 1974).

31 Richard Dawkins, *The God Delusion* (London: Bantam, 2007), p. 287, describes the 'atonement, the central doctrine of Christianity' as 'vicious, sado-masochistic and repellent', not to mention 'barking mad'.

Does Christianity Really Need a Doctrine of the Atonement?

1 Maurice Wiles, 'Christianity without Incarnation?', in *The Myth of God Incarnate* (ed. John Hick; London: SCM, 1977), pp. 1–10.

2 'Crucicentrism' – a focus on the doctrine of the atonement – forms one element of David Bebbington's 'evangelical quadrilateral'. David W. Bebbington, *Evangelicalism in Modern Britain: A History from the 1730s to the 1980s* (London: Unwin Hyman, 1989), pp. 2–17.

3 The early development of Christian art is documented by Robin Jensen, *Face to Face: Portraits of the Divine in Early Christianity* (Grand Rapids, MI: Fortress, 2005). Jensen suggests that the emphasis in these early centuries was on pictures that recalled biblical scenes representing healing and flourishing.

4 *The Passion of the Christ* (2004). A number of commentators pointed to the links between Gibson's violent portrayal of the passion and the violence embodied in medieval passion plays.

5 The Centre for Christianity and Culture at the University of York (http://www.christianityandculture.org.uk/) is the source for *Images of Salvation*, a CD resource relating biblical themes to medieval art.

The medieval developments can be placed in the wider context of the development of Christian art by reference to Neil McGregor and Erika Langmuir, *Seeing Salvation* (London: BBC, 2000).

6   The *Stabat Mater* was written as a Latin hymn in the thirteenth century. It reflects the intensity of Franciscan devotion to the crucified Christ and is usually attributed to Jacopone da Todi (1230–1306).

7   For example, Fanny J. Crosby, 'At the Cross There's Room!' Lyrics: http://www.hymntime.com/tch/htm/a/t/h/athcross.htm (accessed 10 Dec. 2013).

8   Stuart Townend's cross-centred songs, 'How Deep the Father's Love for Us', *Church Hymnal* (Oxford: OUP, 5th edn, 2000), p. 224; and 'In Christ Alone' http://www.stuarttownend.co.uk/song/in-christ-alone/ (accessed 12 Dec. 2013), are currently among the most popular in evangelical and charismatic worship.

9   Jürgen Moltmann, *The Crucified God: The Cross of Christ as the Foundation and Criticism of Christian Theology* (trans. R.A. Wilson and John Bowden; London: SCM, 1974).

10 The phrase was coined by the American biblical commentator and controversialist, Walter Wink.

11 Wilfred Owen, 'At a Calvary near the Ancre' http://www.english.emory.edu/LostPoets /Owen.html (accessed 10 Dec. 2013).

12 Rebecca Ann Parker and Rita Brock, *Saving Paradise: How Christianity Traded Love of This World for Crucifixion and Empire* (Boston: Beacon, 2008).

13 Parker and Brock, *Saving Paradise*, p. ix.

14 Parker and Brock, *Saving Paradise*, p. xix.

15 A.E. Sheckler and M. J. Winn Leith, 'The Crucifixion Conundrum and the Santa Sabina Doors', *Harvard Theological Review* 103.1 (2010): pp. 67–88.

16 R. Stalley, 'European Art and the Irish High Crosses', *Proceedings of the Royal Irish Academy Section C: Archaeology, Celtic Studies, History, Linguistics, Literature* 90C (1990): pp. 135–58.

17 For this reason, I would argue that Anselm's atonement theology is one of the most satisfactory, precisely because, as the title *Cur Deus Homo (Why God Became Human)* suggests, it understands the cross entirely within a discussion of the incarnation. See my 'How Great the Debt We Owe: Can Anselm's *Cur Deus Homo* Say Anything to Contemporary Culture?' *Epworth Review* 36.1 (2009): pp. 18–28.

18 David Bentley Hart, *The Beauty of the Infinite: The Aesthetics of Christian Truth* (Grand Rapids, MI: Eerdmans, 2003), p. 391. The whole of

Hart's lengthy section on salvation is an expression, in the language of rigorous systematic theology, of the traditional Eastern emphasis on the incarnation.

[19] E.g. in Stuart Townend, 'How Deep the Father's Love for Us'.

[20] 'In a word, He died, because it was so expedient, that by His Death He might kill death. God died, that an exchange might be effected by a kind of heavenly contract, that man might not see death. For Christ is God, but He died not in that Nature in which He is God. For the same Person is God and man; for God and man is one Christ. The human nature . . . was assumed, that we might be changed for the better; He did not degrade the Divine . . . Nature down to the lower.' Augustine, *Sermon XXX* http://www.ewtn.com/library/PATRISTC/PNI6-7.TXT (accessed 12 Dec. 2013).

[21] For example, Elizabeth A. Johnson, *She Who Is: The Mystery of God in Feminist Theological Discourse* (New York: Crossroad, 1993). It should also be noted that feminists have been among the fiercest critics of the 'suffering God' theology, pointing out that this can be used to convince women that it is their suffering that links them to God rather than God who liberates them from suffering.

[22] So, e.g., Paul Fiddes, *The Creative Suffering of God* (Oxford: OUP, 1992).

[23] See, e.g., David Bentley Hart, *The Doors of the Sea: Where Was God in the Tsunami?* (Grand Rapids, MI: Eerdmans, 2005).

[24] Kharalambos Anstall, 'Juridical Justification Theology and a Statement of the Orthodox Teaching', in *Stricken by God? Nonviolent Identification and the Victory of Christ* (ed. Brad Jersak and Michael Hardin; Grand Rapids, MI: Eerdmans, 2007), p. 491.

[25] Karl Barth, *Church Dogmatics, Vol. 2: The Doctrine of God Part 2* (ed. G.W. Bromiley and T.F. Torrance; London: T&T Clark, 1957), p. 171.

Reconciliation Between Blame and Lament

[1] James P. Danaher, 'A Contemporary Perspective on Atonement', *Irish Theological Quarterly* 69.3 (2004): pp. 281–94 (281).

[2] Danaher, 'Contemporary Perspective', p. 282.

[3] Danaher, 'Contemporary Perspective', p. 281.

[4] Danaher, 'Contemporary Perspective', p. 282.

[5] Danaher, 'Contemporary Perspective', p. 282.

[6] Danaher, 'Contemporary Perspective', p. 283, quoting Peter Paul

Waldenstrom. See David M. Gustafson, 'J.G. Princell and the Waldenströmian View of the Atonement', in *Trinity Journal* 20.2 (1999): p. 192.

7 Danaher makes a distinction between forgiveness and justice in this regard. In the case of justice the guilty pay for the harm done to the innocent and this may bring restoration of relationship. In the case of forgiveness the innocent relinquish retribution and thus payment is made. He suggests we should understand atonement more in terms of forgiveness than justice. Danaher, 'Contemporary Perspective', p. 286.

8 Hermann Häring, 'Disaster for the World and Human Disaster', *Concilium* (2004) 1: p. 57.

9 Paul Ricoeur, 'Evil as a Challenge to Philosophy and Theology', *Figuring the Sacred* (Minneapolis: Fortress, 1995), pp. 249–61.

10 Ricoeur, 'Evil as a Challenge', p. 249.

11 Cf. Häring, 'Disaster for the World', pp. 57–76.

12 Häring, 'Disaster for the World', p. 64.

13 For an excellent analysis of the relationship between lament and theodicy, cf. John M. Godfrey, *The Place of Lament and the 'Catharsis of the Complaint' in Response to the Problem of Evil* (Braemor Series 2; Dublin: Church of Ireland, 2013).

14 Häring, 'Disaster for the World', p. 65.

15 Ricoeur, 'Evil as a Challenge', p. 250.

16 Ricoeur, 'Evil as a Challenge', p. 250.

17 Ricoeur, 'Evil as a Challenge', p. 250.

18 Ricoeur, 'Evil as a Challenge', p. 250.

19 Lothar Ullrich, 'Reconciliation', in *Handbook of Catholic Theology* (ed. W. Beinert and F. Schüssler Fiorenza; New York: Herder & Herder, 2000), pp. 571–5 (574).

20 Ullrich, 'Reconciliation', p. 574.

21 For one approach, cf. Cathriona Russell, 'Environmental Perspectives on the Genesis Flood Narrative', in *Opening Heaven's Floodgates: The Genesis Flood Narrative, Its Context and Reception* (Biblical Intersections 12; ed. Jason M. Silverman; Piscataway, NJ: Georgias, 2013), pp. 461–87.

22 Jacques Haers SJ, 'Reconciliation in Times of Worldwide Environmental Crisis', *Concilium* (2013) 1: pp. 42–52.

23 Haers, 'Reconciliation', p. 46.

24 Haers, 'Reconciliation', p. 46.

[25] Haers, 'Reconciliation', p. 47.
[26] Haers, 'Reconciliation', p. 48.
[27] Haers, 'Reconciliation', p. 49.
[28] Haers, 'Reconciliation', p. 69.
[29] Haers, 'Reconciliation', p. 72.
[30] Danaher, 'Contemporary Perspective', p. 287.
[31] Danaher, 'Contemporary Perspective', p. 281.

2. The Cross and the Redemption of the Cosmos

[1] Ronald W. Numbers, *The Creationists: From Scientific Creationism to Intelligent Design* (Cambridge, MA: Harvard University Press, 2006).
[2] As noted by M.B. Roberts, 'An Anglican Priest's Perspective on the Doctrine of Creation in the Church Today', in *Geology and Religion: A History of Harmony and Hostility* (Special Publication 310; ed. M. Kölbl-Ebert; London: Geological Society, 2009): pp. 342f. A different view states that 'this curious and disturbing phenomenon . . . is scarcely to be encountered in Britain' (John Polkinghorne, *Reason and Reality: The Relationship Between Science and Theology* [London: SPCK, 2010], p. 60); 'creationism is a fringe movement in Britain which is so small as to be politically insignificant' (Tina Beattie, *The New Atheists: The Twilight of Reason and the War on Religion* [London: Darton, Longman and Todd, 2007], pp. 5f.).
[3] Quoting Psalm 102:25ff. This is part of a passage which is often used as the epistle for Holy Communion on Christmas Day.
[4] Edward H. Bickersteth, 'Peace, Perfect Peace, in This Dark World of Sin?' *Church Hymnal* (Oxford: OUP, 5th edn, 2000), p. 1265.
[5] David Gillett, *Trust and Obey: Explorations in Evangelical Spirituality* (London: Darton Longman & Todd, 1993), p. 30.
[6] Robert Grant, 'O Worship the King, All Glorious Above,' *Church of Ireland Hymnal* (Oxford: OUP, 5th edn, 2000), p. 69.
[7] Ian Fraser, 'Lord, Bring the Day to Pass', *Church of Ireland Hymnal* (Oxford: OUP, 5th edn, 2000), p. 95.
[8] H. Paul Santmire, *The Travail of Nature: The Ambiguous Ecological Promise of Christian Theology* (Minneapolis: Fortress, 1997), pp. 217f.
[9] Ron Elsdon, *Greenhouse Theology: Biblical Perspectives on Caring for Creation* (Eastbourne: Monarch, 1992).
[10] 'A good and broad land, a land flowing with milk and honey' (Exod. 3:8).

[11] This is irrespective of how one understands the hotly debated idea of the 'fallen-ness' of creation.

[12] N.T. Wright, *Colossians and Philemon: An Introduction and Commentary* (Tyndale New Testament Commentaries 12; Downers Grove, IL: IVP, 1986), p. 70.

[13] N.T. Wright, *The Resurrection of the Son of God* (London: SPCK, 2006), p. 606.

[14] Michael S. Northcott, *The Environment and Christian Ethics* (Cambridge: CUP, 1996), pp. 193ff.

[15] E.g. Elsdon, *Greenhouse Theology*, pp. 155–72; Richard Bauckham, *Bible and Ecology: Rediscovering the Community of Creation* (London: Darton, Longman & Todd, 2010), pp. 95–101; Douglas J. Moo, 'Eschatology and Environmental Ethics: On the Importance of Biblical Theology to Creation Care', in *Keeping God's Earth: The Global Environment in Biblical Perspective* (ed. Noah J. Toly and Daniel I. Block; Nottingham: Apollos, 2010), pp. 23–43; Douglas J. Green, 'When the Gardener Returns: An Ecological Perspective on Adam's Dominion', in Toly and Block (eds), *Keeping God's Earth*, pp. 267–75; Tom Wright, *Surprised by Hope* (London: SPCK, 2007).

[16] Colin E. Gunton, *Christ and Creation* (Carlisle: Paternoster, 1992), p. 33.

[17] Andrew T. Lincoln, *Ephesians* (WBC 42; Dallas: Word, 2002), p. 33.

[18] Ralph P. Martin, 'Reconciliation and Forgiveness in Colossians', in *Reconciliation and Hope: New Testament Essays on Atonement and Eschatology Presented to L.L. Morris on His 60th Birthday* (ed. Robert Banks; Grand Rapids, MI: Eerdmans, 1974).

[19] This, of course, also echoes the language of Ephesians 1:10 ('to gather up all things in him, things in heaven and things on earth').

[20] This kind of interpretation is reviewed by Peter T. O'Brien, *Colossians–Philemon* (WBC 44; Dallas: Word, 2002), p. 53.

[21] Martin, 'Reconciliation and Forgiveness', p. 119. Various explanations have been proposed for the nature of a possible Colossian heresy. The details need not concern us here, but are treated in various commentaries and monographs. See, e.g., C.E. Arnold, *The Colossian Syncretism: The Interface between Christianity and Folk Belief at Colossae* (Grand Rapids, MI: Baker, 1996); Vicky S. Balabanski, 'Hellenistic Cosmology and the Letter to the Colossians: Towards an Ecological Hermeneutic', in *Ecological Hermeneutics: Biblical, Historical and Theological Perspectives* (ed. David G. Horrell, Cherryl Hunt, Christopher Southgate and Francesca Stavrakopoulou; London: T&T Clark, 2010), pp. 94–107.

[22] James D.G. Dunn, *The Theology of Paul the Apostle* (Edinburgh: T&T Clark, 1998), pp. 100f.

[23] Cherryl Hunt, David G. Horrell and Christopher Southgate, 'An Environmental Mantra? Ecological Interest in Romans 8:19–23 and a Modest Proposal for Its Narrative Interpretation', *Journal of Theological Studies* 59 (2008): pp. 546–79, esp. 560–63.

[24] C.E.B. Cranfield, 'Some Observations on Romans 8:19–21', in *Reconciliation and Hope* (ed. Banks), p. 226.

[25] Tom Wright, *Virtue Reborn* (London: SPCK, 2010), pp. 79f.

[26] Polkinghorne, *Reason and Reality*, p. 81.

[27] Freeman J. Dyson, *Disturbing the Universe* (New York: Harper & Row, 1979), pp. 225–38.

[28] Dyson, *Disturbing the Universe*, p. 82. He also suggests that modern understandings of the 'togetherness-in-separation' of quantum theory give an 'elementary hint' of what is to come (*Disturbing the Universe*, pp. 94, 103).

[29] One recent discussion focuses in a restricted way on issues of God's omniscience and whether he is 'to blame' for natural evil. John Turl, 'Theodicy and Geodesy: Who Is to Blame?', *Science and Christian Belief* 23 (2011): pp. 49, 66.

[30] 'Earthquakes are signals of activity. They tell us the story of plate tectonics as it is happening today'. Peter J. Wyllie, *The Way the Earth Works: An Introduction to the New Global Geology and Its Revolutionary Development* (New York: John Wiley and Sons, 1976), p. 61.

[31] David Wilkinson, *The Message of Creation* (Leicester: IVP, 2002), p. 234.

[32] John Polkinghorne, 'Scripture and an Evolving Creation', *Science and Christian Belief* 21 (2009): p. 169.

[33] Wright, *Surprised by Hope*, pp. 104–6. James Dunn, however, uses the phrase 'out-of-joint' in a way more directly related to human sinfulness; J.D.G. Dunn, *Romans 1 – 8* (WBC 38A; Waco, TX: Word, 1988), p. 487. See also R.J. Berry, 'Adam or Adamah?', *Science and Christian Belief* 23 (2012): p. 46.

[34] Bauckham, *Bible and Ecology*, p. 60.

[35] Bauckham, *Bible and Ecology*, p. 70.

[36] Bauckham, *Bible and Ecology*, p. 102. 'To speak in this way does not imply the necessary re-creation of everything that was. The anaerobic unicellular life of early Earth was a staging post of biological evolution and we do not have to suppose that it, as such, must reappear somewhere in the new heavens and the new earth. Its good will

be sufficiently preserved in a continuing destiny for that to which it gave rise.'

37 Richard Bauckham and Trevor Hart, *Hope Against Hope: Christian Eschatology in Contemporary Context* (London: Darton, Longman & Todd, 1999), pp. 131f.

38 'Hubble takes us to within a stone's throw of the big bang itself' (Massimo Stiavelli, Space Telescope Science Institute in Baltimore, MD, and HUDF project lead), quoted in 'Hubble's Deepest View Ever of the Universe Unveils Earliest Galaxies' http://hubblesite. org/newscenter/archive/releases/2004/07/text/ (accessed 13 Dec. 2013).

39 Bauckham and Hart, *Hope Against Hope*, p. 107.

40 C.S. Lewis, *The Last Battle* (London: HarperCollins, 2009), p. 224.

3. The Cross and God's Embrace of Suffering

1 E.g. Pss. 6; 7; 13; 22.

2 I have argued this case more fully in Richard Bauckham, *Jesus and the God of Israel: God Crucified and Other Studies on the New Testament's Christology of Divine Identity* (Milton Keynes: Paternoster/Grand Rapids, MI: Eerdmans, 2008), ch. 8 ('God's Self-Identification with the Godforsaken in the Gospel of Mark').

3 Shusaku Endo, *A Life of Jesus* (trans. Richard A. Schuchert; New York: Paulist, 1978), pp. 85–6.

4 Jürgen Moltmann, *The Crucified God* (trans. R.A. Wilson and John Bowden; London: SCM, 1974), p. 46.

5 Emi Mase-Hasegawa, *Christ in Japanese Culture: Theological Themes in Shusaku Endo's Literary Works* (Brill's Japanese Studies Library 28; Leiden: Brill, 2008), p. 78.

6 Shusaku Endo, *Deep River* (trans. Van C. Gessel; London: Hodder & Stoughton, 1995), p. 119.

7 Moltmann, *The Crucified God*, pp. 242–3, and frequently in his later writings.

Spiritual Exercise: Engaging Lament

[1] This exercise is inspired by the Ignatian Examen. For more on the Examen, see http://www.ignatianspirituality.com/ignatian-prayer/the-examen/ (accessed 29 Jan. 2014).

[2] These questions are adapted from http://www.ignatianspirituality.com/ignatian-prayer/the-examen/how-can-i-pray/ (accessed 29 Jan. 2014).

Section 2 – Broken Relationships in a Fractured World

[1] Edward Farley, 'Four Pedagogical Mistakes: *A Mea Culpa*', *Teaching Theology and Religion* 9 (2005): p. 202.

4. The Cross and the Reconciliation of Enemies

[1] The programme offered by the Irish School of Ecumenics, Trinity College Dublin, was launched in Belfast as a Master's programme in Reconciliation Studies in 2001, and was revised into a Conflict Resolution and Reconciliation programme from Sept 2010. A distinctive feature of the programme is that it addresses armed conflict between groups, and especially conflicts in which religious identities may have a role. For more on the programme, see www.tcd.ie/ise/belfast.

[2] On the ambivalence of religion, see Scott R. Appleby, *The Ambivalence of the Sacred: Religion, Violence, and Reconciliation* (Lanham, MD: Rowman & Littlefield, 2000).

[3] Joseph Liechty and Cecelia Clegg, *Moving Beyond Sectarianism: Religion, Conflict and Reconciliation in Northern Ireland* (Dublin: Columba, 2001).

[4] The notions of 'moral imagination' and 'conflict transformation' are key terms in the work of Mennonite scholar and practitioner John Paul Lederach. See especially John Paul Lederach, *The Little Book of Conflict Transformation* (Intercourse, PA: Good Books, 2003); *The Moral Imagination: The Art and Soul of Building Peace* (Oxford: OUP, 2005).

[5] Liechty and Clegg, *Moving Beyond Sectarianism*, pp. 103–7.

[6] Liechty and Clegg, *Moving Beyond Sectarianism*, pp. 185–95. Both the spectrum and the pyramid frameworks can be traced back to

the influential work of others, including the writing of John Paul Lederach. Liechty and Clegg do not claim originality for either tool, but their work in adapting them and developing them as part of an action research project to address sectarianism in Northern Ireland was, and remains, a pioneering achievement.

7 Diagram based on the version presented in Craig Sands, *Moving Beyond Sectarianism: A Resource for Adult Education – Continuing Education* (Dublin and Belfast: Irish School of Ecumenics, 2001), p. 30. Reprinted with permission.

8 See especially the criticisms offered in Joanne Carlson Brown and Carole R. Bohn, eds, *Christianity, Patriarchy, and Abuse: A Feminist Critique* (New York: Pilgrim, 1989).

9 See especially the trilogy, Walter Wink, *Naming the Powers: The Language of Power in the New Testament* (Philadelphia: Fortress, 1984); *Unmasking the Powers: The Invisible Forces that Determine Human Existence* (Philadelphia: Fortress, 1986); *Engaging the Powers: Discernment and Resistance in a World of Dominion* (Minneapolis: Fortress, 1992). See also Walter Wink, *When the Powers Fall: Reconciliation in the Healing of Nations* (Minneapolis: Fortress, 1998); *Jesus and Nonviolence: A Third Way* (Minneapolis: Fortress, 2003).

10 See especially, René Girard, *Violence and the Sacred* (trans. Patrick Gregory; Baltimore: Johns Hopkins, 1979); *Things Hidden since the Foundation of the World* (Stanford, CA: Stanford University Press, 1987); *The Scapegoat* (New York: Athlone, 1988).

11 See, e.g., Mark Heim, *Saved from Sacrifice: A Theology of the Cross* (Grand Rapids, MI: Eerdmans, 2006); and J. Denny Weaver, *The Nonviolent Atonement* (Grand Rapids, MI: Eerdmans, 2001). Heim offers a Girardian critique of sacrifice and an alternative reading of the cross. Weaver offers a sustained critique of Anselmian satisfaction theory and suggests an alternative approach to atonement based on a narrative version of *Christus Victor*.

12 See M. Hengel, *Crucifixion in the Ancient World and the Folly of the Cross* (trans. J. Bowden; Philadelphia: Fortress, 1977 [German orig. 1976]), esp. pp. 22–32. For other recent treatments see R.E. Brown, *Death of the Messiah* (2 vols; Anchor Bible Reference Library; New York: Doubleday, 1994), and the exhaustive bibliography, pp. 885–7.

13 M. Coleman, 'Fatal Charades', *Journal of Roman Studies* 80 (1990): pp. 44–73 (55).

14 Martial, *Lib. spect.* 7 cited in Coleman, 'Fatal Charades', p. 65.

[15] See Richard Harries, *The Passion in Art* (Ashgate Studies in Theology, Imagination and the Arts; Burlington, VT: Ashgate, 2004), pp. 10–11.

[16] For a wider discussion of dehumanization and human evil, see James Dawes, *Evil Men* (Cambridge, MA: Harvard University Press, 2013). For more on humiliation, see William I. Miller, *Humiliation: And Other Essays on Honor, Social Discomfort and Violence* (London: Cornell University Press, 1993).

5. The Cross and the Reconciliation of Gender

[1] Rosemary Radford Ruether, *To Change the World: Christology and Cultural Criticism* (London: SCM, 1981), pp. 45–56.

[2] A reference to the fundamental impossibility of a woman being ordained in Holy Orders, so that even though a church might go through a ceremony which pronounces her a priest, ontologically, she still is not a priest.

[3] CDF, *Declaration on the Question of the Admission of Women to the Ministerial Priesthood* 27, Vatican City, 15 October 1976.

[4] Ruether, *To Change the World*, p. 47.

[5] There were a number of Catholic theologians who had dealt with the issue of women's ordination, but they had rarely considered this problem. See, e.g., Eric Doyle OFM, 'God and the Feminine', *The Clergy Review* 56 (1971).

[6] Rosemary Radford Ruether, 'The Liberation of Christology from Patriarchy', in *Feminist Theology: A Reader* (ed. Ann Loades; Louisville, KY: Westminster John Knox, 1990), p. 140.

[7] See, e.g., Carol Christ and Judith Plaskow, eds, *Womanspirit Rising* (San Francisco: Harper and Row, 1979); and Elisabeth Johnson, *She Who Is: The Mystery of God in Feminist Theological Discourse* (New York: Crossroad, 1993).

[8] Rita Nakashima Brock, 'The Feminist Redemption of Christ', in *Christian Feminism* (ed. Judith Weidman; New York: Harper & Row, 1984), p. 68.

[9] Phyllis Trible, *God and the Rhetoric of Sexuality* (Philadelphia: Fortress, 1978), p. 4.

[10] Helen Sterk, 'Gender Relations and Narrative in a Reformed Church Setting', in *After Eden: Facing the Challenge of Gender Reconciliation* (ed. Mary Stewart Van Leeuwen; Carlisle: Paternoster, 1993), p. 191.

[11] Trible, *God and the Rhetoric of Sexuality*, p. xvi.

[12] Phyllis Trible, 'Depatriarchalizing in Biblical Interpretation', *Journal of the American Academy of Religion* 41.1 (1973): pp. 30–48.

[13] Mary Daly, *Beyond God the Father* (Boston: Beacon, 1973), p. 27.

[14] Letty M. Russell, 'Authority and Challenge of Feminist Interpretation', in *Feminist Interpretation of the Bible* (ed. Letty M. Russell; Oxford: Basil Blackwell, 1985). See also Letty M. Russell, *The Liberating Word: A Guide to Nonsexist Interpretations of the Bible* (Philadelphia: Westminster, 1976).

[15] Phyllis Trible, *Texts of Terror: Literary-Feminist Readings of Biblical Narrative* (Philadelphia: Fortress, 1984).

[16] Virginia R. Mollenkott cited in David E. Anderson, 'Religion in America', *Ludington Daily News*, 29 December 1975.

[17] Virginia R. Mollenkott, *Women, Men and the Bible* (New York: Crossroad, 1989), no page, http://www.ministryforwomen.org/scriptur/mollenk2.asp (accessed 21 Dec. 2013).

[18] See Richard Clark Kroeger and Catherine Clark Kroeger, *I Suffer Not a Woman: Rethinking 1 Timothy 2:11–15 in the Light of Ancient Evidence* (Grand Rapids, MI: Baker Book House, 1992).

[19] Rosemary Radford Ruether, *Sexism and God-Talk: Towards a Feminist Theology* (Boston: Beacon, 1983), p. 14.

[20] Elisabeth Schüssler Fiorenza, 'Feminist Theology as a Critical Theology of Liberation', *TS* 36 (1975): p. 612.

[21] Elisabeth Schüssler Fiorenza, *Bread Not Stone: The Challenge of Feminist Biblical Interpretation* (Boston: Beacon, 1984), pp. xv, 6.

[22] Re-Imagining: A Global Theological Conference by Women: For Men and Women, Minnesota, November 1993.

[23] Daphne Hampson, *Theology and Feminism* (Oxford: Basil Blackwell, 1990), p. 122.

[24] Valerie Saiving, 'The Human Situation: A Feminine View', *Journal of Religion* 40.2 (1960): pp. 100–12.

[25] Anne Wilson Schaef, *Women's Reality: An Emerging Female System in the White Male Society* (San Francisco: Perennial Library, 1985), p. 168.

[26] Grace Jantzen, *Power, Gender and Christian Mysticism* (Cambridge: CUP, 1996), p. 66.

[27] See Dorothee Sölle, *Suffering* (trans. Everett R. Kalin; Philadelphia: Fortress, 1984) and the discussion in Jürgen Moltmann and Elisabeth Moltmann Wendel, *Passion for God: Theology in Two Voices* (Louisville, KY: Westminster John Knox, 2003), pp. 82–3.

28 Ruether, *To Change the World*, pp. 27–8.
29 Ruether, *Sexism*, p. 131.
30 Mary Grey, *Redeeming the Dream: Feminism, Redemption and Christian Tradition* (London: SPCK, 1989), p. 175.

Group Activity: Letter Writing

1 While this exercise is designed as a group activity, individuals may find it useful as well.

6. The Cross and Our Aspiration for a Common Doctrine of Redemption: A Dialogue

1 G.K. Chesterton, 'The Secret Garden', *The Complete Father Brown Stories* (London: Wordsworth, 2006), p. 33.
2 Steve Chalke and Alan Mann, *The Lost Message of Jesus* (Grand Rapids, MI: Zondervan, 2003), p. 182.
3 Irenaeus, *Adv. Haer.* 4.6.5.

7. The Cross and Eucharistic Sacrifice: A Personal Reflection on an Ecumenical Struggle

1 John Calvin, *Institutes of the Christian Religion* 4.18.1 (trans. Henry Beveridge; London: James Clarke & Co., 1962), 2:607.
2 Calvin, *Institutes*, 2:609.
3 World Council of Churches, *Baptism, Eucharist and Ministry* (Geneva: WCC, 1982).
4 George H. Tavard, 'The Anglican–Roman Catholic Agreed Statements and Their Reception', *TS* 41.1 (1980): pp. 94–5.
5 E.g. Christopher Cocksworth, 'Holding Together: Catholic Evangelical Worship in the Spirit', *Anvil* 22.1 (2004): p. 9.
6 I am aware that the notion of Christ's real presence in the Eucharist also represents a significant ecumenical barrier to many Protestants. However, this notion was less problematic to the Reformers than the idea of eucharistic sacrifice. To this extent, the latter doctrine operates as a more serious obstacle to theological rapprochement.

7   Leonardo De Chirico, 'The Cross and the Eucharist: The Doctrine of the Atonement According to the Catholic Church', *European Journal of Theology* 8.1 (1999): p. 55.

8   De Chirico, 'Cross and Eucharist', p. 58.

9   Leonardo De Chirico, *Evangelical Theological Perspectives on Post-Vatican II Roman Catholicism* (Oxford: Peter Lang, 2003).

10 John Stott, *Evangelical Truth: A Plea for Unity* (Leicester: IVP, 1999).

11 Stott, *Evangelical Truth*, pp. 40–41.

12 De Chirico, *Evangelical Theological Perspectives*, p. 275.

13 Leonardo De Chirico, 'The Blurring of Time Distinctions in Roman Catholicism', *Themelios* 29.2 (2004): p. 41.

14 *Catechism of the Catholic Church* (London: Geoffrey Chapman, 1994).

15 While fewer than thirty paragraphs are dedicated to the atonement, almost 100 paragraphs treat the sacrament of the Eucharist. See De Chirico, 'Cross and Eucharist', p. 54.

16 De Chirico, 'Cross and Eucharist', p. 54.

17 De Chirico, 'Cross and Eucharist', p. 56. See also *Catechism of the Catholic Church*, p. 141.

18 De Chirico, 'Cross and Eucharist', p. 56.

19 De Chirico, 'Blurring of Time Distinctions', p. 44. See also *Catechism of the Catholic Church*, pp. 306–7.

20 De Chirico, 'Blurring of Time Distinctions', p. 46.

21 Roger Beckwith does define the basic argument against an ARCIC-type interpretation of *anamnesis*. Beckwith argues that *anamnesis* etymologically has nothing to do with the sort of mystical 'remembrance' suggested by theologians such as Odo Casel and Gregory Dix. Its meaning is much more prosaic and he claims the elaborate conjectures of Dix et al. are unscientific and fanciful. Beckwith suggests that the first-century mystery religions are the more likely source for the sort of notion promoted by supporters of eucharistic sacrifice and that ideas emanating from that source have been transposed into an imaginary first-century Jewish Passover context. Thus the scholarly basis for such an involved reading of *anamnesis* as that suggested by ARCIC is deemed to be relatively weak. See R.T. Beckwith, *Christ's Presence and Sacrifice: The Agreed Statement on Eucharistic Doctrine with a Response* (London: The Church Book Room, 1973).

22 'Joint Declaration on the Doctrine of Justification by the Lutheran World Federation and the Catholic Church', para. 15 http://www.

vatican.va/roman_curia/pontifical_councils/chrstuni/documents/ rc_pc_chrstuni_doc_31101999 (accessed 29 Dec. 2013).

23 Tracey Rowland, *Benedict XVI: A Guide for the Perplexed* (London: Continuum, 2010), p. 139.

24 See the forthcoming monograph, Patrick G. McGlinchey, *Ratzinger's Augustinianism and Evangelicalism* (Milton Keynes: Paternoster, 2017).

25 Congregation for the Doctrine of the Faith, *Dominus Iesus* (London: Catholic Truth Society, 2000), para. 17.

26 For a positive Protestant assessment of *Dominus Iesus* see Timothy George, 'Symposium on the Declaration *Dominus Iesus*', *Pro Ecclesia* 10.1 (2001): p. 8.

27 Joseph Ratzinger, 'Luther and the Unity of the Churches', *Communio: International Catholic Review* 11 (1984): pp. 210–26.

28 Ratzinger, 'Luther', pp. 215–16.

29 Joseph Ratzinger, 'Is the Eucharist a Sacrifice?' *Concilium* 4.3 (1967): pp. 35–40; and John Jay Hughes, 'Eucharistic Sacrifice: Transcending the Reformation Deadlock', *Worship* 43.9 (1969): pp. 532–44.

30 Ratzinger, 'Is the Eucharist a Sacrifice?', p. 35.

31 Ratzinger, 'Is the Eucharist a Sacrifice?', p. 35.

32 Ratzinger, 'Is the Eucharist a Sacrifice?', p. 36.

33 Ratzinger, 'Is the Eucharist a Sacrifice?', p. 36.

34 Ratzinger, 'Is the Eucharist a Sacrifice?', p. 36.

35 Ratzinger, 'Is the Eucharist a Sacrifice?', p. 36.

36 Ratzinger, 'Is the Eucharist a Sacrifice?', p. 36.

37 The second 'take-off' point is the centrality of thanksgiving to the Eucharist, and the argument which Ratzinger pursues in the light of this depends on the very same concept or notion that undergirds everything he says about the first 'take-off' point. I have chosen therefore not to dwell upon it.

38 Ratzinger, 'Is the Eucharist a Sacrifice?', p. 36.

39 Ratzinger, 'Is the Eucharist a Sacrifice?', p. 36.

40 Martin Luther, *Martin Luthers Werke* (Weimar: Weimerer Ausgabe, no year), 18:205. Cited in Ratzinger, 'Is the Eucharist a Sacrifice?', p. 36.

41 Ratzinger, 'Is the Eucharist a Sacrifice?', p. 39.

42 Ratzinger, 'Is the Eucharist a Sacrifice?', p. 39.

43 Hughes, 'Transcending the Deadlock', p. 538.

44 Ratzinger, 'Is the Eucharist a Sacrifice?', p. 36.

[45] Pope Francis, 'Easter Vigil Homily' http://www.catholicherald.co.uk/news/2013/03/30/full-text-of-pope-franciss-homily-at-the-easter-vigil/ (accessed 27 Nov. 2013).

[46] De Chirico, 'Blurring of Time Distinctions', p. 44.

[47] The phrase in the *Catechism* cited by De Chirico to illustrate the church's monopoly on the cross. *Catechism of the Catholic Church*, pp. 306–7.

[48] *Catechism of the Catholic Church*, p. 141, italics mine.

[49] Alasdair Heron, *Table and Tradition: Towards an Ecumenical Understanding of the Eucharist* (Edinburgh: Handsel, 1983), pp. 169–70; cf. Joseph Ratzinger, *God Is Near Us: The Eucharist, the Heart of Life* (San Francisco: Ignatius, 2003), pp. 48–50.

[50] This is the view of dissenting Lutheran scholar Robert A.D. Clancy, 'The Old Testament Roots of Remembrance in the Lord's Supper', *Concordia Journal* (1993): pp. 35–6. Clancy further cites eminent Old Testament scholars such as B.S. Childs, *Memory and Tradition* (Naperville, IL: Alec R. Allenson, 1961); and W. Schottroff, *'Gedenken' im Alten Orient und im Alten Testament* (Neukirchen-Vluyn: Neukirchener Verlag, 1964) who also understand *anamnesis* in the sense of 'actualization'.

[51] Anthony Thiselton, *First Epistle to the Corinthians* (NIGTC; Grand Rapids, MI: Eerdmans, 2013), p. 879.

[52] Thiselton, *First Epistle to the Corinthians*, p. 879.

[53] F.F. Bruce, *1 & II Corinthians* (NCB; London: Marshall, Morgan & Scott, 1971), pp. 111–12.

[54] Gordon Fee, *First Epistle to the Corinthians* (NICNT; Grand Rapids, MI: Eerdmans, 1991), p. 558, while warning against individualism in the Lord's Supper, nevertheless seems to endorse a strongly realistic understanding of what is happening in the Supper. 'It is easy for us to miss Paul's concern in the argument for our own concern in "actualizing" the Lord's Supper for ourselves. The latter is certainly legitimate, if for no other reason than that the whole paragraph serves as a kind of paradigm of such actualizing for the Corinthian community. The Lord's Supper is not simply a memorial of the Last Supper . . . It is a constant, repeated reminder – and experience – of the efficacy of that death for us.'

Section 3: Re-Imagining the Self in the Light of the Cross

[1] Nicholas Wolterstorff, 'To Theologians: From One Who Cares about Theology but Is Not One of You', *Theological Education* 40 (2005): p. 85.

8. The Cross and Our Captivity to Shame

[1] Gerhard Johannes Botterweck, Helmer Ringgren, Heinz-Josef Fabry et al., *Theological Dictionary of the Old Testament* (15 vols; Grand Rapids, MI: Eerdmans, 1975), 2:52.

[2] Dietrich Bonhoeffer, *Creation and Fall: A Theological Interpretation of Genesis 1 – 3* (New York: Macmillan, 1964), p. 63.

[3] Dietrich Bonhoeffer, *Ethics* (New York: Macmillan, 1955), p. 20.

[4] Kenneth E. Bailey, *Jesus through Middle Eastern Eyes: Cultural Studies in the Gospels* (Downers Grove, IL: IVP, 2008), p. 173.

[5] Rom. 3:19 (NIV): 'Now we know that whatever the law says, it speaks to those who are under the law, so that every mouth may be silenced, and the whole world held accountable (*hupodikos*) to God.'

[6] J.E. Lendon, *Empire of Honour: The Art of Government in the Roman World* (Oxford: OUP, 2001), p. 13.

[7] Robert Jewett, *Romans* (Hermeneia; Minneapolis: Fortress, 2008), p. 49, citing Lendon, *Empire of Honour*.

[8] Jewett, *Romans*, p. 53.

[9] Jewett, *Romans*, p. 136.

[10] Jewett, *Romans*, p. 137.

[11] E.g. Acts 2:33: 'Being therefore exalted at the right hand of God, and having received from the Father the promise of the Holy Spirit, he has poured out this that you both see and hear.'

Exercise: Bibliodrama

[1] As a creative process, bibliodrama takes many forms. There are a wide variety of approaches available, and the suggestions made here were part of our own experience of introducing students to this form of imaginative engagement and drew heavily on practices familiar to our faith community. See Denise Dombkowski Hopkins and Michael

S. Koppel, *Grounded in the Living Word: The Old Testament and Pastoral Care Practices* (Cambridge: Eerdmans, 2010), pp. 50–51.

[2] This exercise is adapted from Anneliese Hecht, 'Bibliodrama and Exegesis', *Bulletin Dei Verbum* 66/67 (2003): pp. 6–10 http://www.deiverbum2005.org/Bulletin/BDV%206667_e.pdf (accessed 4 Nov. 2013).

[3] Hecht, 'Bibliodrama and Exegesis', p. 8.

[4] Hecht, 'Bibliodrama and Exegesis', p. 8, and building upon commonalities with a *Lectio Divina* approach to engagement with Scripture. Cf. Rudi Pöhl, 'Bibliodrama Is *Lectio Divina* on Stage', *Bulletin Dei Verbum* 66/67 (2003): pp. 2–22 http://www.deiverbum2005.org/Bulletin/BDV%206667_e.pdf (accessed 4 Nov. 2013).

[5] This step of the group process is based on common approaches to leading groups in Ignatian contemplation.

[6] This step is based on a combination of typical Ignatian contemplation practice and the suggestions of Hecht, 'Bibliodrama and Exegesis', p. 9.

[7] Several of these texts were used during the seminar in small groups immediately following Robin Stockitt's lecture.

9. The Cross and the Poetic Imagination

[1] This description of christological reading is the one I affirm as appropriate. I expect that Old Testament texts were meaningful in their original context and that this primary meaning still attaches to them. However, to the extent that belated readers find in these texts words which give voice to their beliefs, or express their experience of God, they may appropriate them into their own telling and add to the layers of meaning the text conveys. I do not reject the additional possibility suggested by Nicholas Wolterstorff, *Divine Discourse: Philosophical Reflections on the Claim that God Speaks* (New York: CUP, 1995), p. 56, that the text may be 'a medium of *contemporary* divine discourse' nor that God might now be saying something different through this text than its original authors may have intended.

[2] The focus within this chapter on the use of Isa 52:13 – 53:13 in atonement-centred Christian worship is not an indication that the text might not be a poetic, transformative encounter when read in Jewish worship, or that the text does not confront the Christian reader aside from any christological frame. However, for my present purposes within a volume

devoted to the Christian doctrine of the atonement, the common christological assumptions of many readers and the New Testament's validation of such readings will be taken as relevant context for the public
reading of this passage in Christian liturgical settings.

[3] Cf. Ellen F. Davis, *Wondrous Depth: Preaching the Old Testament* (Louisville, KY: Westminster John Knox, 2005), p. 17.

[4] John Wesley, 'Preface', *Sermons on Several Occasions* (Grand Rapids,
MI: Christian Classics Ethereal Library), p. 14 http://www.ccel.org/
ccel/wesley/sermons.pdf (accessed 21 Dec. 2013). However, it should
be noted that Wesley's own aversion to flowery speech was apparently not in conflict with his sense of the value of religious poetry and
hymnody for communicating theological truths as he was actively
involved in the publication and promotion of his brother Charles'
hymns and poems.

[5] See Patrick D. Miller, *Interpreting the Psalms* (Philadelphia: Fortress,
1986), p. 17; and David J.A. Clines, *I, He, We, and They: A Literary
Approach to Isaiah 53* (JSOTSup 1; Sheffield: *JSOT*, 1976), p. 25.

[6] See, e.g., the discussions in Joseph Blenkinsopp, *Isaiah 40 – 55* (AB19A;
New York: Doubleday, 2000), p. 349; and Klaus Baltzer, *Deutero-Isaiah*
(trans. Margaret Kohl; Hermeneia; Minneapolis: Fortress, 2001), p. 19.

[7] Clines, *I, He, We, and They*, p. 25.

[8] Classically, literary theorists divide poetry into three types: lyric,
dramatic and epic. Of these three, lyric is the non-narrative category.
On biblical Hebrew poetry as lyric see S.R. Driver, *An Introduction to
the Literature of the Old Testament* (New York: Meridian Library, 1957),
p. 360; F.W. Dobbs-Allsopp, 'The Psalms and Lyric Verse', in *The
Evolution of Rationality: Interdisciplinary Essays in Honor of J. Wetzel van
Huyssteen* (ed. F. LeRon Shuts; Grand Rapids, MI: Eerdmans, 2006);
and Katie M. Heffelfinger, *I Am Large, I Contain Multitudes: Lyric Cohesion and Conflict in Second Isaiah* (Leiden: Brill, 2011).

[9] See further Heffelfinger, *I Am Large*, pp. 37–81.

[10] Jonathan Culler, *Literary Theory* (A Very Short Introduction Series;
New York: OUP, 1997), p. 75.

[11] Davis, *Wondrous Depth*, p. 17.

[12] Wayne C. Booth, *The Company We Keep: An Ethics of Fiction* (London:
University of California Press, 1988), p. 298.

[13] Simone Weil, 'Reflections on the Right Use of School Studies with a
View to the Love of God', p. 1 http://www.uwo.ca/chaplain/crc/
articles/right_use.pdf (accessed 21 Dec. 2013).

[14] This idea is fairly obviously dependent upon the ethics of Emmanuel Levinas. See especially his *Entre Nous: Thinking-of-the-Other* (trans. Michael B. Smith and Barbara Harshav; New York: Columbia University Press, 1998), pp. 4–11.

[15] Weil, 'Reflections on the Right Use', pp. 5–6.

[16] Mary Kinzie, *The Cure of Poetry in an Age of Prose: Moral Essays on the Poet's Calling* (Chicago: University of Chicago Press, 1993), p. 291.

[17] Roland Greene, *Post Petrarchism: Origins and Innovations of the Western Lyric Sequence* (Princeton: Princeton University Press, 1991), p. 5.

[18] See F.W. Dobbs-Allsopp, *Lamentations* (IBC; Louisville, KY: Westminster John Knox, 2002), p. 39; and Adele Berlin, *Lamentations* (OTL; Louisville, KY: Westminster John Knox, 2002), p. 49.

[19] Ten of the twenty-one verbs in these verses are in the passive voice.

[20] Booth, *The Company We Keep*, p. 298.

[21] See, e.g., S.T. Kimbrough Jr, 'Lyrical Theology: Theology in Hymns', *Theology Today* 63 (2006): pp. 22–37.

[22] Bernd Janowski, '"He Bore Our Sins": Isaiah 53 and the Drama of Taking Another's Place', in *The Suffering Servant: Isaiah 53 in Jewish and Christian Sources* (ed. Bernd Janowski and Peter Stuhlmacher; Cambridge: Eerdmans, 2004), p. 64, points out the way that the song begins and ends with the divine perspective.

[23] Clutterbuck, 'Does Christianity Really Need a Doctrine of the Atonement?', p. 23.

[24] See Alistair James Morrison, *The New Masculinity Movement: A Viable Model for Engaging Men with God and the Church?* (Braemor Studies Series 3; Dublin: Church of Ireland, 2013).

[25] See Janowski, 'He Bore Our Sins', p. 65, on the text as presenting the servant's suffering as an aspect of divine plan.

[26] Kieran O'Mahony, 'To Tear Down and to Build: Replacing Anselm, Reading Paul and John', lecture to the Trinity College Dublin Biblical Studies Seminar, 15 November 2013.

[27] *Book of Common Prayer* (Dublin: Columba, 2004), p. 208.

[28] Cf. the connection drawn between Jesus as 'Lamb of God' and 'bearer of our sins', by the parallel construction of section 5 of 'The Litany Two', *Book of Common Prayer*, p. 178.

[29] Charles Wesley, 'Christ the Lord Is Risen Today'.

[30] Jeremy S. Begbie, 'Faithful Feelings: Music and Emotion in Worship', in *Resonant Witness: Conversations between Music and Theology* (ed.

Jeremy S. Begbie and Steven R. Guthrie; Grand Rapids, MI: Eerdmans, 2011), p. 337.

[31] Walter Brueggemann, *The Book that Breathes New Life: Scriptural Authority and Biblical Theology* (Minneapolis: Fortress, 2005), p. 18.

10. The Cross and the Healing of the Self

[1] Tapio Luoma, *Incarnation and Physics: Natural Science in the Theology of Thomas F. Torrance* (Oxford: OUP, 2002), p. 18.

[2] Gerard Loughlin, *Telling God's Story: Bible, Church and Narrative Theology* (Cambridge: CUP, 1999), p. 8.

[3] Martha C. Nussbaum, *Love's Knowledge: Essays on Philosophy and Literature* (Oxford: OUP, 1990), p. 5.

[4] John Swinton, *Raging with Compassion: Pastoral Responses to the Problem of Evil* (Grand Rapids, MI: Eerdmans, 2007), p. 71.

[5] William H. Willimon, *Who Will Be Saved?* (Nashville: Abingdon, 2008), p. 67.

[6] See this repeated emphasis in Rowan Williams, *The Wound of Knowledge* (London: Darton, Longman & Todd, 1990), pp. 1–24.

[7] Ellen Charry, *By the Renewing of Your Minds: The Pastoral Function of Christian Doctrine* (New York: OUP, 1997), p. 173.

[8] See Steve Chalke and Alan Mann, *The Lost Message of Jesus* (Grand Rapids, MI: Zondervan, 2003), p. 182.

[9] *The Apostles' Creed.*

[10] Stanley Hauerwas, *A Cross-Shattered Church: Reclaiming the Theological Heart of Preaching* (Grand Rapids, MI: Brazos, 2009), p. 72.

[11] John Wesley, *The Journal of John Wesley* (Chicago: Moody, 1974), p. 64.

[12] John Wesley, *The Works of the Rev. John Wesley* (14 vols; London: John Mason, 1831), 13:449.

[13] Harold's Cross is a village only a few miles from the Church of Ireland Theological Institute where the original lecture that forms the basis of this chapter was given.

[14] Alastair V. Campbell, *Rediscovering Pastoral Care* (Louisville, KY: Westminster John Knox, 1981), p. 38.

[15] Dietrich Bonhoeffer, *Letters and Papers from Prison* (London: SCM, 2002), p. 134.

[16] See Jürgen Moltmann, *The Crucified God* (London: SCM, 1974), p. 170.

17 Serene Jones, *Trauma and Grace: Theology in a Ruptured World* (Louisville, KY: Westminster John Knox, 2009), p. xiii.

18 Charry, *By the Renewing of Your Minds*, p. 193.

19 Henri Nouwen, *The Wounded Healer* (New York: Doubleday, 1972), p. 94.

20 Reading with NRSV's footnote. Wesley Carr, *The Pastor as Theologian: The Integration of Pastoral Ministry, Theology and Discipleship* (London: SPCK, 1989), p. 127.

21 Alister McGrath and Joanne McGrath, *The Dilemma of Self-Esteem: The Cross and Christian Confidence* (Wheaton, IL: Crossway, 1992), p. x.

22 Frank Lake, 'The Theology of Pastoral Counselling', in *Spiritual Dimensions of Pastoral Care: Practical Theology in a Multidisciplinary Context* (ed. David Willows and John Swinton; London: Jessica Kingsley, 2000), p. 135.

Exercise: Prayer Clinic

1 This meditation is based in part on the story of Julian of Norwich's meditation on the cross (*Revelations of Divine Love* [trans. Grace Warrack; Grand Rapids, MI: Christian Classics Ethereal Library], pp. 36–44 http://www.ccel.org/ccel/julian/revelations.pdf (accessed 23 Dec. 2013) and the advice to 'fix your eyes on the Crucified', given by Teresa of Avila, *Interior Castle* (ed. Benedict Zimmerman; Grand Rapids, MI: Christian Classics Ethereal Library), p. 173 http://www.ccel.org/ccel/teresa/castle2.pdf (accessed 23 Dec. 2013).

2 This approach is adapted from 'Draw a Hope, Pain, Thanks or Joy' www.creativeprayer.com (accessed 4 Nov. 2013).

3 This activity is adapted from 'To Be Broken' www.creativeprayer.com (accessed 4 Nov. 2013).

4 This activity is adapted from 'Blessing Our Enemies' www.creativeprayer.com (accessed 4 Nov. 2013).

5 *Lectio Divina* is a contemplative approach to devotional reading of the Scriptures that grows out of monastic practice. It typically progresses according to the following steps: stilling ourselves, reading the text slowly and lovingly expecting it to speak to us, choosing a word or phrase from the text to chew over and ponder, expressing our worship back to God, and resting in the presence of God. See further Marjorie J. Thompson, *Soul Feast: An Invitation to the Christian Spiritual Life* (Louisville, KY: Westminster John Knox,

1995), pp. 22–5; and http://daily.upperroom.org/?page_id=19 (accessed 4 Nov. 2013).

Suggestions for the Use of Integrative Silence

[1] See the footnote details about *Lectio Divina* and resources for it in the Prayer Clinic if you are unfamiliar with this practice.

Responses to the Chapters

[1] Bauckham refers to such theories as 'degenerate'.

[2] See Joseph Ratzinger, *Introduction to Christianity* (San Francisco: Ignatius, 1990), pp. 213ff.

[3] Karl Barth, *Church Dogmatics, Vol. 4.1: The Doctrine of Reconciliation* (ed. G.W. Bromiley and T.F. Torrance; 14 vols; London: T&T Clark, 1957).

[4] John Stott, *The Cross of Christ* (Leicester: IVP, 1986), p. 151. For a succinct overview of John Stott's engagement with the doctrine of penal substitution see Christina A. Baxter, 'Cursed Beloved', in *Atonement Today* (ed. John Goldingay; London: SPCK, 1995), pp. 54–72.

[5] See, e.g., the liturgy of the Episcopal Church USA as represented in 'Holy Eucharist II: Eucharistic Prayer C', *The Book of Common Prayer*, p. 370 http://justus.anglican.org (accessed 29 Nov. 2013).

[6] Elsdon is referring here to the ways that the naturally evolving world both makes life possible and produces destructive natural phenomena.

Conclusion: Continuing the Conversation

[1] See, e.g., Sue Pickering, *Creative Retreat Ideas: Resources for Short Day and Weekend Retreats* (Norwich: Canterbury, 2010), pp. 34–5; Walter Brueggemann, *The Psalms and the Life of Faith* (Minneapolis: Fortress, 1995); and Paul Bradbury, *Sowing in Tears: How to Lament in a Church of Praise* (Cambridge: Grove, 2007).

[2] Relevant liturgical resources include: Robin Stockitt, *Restoring the Shamed: Towards a Theology of Shame* (Eugene, OR: Cascade, 2012), pp. 160–61; United Methodist General Board of Discipleship Website

http://www.gbod.org/live-the-um-way/responding-to-world-events (accessed 29 Dec. 2013); and Kathy Galloway, ed. *The Pattern of Our Days: Liturgies and Resources for Worship* (Glasgow: Wild Goose, 1996).

[3] Edward Farley, 'Four Pedagogical Mistakes: *A Mea Culpa*', *Teaching Theology and Religion* 8 (2005): p. 201.

General Index

A

Abelard, Peter 5–6, 18, 24–25, 28, 30
Adam 6, 35, 42, 136ff., 149, 170
aesthetics 98ff., 102–103
anamnesis 119, 124ff., 130–131
Anselm 5, 13, 18, 20, 24ff., 28, 30, 96, 171
Aulen, Gustav 4ff.
Augustine 22, 26ff.
ARCIC 108–109, 115, 119, 130
Aquinas, Thomas 24–25

B

Barth, Karl 10, 23, 186
Bentley Hart, David 100
Bonhoeffer, Dietrich, 138–139
Brunner, Emil 10, 186

C

Calvin, John 9, 18, 109–110, 114–115
Caravaggio 99
Chagall, Marc 63
Chalke, Steve xix, 105
Chesterton, G.K. 99–100
Christus Victor 5, 24, 30, 95–98
Church Fathers 5, 24, 96, 188
Clegg, Cecilia 67–70
cosmic child abuse xix, 8, 171
cosmos and environment 29, 35ff., 45, 189–190, 197–198
crucifixion 19–20, 77–78, 141–142, 146–149, 160, 192–193
Cyril of Alexandria 58

D

Dali, Salvador 63
Dawkins, Richard 26
dehumanization 76, 78
Denney, James 10, 102–103, 186
Devil/Satan 5, 24–25, 30, 96–97

E

emotion 153–156, 164–166, 188
eucharist 101–103, 109–111, 114–131, 123, 152, 164
evil 25–28, 30, 50, 96–97

F

feminist theology xxiii, 7, 23, 79, 82, 85ff., 189, 191
forgiveness 11–12, 30, 38, 53, 55, 90–91, 105, 135, 142–143, 174, 195
Francis, Pope 128

G

Girard, René 8, 74
Gnosticism 32, 41
Gregory of Nazianzus 21, 188

H

Hart, Trevor 47
healing xxiii–xxiv, iv, 20, 33, 43, 53, 55, 88, 140, 158, 167, 169, 171, 174ff., 179, 180, 192–193, 195–197
honour 13, 18, 25, 30, 76, 136, 143–148, 161

I

Incarnation xxiii, 5, 16–17, 21–22, 36, 54, 58, 59, 80, 117, 164, 166, 185, 187 ff., 192, 194, 198

imagination xvi, xxiv, 12, 15, 48, 68, 98, 73, 153, 155–157, 160–161, 166, 192–194, 196

impassibility 57 ff.

Irenaeus 21, 37, 108, 188,

J

Japan 46, 49 ff., 55 ff.

Julian of Norwich 17–18, 20, 175

L

lament xxiii, 24 ff., 53–54, 61–62, 118, 156–157, 181, 197

Leibnitz, Gottfried 50

Lewis, C.S. xi, 48

liberation theology 7, 56–57, 87

Liechty, Joseph 67 ff.

Luther, Martin 5, 18, 25, 98, 104, 110, 121–125, 129, 131, 172

Lloyd–Jones, Martin 10

M

McGrath, Alister 175

memorialism 101

Moltmann, Jürgen 18, 23, 56, 58, 174

Mollenkott, Virginia 83

moral imagination 68, 73 ff., 76, 192

N

natural evil xxiii, 45 ff., 50, 189–190

New Atheism 3–4, 8, 26, 52

New Testament xviii ff., 5–6, 10, 15, 35 ff., 42–43, 53, 85, 102, 104, 108, 122–123, 127–128, 131, 140, 146, 153

O

Old Testament xxiv, 35, 40, 42, 47, 51, 124, 137

'other', the xxiii, 71–72, 74–75, 78, 136 ff., 156, 193

P

penal substitution xix, xxii, 5–15, 25–26, 28, 98, 105, 108, 185–186

Percy, Walker 99

Polkinghorne, John 45–47

R

Radford Ruether, Rosemary 79 ff., 84–85, 87

Ratzinger, Joseph xxiii, 116, 120–128, 131, 186

reconciliation xvi, xxi, xxiii, 5, 12, 24 ff., 28 ff., 39 ff., 67 ff., 78–79, 87, 89 ff., 129, 132, 159, 169, 188, 190, 192, 197–198

Reformation/Counter–Reformation 99, 103–104, 111, 114, 121–122, 124, 126, 131,188

resurrection xv, xix, 5, 19, 21, 23, 36, 51, 57, 78, 92, 102, 141, 145–146, 160, 164, 168, 174, 188–189, 193

Ricoeur, Paul 26 ff., 96

S

sacrifice 23, 69, 84, 87, 164, 171, 175, 187, 194

sacrifice, eucharistic xxiii, 21, 101, 109–110, 114 ff.

salvation xx, xxii, 15, 19 ff., 28, 33, 38, 74, 86–87, 89, 116–117, 122, 124, 126, 130, 141, 145, 149, 159, 162, 171 ff., 195

Satisfaction Theory 4 ff., 18, 24, 28

Schüssler Fiorenza, Elisabeth 84–85

sectarianism 67 ff., 70–71

secularization 128

shame xvi–xvii, xxi, xxiii, 76 ff., 135 ff., 151, 170, 191 ff., 195, 197

sin xvi, 4 ff., 24 ff., 33, 37 ff., 41 ff., 45–46, 51, 53 ff., 73, 79–80, 86–87, 89 ff., 96–97, 100–101, 105 ff., 129, 135, 137–138, 140–141, 163–164, 169 ff., 187, 189, 192, 195

Stott, John 10, 116, 186

subjective view of the atonement 5

suffering xxi, xxiii, 8, 17 ff., 20, 22–23,

25ff., 42, 46–47, 49ff., 63, 85, 87,
90–91, 106–107, 148–149, 152–153,
157ff., 165–166, 170–171, 173–174,
181, 186ff., 197

T
Trible, Phyllis 81, 83
Trinity 10ff., 20, 22, 58, 105, 108–116,
162, 171, 185–187, 194, 198

V
violence xxiiff., 7–8, 11, 13ff., 17ff.,
23ff., 67ff., 76, 87, 89ff., 97, 106, 135,
140, 162, 171, 189, 191–192, 194

W
Wesley, John 153, 171–172
Wink, Walter 74
worship/liturgy xviii, 34, 111, 115,
122–124, 126, 130–132, 152–153,
156, 158–162, 164–166, 178, 197–198
wound xxi, 85, 89, 162, 165, 172–177,
179, 196
Wright, N.T. 36, 43, 46

Z
Zwingli, Ulrich 104, 109